LLEWELLYN'S 2014

Daily Planetary Guide

ISBN: 978-0-7387-2151-4. Astrological calculations compiled and programmed by Rique Pottenger based on the earlier work of Neil F. Michelsen.

Astrological proofreading by Jim Shawvan
Cover design by Lisa Novak
Edited by Andrea Neff

Cover images: Jupiter: Victor Habbick Visions/Science Photo Library/PunchStock
          Top star field: iStockphoto.com/Phil Johnston
          Bottom star field: iStockphoto.com/Amanda Rohde

Llewellyn Worldwide Ltd.
2143 Wooddale Drive
Woodbury, MN 55125-2989
www.llewellyn.com

Printed in the United States of America

2013

SEPTEMBER
S	M	T	W	T	F	S
1	2	3	4	5	6	7
8	9	10	11	12	13	14
15	16	17	18	19	20	21
22	23	24	25	26	27	28
29	30					

OCTOBER
S	M	T	W	T	F	S
		1	2	3	4	5
6	7	8	9	10	11	12
13	14	15	16	17	18	19
20	21	22	23	24	25	26
27	28	29	30	31		

NOVEMBER
S	M	T	W	T	F	S
					1	2
3	4	5	6	7	8	9
10	11	12	13	14	15	16
17	18	19	20	21	22	23
24	25	26	27	28	29	30

DECEMBER
S	M	T	W	T	F	S
1	2	3	4	5	6	7
8	9	10	11	12	13	14
15	16	17	18	19	20	21
22	23	24	25	26	27	28
29	30	31				

2014

JANUARY
S	M	T	W	T	F	S
			1	2	3	4
5	6	7	8	9	10	11
12	13	14	15	16	17	18
19	20	21	22	23	24	25
26	27	28	29	30	31	

FEBRUARY
S	M	T	W	T	F	S
						1
2	3	4	5	6	7	8
9	10	11	12	13	14	15
16	17	18	19	20	21	22
23	24	25	26	27	28	

MARCH
S	M	T	W	T	F	S
						1
2	3	4	5	6	7	8
9	10	11	12	13	14	15
16	17	18	19	20	21	22
23	24	25	26	27	28	29
30	31					

APRIL
S	M	T	W	T	F	S
		1	2	3	4	5
6	7	8	9	10	11	12
13	14	15	16	17	18	19
20	21	22	23	24	25	26
27	28	29	30			

MAY
S	M	T	W	T	F	S
				1	2	3
4	5	6	7	8	9	10
11	12	13	14	15	16	17
18	19	20	21	22	23	24
25	26	27	28	29	30	31

JUNE
S	M	T	W	T	F	S
1	2	3	4	5	6	7
8	9	10	11	12	13	14
15	16	17	18	19	20	21
22	23	24	25	26	27	28
29	30					

JULY
S	M	T	W	T	F	S
		1	2	3	4	5
6	7	8	9	10	11	12
13	14	15	16	17	18	19
20	21	22	23	24	25	26
27	28	29	30	31		

AUGUST
S	M	T	W	T	F	S
					1	2
3	4	5	6	7	8	9
10	11	12	13	14	15	16
17	18	19	20	21	22	23
24	25	26	27	28	29	30
31						

SEPTEMBER
S	M	T	W	T	F	S
	1	2	3	4	5	6
7	8	9	10	11	12	13
14	15	16	17	18	19	20
21	22	23	24	25	26	27
28	29	30				

OCTOBER
S	M	T	W	T	F	S
			1	2	3	4
5	6	7	8	9	10	11
12	13	14	15	16	17	18
19	20	21	22	23	24	25
26	27	28	29	30	31	

NOVEMBER
S	M	T	W	T	F	S
						1
2	3	4	5	6	7	8
9	10	11	12	13	14	15
16	17	18	19	20	21	22
23	24	25	26	27	28	29
30						

DECEMBER
S	M	T	W	T	F	S
	1	2	3	4	5	6
7	8	9	10	11	12	13
14	15	16	17	18	19	20
21	22	23	24	25	26	27
28	29	30	31			

2015

JANUARY
S	M	T	W	T	F	S
				1	2	3
4	5	6	7	8	9	10
11	12	13	14	15	16	17
18	19	20	21	22	23	24
25	26	27	28	29	30	31

FEBRUARY
S	M	T	W	T	F	S
1	2	3	4	5	6	7
8	9	10	11	12	13	14
15	16	17	18	19	20	21
22	23	24	25	26	27	28

MARCH
S	M	T	W	T	F	S
1	2	3	4	5	6	7
8	9	10	11	12	13	14
15	16	17	18	19	20	21
22	23	24	25	26	27	28
29	30	31				

APRIL
S	M	T	W	T	F	S
			1	2	3	4
5	6	7	8	9	10	11
12	13	14	15	16	17	18
19	20	21	22	23	24	25
26	27	28	29	30		

MAY
S	M	T	W	T	F	S
					1	2
3	4	5	6	7	8	9
10	11	12	13	14	15	16
17	18	19	20	21	22	23
24	25	26	27	28	29	30
31						

JUNE
S	M	T	W	T	F	S
	1	2	3	4	5	6
7	8	9	10	11	12	13
14	15	16	17	18	19	20
21	22	23	24	25	26	27
28	29	30				

JULY
S	M	T	W	T	F	S
			1	2	3	4
5	6	7	8	9	10	11
12	13	14	15	16	17	18
19	20	21	22	23	24	25
26	27	28	29	30	31	

AUGUST
S	M	T	W	T	F	S
						1
2	3	4	5	6	7	8
9	10	11	12	13	14	15
16	17	18	19	20	21	22
23	24	25	26	27	28	29
30	31					

Contents

Introduction to Astrology

by Kim Rogers-Gallagher

Your horoscope is calculated using the date and time you were born from the perspective of your birth location. From this information, a clock-like diagram emerges that shows where every planet was located at the moment you made your debut. Each chart is composed of the same elements, rearranged, so everyone has one of everything, but none are exactly alike. I think of planets, signs, houses, and aspects as the four astrological building blocks. Each block represents a different level of human existence.

The eight planets along with the Sun and Moon are actual physical bodies. They represent urges or needs we all have. Chiron also falls into this category. The twelve signs of the zodiac are sections of the sky, and each is 30 degrees. The signs describe the behavior a planet or house will use to express itself. The twelve houses in a chart tell us where our planets come to life. Each house represents different life concerns—values, communication, creativity, and so on—that we must live through as life and time progress.

Basically, aspects are angles. Some of the planets will be positioned an exact number of degrees apart, forming angles to one another. For example, 180 degrees is a circle divided by two and is called an opposition. A square is 90 degrees and divides the circle by four. A trine is 120 degrees and divides the circle by three, and so forth. Aspects show which planets will engage in constant dialogue with one another. The particular aspect that joins them describes the nature of their "conversation." Not all planets will aspect all other planets in the houses.

Planets: The First Building Block

Each planet acts like the director of a department in a corporation, and the corporation is, of course, you. For example, Mercury directs your Communications Department and Jupiter oversees your Abundance and Growth Department. When you have the need to communicate, you call on your Mercury; when it's time to take a risk or grow, you use your Jupiter. Let's meet each of the planets individually and take a look at which job duties fall under each planet's jurisdiction.

The Sun

⊙ Every corporation needs an executive director who makes the final decisions. The Sun is your Executive Director. The Sun in your chart is your core, your true self. Although each of the planets in your chart is important in its own right, they all "take their orders," figuratively speaking, from the Sun.

Everyone's Sun has the same inner goal: to shine. The house your Sun is in shows where you really want to do good, where you want to be appreciated and loved. Your Sun is your inner supply of pride and confidence, your identity. The Sun is you at your creative best, enjoying life to the fullest.

The Sun shows the focus of the moment, where the world's attention will be directed on that particular day. In fact, in horary and electional astrology, the two branches that pertain most to timing and prediction, the Sun represents the day, the Moon the hour, and the Midheaven the moment. In the physical body, the Sun rules the heart, upper back, and circulatory system.

The Moon

☽ Speaking of the Moon, a good place to meet her and begin to understand her qualities is by the water on a clear night when she's full. Whether you're looking up at her or at that silvery patch she creates that shivers and dances on the water, take a deep breath and allow yourself to be still. She represents the soft interior of each of us that recalls memories, that fears and dreams.

She's a lovely lady who oversees the Department of Feelings; she's the bringer of "moods" (a great Moon word). Her house and placement in your chart reveal how your intuition works, what your emotional needs are, and how you want your needs met. She is the ultimate feminine energy, the part of you that points both to how you were nurtured and to how you will nurture others. In the body, the Moon has jurisdiction over the breasts, ovaries, and womb. She also rules our body fluids, the internal ocean that keeps us alive.

Mercury

♀ Back when gods and goddesses were thought to be in charge of the affairs of humanity, Mercury shuttled messages between the gods and mortals. In today's world, Mercury is the computer, the telephone, and the Internet. He's the internal computer that constantly feeds you data about the world. His position and house in your chart show how you think and reason, and how you express yourself to others. You'll recognize him in your speech patterns, in your handwriting, and in the way you walk, because moving through your environment means communicating with it. He operates through your five senses and your brain, and makes you conscious of opposites—light and dark, hot and cold, up and down. He's what you use when you have a conversation, exchange a glance, gesture, or interpret a symbol. Mercury represents the side of you living totally in the present.

If you've ever tried to collect mercury after it escaped from a broken thermometer, you've learned something about Mercury. Just as your Mercury never stops collecting data, those tiny beads you tried so hard to collect brought back a bit of everything they contacted—dog hair, crumbs, and grains of dirt. In the body, Mercury also acts as a messenger. He transmits messages through his function as the central nervous system that lets your eyes and hands collaborate, your eyes blink, and breathing continue.

Venus

♀ Venus spends her energy supplying you with your favorite people, places, and things. If you want chocolate, music, flannel sheets, or the coworker you've got a mad crush on, it's your Venus that tells you how to get it. Venus enjoys beauty and comfort. She shows how to attract what you love, especially people. When you're being charming, whether by using your manners or by adorning yourself, she's in charge of all behavior that is pleasing to others—social chitchat, smiles, hugs, and kisses. Whenever you're pleased, satisfied, or content enough to purr, it's your Venus who made you feel that way. Since money is one of the ways we draw the objects we love to us, she's also in charge of finances. Venus relates to your senses—sight, smell, taste, touch, and sound—the body's receptors.

After all, it's the senses that tell us what feels good and what doesn't. Venus responds to your desire for beautiful surroundings, comfortable clothing, and fine art.

Mars

♂ Mars is in charge of your Self-Defense and Action Department. He's the warrior who fights back when you're attacked—your own personal SWAT team. Your Mars energy makes you brave, courageous, and daring. His placement in your chart describes how you act on your own behalf. He's concerned only with you, and he doesn't consider the size, strength, or abilities of whomever or whatever you're up against. He's the side of you that initiates all activity. He's also in charge of how you assert yourself and how you express anger.

"Hot under the collar," "seeing red," and "all fired up" are Mars phrases. Mars is what you use to be passionate, adventurous, and bold. But he can be violent, accident-prone, and cruel, too. Wherever he is in your chart, you find constant action. Mars pursues. He shows how you "do" things. He charges through situations. This "headstrong" planet corresponds to the head, the blood, and the muscles.

Jupiter

♃ Jupiter is called "the Greater Benefic," and he heads the Department of Abundance and Growth. He's the side of you that's positive, optimistic, and generous. He's where you keep your supply of laughter, enthusiasm, and high spirits. It's Jupiter's expansive, high-spirited energy that motivates you to travel, take classes, and meet new people. Wherever he is in your chart is a place where you'll have an extensive network of friends and associates—folks you can visit, count on, and learn from. Jupiter is the side of you that will probably cause you to experience the "grass is greener" syndrome. Your Jupiter is also what you're using when you find yourself being excessive and wasteful, overdoing, or blowing something out of proportion. Words like "too" and "always" are the property of Jupiter, as are "more" and "better." In general, this planet just loves to make things bigger. In the body, Jupiter corresponds with the liver, the organ that filters what you take in and rids your body of excess. Jupiter also handles physical growth.

Saturn

♄ Saturn represents withholding and resistance to change. He heads the Boundaries and Rules Department. Locate Saturn in your chart to find out where you'll build walls to keep change out, where you may segregate yourself at times, where you'll be most likely to say no. Your Saturn is the authority inside you, the spot where you may inhibit or stall yourself throughout life—most often because you fear failure and would rather not act at all than act inappropriately. This planet teaches you to respect your elders, follow the rules, and do things right the first time. Wherever Saturn is in your chart is a place where you'll feel respectful, serious, and conservative. Your Saturn placement is where you'll know that you should never embellish the facts and never act until you're absolutely sure you're ready. Here is where you won't expect something for nothing. Saturn is also where you're at your most disciplined, where you'll teach yourself the virtues of patience, endurance, and responsibility. Because this planet is so fond of boundaries, it's also the planet in charge of organization, structures, and guidelines. In the physical body, Saturn correlates with the bones and the skin, those structures that hold your body together.

Uranus

♅ There's a spot in everyone's chart where independence is the order of the day, where rules are made specifically to be broken, and where personal freedom is the only way to go, regardless of the consequences. Here's where you'll surprise even yourself at the things you say and do. Meet Uranus, head of the Department of One Never Knows, the place in your chart where shocks, surprises, and sudden reversals are regular fare.

Your Uranus energy is what wakes you up to how confined you feel, breaks you out of the rut you're in, and sets you free. He's a computer wizard and involved in mass communications. Where he's strong in your chart, you will be strong, too. Here is where you'll have genius potential, where you'll be bold enough to ignore the old way to solve a problem and instead find a whole new way. Major scientific and technological breakthroughs like the space program and the Internet were inspired by Uranus. In the body, Uranus rules the lower part of the legs, including the calves and ankles, and he co-rules with Mercury the central nervous system.

Neptune

♆ Next time you hear yourself sigh or feel yourself slip into a daydream, think of Neptune. This is the planet in charge of romance, nostalgia, and magic. Although her official title is head of the Department of Avoidance and Fantasy, she's also one of the most creative energies you own. Wherever she is in your chart is where you're psychic. It's also where you're capable of amazing compassion and sensitivity for beings and creatures less fortunate than yourself. It's where you'll be drawn into charity or volunteer work because you realize that we're all part of a bigger plan, that there are no boundaries between you and what's out there.

This combination of sensitivity and harsh reality doesn't always mix well. This may also be a place where you'll try to escape. Sleep, meditation, and prayer are the highest uses of her energies, but alcohol and drugs are also under her jurisdiction. Neptune's place in your chart is where you're equally capable of fooling all of the people all of the time, and of being fooled yourself. In the body, Neptune and the Moon co-rule fluids. Neptune also has a connection with poisons and viruses that invisibly infiltrate our bodies and with the body's immune system, which is how we keep our barriers intact.

Pluto

♇ Pluto is head of the Department of Death, Destruction, and Decay. He's in charge of things that have to happen, and he disposes of situations that have gone past the point of no return, where the only solution is to "let go." He also oversees sex, reincarnation, recycling, regeneration, and rejuvenation. Pluto's spot in your chart is a place where intense, inevitable circumstances will arrive to teach you about agony and ecstasy. Pluto's place in your chart is where you'll be in a state of turmoil or evolution, where there will be ongoing change. This is the side of you that realizes that, like it or not, life goes on after tremendous loss. It is the side of you that will reflect on your losses down the road and try to make sense of them. Most importantly, since Pluto rules life, death, and rebirth, here's where you'll understand the importance of process. You'll be amazingly strong where your Pluto is—he's a well of concentrated, transforming energy. In the body, Pluto is associated with the reproductive organs since here is where the invisible process of life and death begins. He is also in charge of puberty and sexual maturity. He corresponds with plutonium.

Signs: The Second Building Block

Every sign is built of three things: an element, a quality, and a polarity. Understanding each of these primary building blocks gives a head start toward understanding the signs themselves, so let's take a look at them.

The Polarities: Masculine and Feminine

The words "masculine" and "feminine" are often misunderstood or confused in the context of astrology. In astrology, masculine means that an energy is assertive, aggressive, and linear. Feminine means that an energy is receptive, magnetic, and circular. These terms should not be confused with male and female.

The Qualities: Cardinal, Fixed, and Mutable

Qualities show the way a sign's energy flows. The cardinal signs are energies that initiate change. Cardinal signs operate in sudden bursts of energy. The fixed signs are thorough and unstoppable. They're the energies that endure. They take projects to completion, tend to block change at all costs, and will keep at something regardless of whether or not it should be terminated. The mutable signs are versatile, flexible, and changeable. They can be scattered, fickle, and inconstant.

The Elements: Fire, Earth, Air, and Water

The fire signs correspond with the spirit and the spiritual aspects of life. They inspire action, attract attention, and love spontaneity. The earth signs are solid, practical, supportive, and as reliable as the earth under our feet. The earth signs are our physical envoys and are concerned with our tangible needs, such as food, shelter, work, and responsibilities. Air signs are all about the intellectual or mental sides of life. Like air itself, they are light and elusive. They love conversation, communication, and mingling. The water signs correspond to the emotional side of our natures. As changeable, subtle, and able to infiltrate as water itself, water signs gauge the mood in a room when they enter, and operate on what they sense from their environment.

Aries: Masculine, Cardinal, Fire

♈ Aries is ruled by Mars and is cardinal fire—red-hot, impulsive, and ready to go. Aries planets are not known for their patience, and they ignore obstacles, choosing instead to focus on the shortest distance between where they are and where they want to be. Planets in Aries are brave, impetuous, and direct. Aries planets are often very good at initiating projects. They are not, however, as eager to finish, so they will leave projects undone. Aries planets need physical outlets for their considerable Mars-powered energy; otherwise their need for action can turn to stress. Exercise, hard work, and competition are food for Aries energy.

Taurus: Feminine, Fixed, Earth

♉ Taurus, the fixed earth sign, has endless patience that turns your Taurus planet into a solid force to be reckoned with. Taurus folks never, ever quit. Their reputation for stubbornness is earned. They're responsible, reliable, honest as they come, practical, and endowed with a stick-to-it attitude other planets envy. They're not afraid to work hard. Since Taurus is ruled by Venus, it's not surprising to find that these people are sensual and luxury-loving, too. They love to be spoiled with the best—good food, fine wine, or even a Renoir painting. They need peace and quiet like no other, and don't like their schedules to be disrupted. However, they may need a reminder that comfortable habits can become ruts.

Gemini: Masculine, Mutable, Air

♊ This sign is famous for its duality and love of new experiences, as well as for its role as communicator. Gemini is mutable air, which translates into changing your mind, so expect your Gemini planet to be entertaining and versatile. This sign knows a little bit about everything. Gemini planets usually display at least two distinct sides to their personalities, are changeable and even fickle at times, and are wonderfully curious. This sign is ruled by Mercury, so if what you're doing involves talking, writing, gesturing, or working with hand-eye coordination, your Gemini planet will love it. Mercury also rules short trips, so any planet in Gemini is an expert at how to make its way around the neighborhood in record time.

Cancer: Feminine, Cardinal, Water

Cancer is cardinal water, so it's good at beginning things. It's also the most privacy-oriented sign. Cancer types are emotionally vulnerable, sensitive, and easily hurt. They need safe "nests" to return to when the world gets to be too much. Cancer types say "I love you" by tending to your need for food, warmth, or a place to sleep. The problem is that they can become needy, dependent, or unable to function unless they feel someone or something needs them. Cancer rules the home and family. It's also in charge of emotions, so expect a Cancer to operate from his or her gut most of the time.

Leo: Masculine, Fixed, Fire

Leo is fixed fire, and above all else represents pride and ego. Sun-ruled Leo wants to shine and be noticed. Natural performers, people in this sign are into drama and attract attention even when they don't necessarily want it. Occasionally your Leo friends may be touchy and high maintenance. Still, they are generous to a fault. Leo appreciates attention and praise with lavish compliments, lovely gifts, and creative outings designed to amaze and delight. Leo's specialties are having fun, entertaining, and making big entrances and exits.

Virgo: Feminine, Mutable, Earth

Virgo may seem picky and critical, but that may be too simplistic. As a mutable earth sign, your Virgo planet delights in helping, and it's willing to adapt to any task. Having a keen eye for details may be another way to interpret a Virgo planet's automatic fault-finding ability. When Virgo's eye for detail combines with the ability to fix almost anything, you have a troubleshooter extraordinaire. This sign practices discrimination—analyzing, critiquing, and suggesting remedies to potential problems. This sign is also wonderful at lists, agendas, and schedules. Keep your Virgo planet happy by keeping it busy.

Libra: Masculine, Cardinal, Air

Libra adores balance, harmony, and equal give and take—no easy task. A more charming sign would be difficult to find, though. Libra's cardinal airy nature wants to begin things, and entertaining and socializing are high priorities. These expert people-pleasing Venus-ruled planets specialize in manners, courtesy, and small talk. Alone time may be shunned, and because they're gifted with the ability to pacify, they may sell out their own needs, or the truth, to buy peace and companionship. Seeing both sides of a situation, weighing the options, and keeping their inner balance by remaining honest may be Libra's hardest tasks.

Scorpio: Feminine, Fixed, Water

Planets in this sign are detectives, excelling at the art of strategy. Your Scorpio planets sift through every situation for subtle clues, which they analyze to determine what's really going on. They're also gifted at sending subtle signals back to the environment, and at imperceptibly altering a situation by manipulating it with the right word or movement. Scorpio planets are constantly searching for intimacy. They seek intensity and may be crisis-oriented. They can be relentless, obsessive, and jealous. Remember, this is fixed water. Scorpios feel things deeply and forever. Give your Scorpio planets the opportunity to fire-walk, to experience life-and-death situations.

Sagittarius: Masculine, Mutable, Fire

The enthusiasm of this mutable fire sign, ruled by Jupiter, spreads like a brushfire. These planets tend to never feel satisfied or content, and to always wonder if there's something even more wonderful over the next mountain. Your Sagittarius planets are bored by routine; they're freedom-oriented, generous, and optimistic to a fault. They can be excessive and overindulgent. They adore outdoor activities and foreign places and foreign people. They learn by first having the big picture explained. They're only too happy to preach, advertise, and philosophize. Sagittarius planets can be quite prophetic, and they absolutely believe in the power of laughter, embarrassing themselves at times to make someone laugh.

Capricorn: Feminine, Cardinal, Earth

♑ Your Capricorn planets, ruled by Saturn, have a tendency to build things, such as erecting structures and creating a career for you. Saturn will start up an organization and turn it into the family business. These planets automatically know how to run it no matter what it is. They're authority figures. They exercise caution and discipline, set down rules, and live by them. Capricorn is the sign with the driest wit. Here's where your sense of propriety and tradition will be strong, where doing things the old-fashioned way and paying respect to the elders will be the only way to go. They want a return for the time they invest, and don't mind proving how valuable they are.

Aquarius: Masculine, Fixed, Air

♒ Aquarian planets present some unexpected contradictions because they are fixed air and unpredictable. This sign's ruler, Uranus, gets the credit for Aquarius's tumultuous ways. Aquarian energy facilitates invention and humanitarian conquests, to the amazement of the masses, and planets in this sign are into personal freedom like no other. They create their own rules, fight city hall whenever possible, and deliberately break tradition. They adore change. Abrupt reversals are their specialty, so others often perceive them as erratic, unstable, or unreliable. But when Aquarius energy activates, commitment to a cause or an intellectual ideal has a steadfastness like no other sign possesses.

Pisces: Feminine, Mutable, Water

♓ Mutable Pisces can't separate itself emotionally from whatever it's exposed to. While this is the source of Pisces' well-deserved reputation for compassion, it's also the source of a desire to escape reality. Planets in this sign feel everything—for better or worse—so they need time alone to unload and reassemble themselves. Exposure to others, especially in crowds, is exhausting to your Pisces planets. Here is where you may have a tendency to take in stray people and animals and where you'll need to watch for the possibility of being victimized or taken advantage of in some way. Pisces planets see the best in people or situations, and they can be disappointed when reality sets in. These planets are the romantics of the zodiac. Let them dream in healthy ways.

Houses: The Third Building Block

Houses are represented by twelve pie-shaped wedges in a horoscope chart. (See blank chart on page 191.) They're like rooms in a house, and each reflects the circumstances we create and encounter in a specific area of life. One room, the Sixth House, relates to our daily routine and work, while the Eleventh House relates to groups we may be affiliated with, for example. The sign (Aries, Taurus, etc.) on the cusp of each house tells us something about the nature of the room behind the door. Someone with Leo on the Sixth House cusp will create different routines and work habits than a person with Capricorn on that cusp. The sign influences the type of behavior you'll exhibit when those life circumstances turn up. Since the time of day you were born determines the sign on each of the houses, an accurate birth time will result in more accurate information from your chart.

The Twelve Houses

The First House

The First House shows the sign that was ascending over the horizon at the moment you were born. Let's think again of your chart as one big house and of the houses as "rooms." The First House symbolizes your front door. The sign on this house cusp (also known as the Rising Sign or Ascendant) describes the way you dress, move, and adorn yourself, and the overall condition of your body. It relates to the first impression you make on people.

The Second House

This house shows how you handle the possessions you hold dear. That goes for money, objects, and the qualities you value in yourself and in others. This house also holds the side of you that takes care of what you have and what you buy for yourself, and the amount of money you earn. The Second House shows what you're willing to do for money, too, so it's also a description of your self-esteem.

The Third House

This house corresponds to your neighborhood, including the bank, the post office, and the gym where you work out. This is the side of you that performs routine tasks without much conscious thought. The Third House also refers to childhood and grammar school, and it shows your relationships with siblings, your communication style, and your attitude toward short trips.

The Fourth House

This house is the symbolic foundation brought from your childhood home, your family, and the parent who nurtured you. Here is where you'll find the part of you that decorates and maintains your nest. It decides what home in the adult world will be like and how much privacy you'll need. The Fourth House deals with matters of real estate. Most importantly, this house contains the emotional warehouse of memories you operate from subconsciously.

The Fifth House

Here's the side of you that's reserved for play, that only comes out when work is done and it's time to party and be entertained. This is the charming, creative, delightful side of you, where your hobbies, interests, and playmates are found. If it gives you joy, it's described here. Your Fifth House shines when you are creative, and it allows you to see a bit of yourself in those creations—anything from your child's smile to a piece of art. Traditionally this house also refers to speculation and gambling.

The Sixth House

This house is where you keep the side of you that decides how you like things to go along over the course of a day, the side of you that plans a schedule. Since it describes the duties you perform on a daily basis, it also refers to the nature of your work, your work environment, and how you take care of your health. It's how you function.

Pets are also traditionally a Sixth House issue, since we tend to them daily and incorporate them into our routine.

The Seventh House

Although it's traditionally known as the house of marriage, partnerships, and open enemies, the Seventh House really holds the side of you that only comes out when you're in the company of just one other person. This is the side of you that handles relating on a one-to-one basis. Whenever you use the word "my" to describe your relationship with another, it's this side of you talking.

The Eighth House

Here's the crisis expert side of you that emerges when it's time to handle extreme circumstances. This is the side of you that deals with agony and ecstasy, with sex, death, and all manner of mergers, financial and otherwise. The Eighth House also holds information on surgeries, psychotherapy, and the way we regenerate and rejuvenate after loss.

The Ninth House

This house holds the side of you that handles new experiences, foreign places, long-distance travel, and legal matters. Higher education, publishing, advertising, and forming opinions are handled here, as are issues involving the big picture, such as politics, religion, and philosophy.

The Tenth House

This spot in your chart describes what the public knows about you. Your career, reputation, and social status are found here. This is the side of you that takes time to learn and become accomplished. It describes the behavior you'll exhibit when you're in charge, and also the way you'll act in the presence of an authority figure. Most importantly, the Tenth House describes your vocation or life's work—whatever you consider your "calling."

The Eleventh House

Here's the team player in you, the side of you that helps you find your peer groups. The Eleventh House shows the types of organizations you're drawn to join, the kind of folks you consider kindred spirits, and how you'll act in group situations. It also shows the causes and social activities you hold near and dear.

The Twelfth House

This is the side of you that only comes out when you're alone, or in the mood to retreat and regroup. Here's where the secret side of you lives, where secret affairs and dealings take place. Here, too, is where matters like hospital stays are handled. Most importantly, the Twelfth House is the room where you keep all the traits and behaviors that you were taught early on to stifle, avoid, or deny—especially in public. This side of you is very fond of fantasy, illusion, and pretend play.

Aspects and Transits: The Fourth Building Block

Planets form angles to one another as they move through the heavens. If two planets are 90 degrees apart, they form a square. If they're 180 degrees apart, they're in opposition. Planets in aspect have twenty-four-hour communication going on. The particular angle that separates any two planets describes the nature of their conversation. Astrologers use six angles most often, each of which produces a different type of relationship or "conversation" between the planets they join. Let's go over the meaning of each of the aspects.

Ptolemic Aspects

The Conjunction: (0–8 degrees)

♂ When you hear that two things are operating "in conjunction," it means they're operating together. This holds true with planets as well. Two (or more) planets conjoined are a team, but some planets pair up more easily than others. Venus and the Moon work well together because both are feminine and receptive, but the Sun and Mars are both pretty feisty by nature, and may cause conflict. Planets in conjunction are usually sharing a house in your chart.

The Sextile: (60 degrees)

✳ The sextile links planets in compatible elements. That is, planets in sextile are either in fire and air signs or earth and water signs. Since these pairs of elements get along well, the sextile encourages an active exchange between the two planets involved, so these two parts of you will be eager to work together.

The Square: (90 degrees)

☐ A square aspect puts planets at cross-purposes. Friction develops between them and one will constantly challenge the other. You can see squares operating in someone who's fidgety or constantly restless. Although they're uncomfortable and even aggravating at times, your squares point to places where tremendous growth is possible.

The Trine: (120 degrees)

△ Trines are usually formed between planets of the same element, so they understand each other. They show an ease of communication not found in any of the other aspects, and they're traditionally thought of as "favorable." Of course, there is a downside to trines. Planets in this relationship are so comfortable that they can often get lazy and spoiled. (Sometimes they get so comfy they're boring.) Planets in trine show urges or needs that automatically support each other. The catch is that you've got to get them operating.

The Quincunx: (150 degrees)

⚻ This aspect joins two signs that don't share a quality, element, or gender, which makes it difficult for them to communicate with each other. It's frustrating. For that reason, this aspect has always been considered to require an adjustment in the way the two planets are used. Planets in quincunx often feel pushed, forced, or obligated to perform. They seem to correspond to health issues.

The Opposition: (180 degrees)

☍ When two planets are opposed, they work against each other. For example, you may want to do something, and if you have two opposing planets you may struggle with two very different approaches to getting the job done. If Mars and Neptune are opposing, you may struggle between getting a job done the quick, easy way or daydreaming about all the creative possibilities open to you. It's as if the two are standing across from one another with their arms folded, involved in a debate, neither willing to concede an inch. They can break out of their standoff only by first becoming aware of one another and then compromising. This aspect is the least difficult of the traditionally known "hard" aspects because planets "at odds" with one another can come to some sort of compromise.

Transits

While your horoscope (natal chart) reflects the exact position of planets at the time of your birth, the planets, as you know, move on. They are said to be "transiting." We interpret a transit as a planet in its "today" position making an aspect to a planet in your natal chart. Transiting planets represent incoming influences and events that your natal planets will be asked to handle. The nature of the transiting planet describes the types of situations that will arise, and the nature of your natal planet tells which "piece" of you you're working on at the moment. When a planet transits through a house or aspects a planet in your chart, you will have opportunities for personal growth and change. Every transit you experience adds knowledge to your personality.

Sun Transit

A Sun transit points to the places in your chart where you'll want special attention, pats on the back, and appreciation. Here's where you want to shine. These are often times of public acclaim, when we're recognized, congratulated, or applauded for what we've done. Of course, the ultimate Sun transit is our birthday, the day when we're all secretly sure that we should be treated like royalty.

Moon Transit

When the Moon touches one of the planets in our natal chart, we react from an emotional point of view. A Moon transit often corresponds to the highs and lows we feel that last only a day or two. Our instincts are on high during a Moon transit and we're more liable to sense what's going on around us than to consciously know something.

Mercury Transit

Transiting Mercury creates activity in whatever area of life it visits. The subject is communication of all kinds, so conversation, letters, and quick errands take up our time now. Because of Mercury's love of duality, events will often occur in twos—as if Hermes the trickster were having some fun with us—and we're put in the position of having to do at least two things at once.

Venus Transit

Transiting Venus brings times when the universe gives us a small token of warmth or affection or a well-deserved break. These are often sociable, friendly periods when we do more than our usual share of mingling and are more interested in good food and cushy conditions than anything resembling work. A Venus transit also shows a time when others will give us gifts. Since Venus rules money, this transit can show when we'll receive financial rewards.

Mars Transit

Mars transiting a house can indicate high-energy times. You're stronger and restless, or maybe you're cranky, angry, accident-prone, or violent. When Mars happens along, it's best to work or exercise hard to use up this considerable energy. Make yourself "too tired to be mad." These are ideal times to initiate projects that require a hard push of energy to begin.

Jupiter Transit

Under this transit you're in the mood to travel, take a class, or learn something new about the concerns of any house or planet Jupiter visits. You ponder the big questions. You grow under a Jupiter transit, sometimes even physically. Now is the time to take chances or risk a shot at the title. During a Jupiter transit you're luckier, bolder, and a lot more likely to succeed. This transit provides opportunities. Be sure to take advantage of them.

Saturn Transit

When Saturn comes along, we see things as they truly are. These are not traditionally great times, but they are often times when your greatest rewards appear. When Saturn transits a house or planet, he checks to see if the structure is steady and will hold up. You are then tested, and if you pass, you receive a symbolic certificate of some kind—and sometimes a real one, like a diploma. We will always be tested, but if we fail, life can feel very difficult. Firming up our lives is Saturn's mission. This is a great time to tap into Saturn's will-power and self-discipline to stop doing something. It is not traditionally a good time to begin new ventures, though.

Uranus Transit

The last thing in the world you'd ever expect to happen is exactly what you can expect under a Uranus transit. This is the planet of last-minute plan changes, reversals, and shock effects. So if you're feeling stuck in your present circumstances, when a Uranus transit happens along you won't be stuck for long. "Temporary people" often enter your life at these times, folks whose only purpose is to jolt you out of your present circumstances by appearing to provide exactly what you were sorely missing. That done, they disappear, leaving you with your life in a shambles. When these people arrive, enjoy them and allow them to break you out of your rut—just don't get comfortable.

Neptune Transit

A Neptune transit is a time when the universe asks only that you dream and nothing more. Your sensitivity heightens to the point that harsh sounds can actually make you wince. Compassion deepens, and psychic moments are common. A Neptune transit inspires divine discontent. You sigh, wish, feel nostalgic, and don't see things clearly at all. At the end of the transit, you realize that everything about you is different, that the reality you were living at the beginning of the transit has been gradually eroded or erased right from under your feet, while you stood right there upon it.

Pluto Transit

A Pluto transit is often associated with obsession, regeneration, and inevitable change. Whatever has gone past the point of no return, whatever is broken beyond repair, will pass from your life now. As with a Saturn transit, this time is not known to be wonderful, but when circumstances peel away everything from us and we're forced to see ourselves as we truly are, we do learn just how strong we are. Power struggles often accompany Pluto's visit, but being empowered is the end result of a positive Pluto transit. The secret is to let go, accept the losses or changes, and make plans for the future.

Retrograde Planets

Retrograde literally means "backwards." Although none of the planets ever really throw their engines in reverse and move backward, all of them, except the Sun and Moon, appear to do so periodically from our perspective here on Earth. What's happening is that we're moving either faster or slower than the planet that's retrograde, and since we have to look over our shoulder to see it, we refer to it as retrograde.

Mercury Retrograde: A Communication Breakdown

The way retrograde planets seem to affect our affairs varies from planet to planet. In Mercury's case, it means often looking back at Mercury-ruled things—communications, contracts, and so on. Keep in mind that Mercury correlates with Hermes, the original trickster, and you'll understand how cleverly disguised some of these errors can be. Communications become confused or are delayed. Letters are lost or sent to Auckland instead of Oakland, or they end up under the car seat for three weeks. We sign a contract or agreement and find out later that we didn't have all the correct information and what we signed was misleading in some way. We try repeatedly to reach someone on the telephone but can never catch them, or our communications devices themselves break down or garble information in some way. We feel as if our timing is off, so short trips often become more difficult. We leave the directions at home or write them down incorrectly. We're late for appointments due to circumstances beyond our control, or we completely forget about them.

Is there a constructive use for this time period? Yes. Astrologer Erin Sullivan has noted that the ratio of time Mercury spends moving retrograde (backward) and direct (forward) corresponds beautifully with the amount of time we humans spend awake and asleep—about a third of our lives. So this period seems to be a time to take stock of what's happened over the past three months and assimilate our experiences.

A good rule of thumb with Mercury retrograde is to try to confine activities to those that have "re" attached to the beginning of a word: reschedule, repair, return, rewrite, redecorate, restore, replace, renovate, or renew, for example.

Retrogrades of the Other Planets

With Venus retrograde every eighteen months for six weeks, relationships and money matters are delayed or muddled.

With Mars retrograde for eleven weeks and then direct for twenty-two months, actions initiated are often rooted in confusion or end up at cross-purposes to our original intentions. Typically under a Mars retrograde, the aggressor or initiator of a battle is defeated.

Jupiter retrogrades for four months and is direct for nine months. Saturn retrogrades for about the same amount of time. Each of the outer planets—Uranus, Neptune, and Pluto—stays retrograde for about six or seven months of every year. In general, remember that actions ruled by a particular planet quite often need to be repeated or done over when that planet is retrograde. Just make sure that whatever you're planning is something you don't mind doing twice.

Moon Void-of-Course

The Moon orbits Earth in about twenty-eight days, moving through each of the signs in about two days. As she passes through the thirty degrees of each sign, she visits with the planets in order by forming angles, or aspects, with them. Because she moves one degree in just two to two and a half hours, her influence on each planet lasts only a few hours. As she approaches the late degrees of the sign she's passing through, she eventually forms what will be her final aspect to another planet before leaving the sign. From this point until she actually enters the new sign, she is referred to as being "void-of-course (v/c)."

The Moon symbolizes the emotional tone of the day, carrying feelings of the sign she's "wearing" at the moment. She rules instincts. After she has contacted each of the planets, she symbolically "rests" before changing her costume, so her instincts are temporarily on hold. It's during this time that many people feel fuzzy, vague, or scattered. Plans or decisions do not pan out. Without the instinctual knowing the Moon provides as she touches each planet, we tend to be unrealistic or exercise poor judgment. The traditional definition of the void-of-course Moon is that "nothing will come of this," and it seems to be true. Actions initiated under a void-of-course Moon are often wasted, irrelevant, or incorrect—usually because information needed to make a sound decision is hidden or missing or has been overlooked.

Now, although it's not a good time to initiate plans when the Moon is void, routine tasks seem to go along just fine. However, this period is really ideal for what the Moon does best: reflection. It's at this time that we can assimilate what has occurred over the past few days. Use this time to meditate, ponder, and imagine. Let your conscious mind rest and allow yourself to feel.

On the lighter side, remember that there are other good uses for the void-of-course Moon. This is the time period when the universe seems to be most open to loopholes. It's a great time to make plans you don't want to fulfill or schedule things you don't want to do. In other words, like the saying goes, "To everything, there is a season." Even void-of-course Moons.

The Moon's Influence

As the Moon goes along her way, she magically appears and disappears, waxing to full from the barest sliver of a crescent just after she's new, then waning back to her invisible new phase again. The four quarters—the New Moon, the second quarter, the Full Moon, and the fourth quarter—correspond to the growth cycle of every living thing.

The Quarters

First Quarter

This phase begins when the Moon and the Sun are conjunct one another in the sky. At the beginning of the phase, the Moon is invisible, hidden by the brightness of the Sun as they travel together. The Moon is often said to be in her "dark phase" when she is just new. The New Moon can't actually be seen until 5½ to 12 hours after its birth. Toward the end of the first-quarter phase, as the Moon pulls farther away from the Sun and begins to wax toward the second quarter stage, a delicate silver crescent appears. This time corresponds to all new beginnings; this is the best time to begin a project.

Second Quarter

The second quarter begins when the Moon has moved 90 degrees away from the Sun. At this point the waxing Moon rises at about noon and sets at about midnight. It's at this time that she can be seen in the western sky during the early evening hours, growing in size from a crescent to her full beauty. This period corresponds to the development and growth of life, and with projects that are coming close to fruition.

Third Quarter

This phase begins with the Full Moon, when the Sun and Moon are opposite one another in the sky. It's now that the Moon can be seen rising in the east at sunset, a bit later each night as this phase progresses. This time corresponds to the culmination of plans and to maturity.

Fourth Quarter

This phase occurs when the Moon has moved 90 degrees past the full phase. She is decreasing in light, rises at midnight, and can be seen now in the eastern sky during the late evening hours. She doesn't reach the highest point in the sky until very early in the morning. This period corresponds to "disintegration"—a symbolic "drawing back" to reflect on what's been accomplished. It's now time to reorganize, clear the boards, and plan for the next New Moon stage.

The Moon Through the Signs

The signs indicate how we'll do things. Since the Moon rules the emotional tone of the day, it's good to know what type of mood she's in at any given moment. Here's a thumbnail sketch to help you navigate every day by cooperating with the Moon no matter what sign she's in.

Aries

The Moon in Aries is bold, impulsive, and energetic. It's a period when we feel feisty and maybe a little argumentative. This is when even the meekest aren't afraid to take a stand to protect personal feelings. Since Aries is the first sign of the zodiac, it's a natural starting point for all kinds of projects, and a wonderful time to channel all that "me first" energy to initiate change and new beginnings. Just watch out for a tendency to be too impulsive and stress-oriented.

Taurus

The Moon in Taurus is the Lady at her most solid and sensual, feeling secure and well rooted. There's no need to stress or hurry—and definitely no need to change anything. We tend to resist change when the Moon is in this sign, especially change that's not of our own making. We'd rather sit still, have a wonderful dinner, and listen to good music. Appreciating the beauty of the earth, watching a sunset, viewing some lovely art, or taking care of money and other resources are Taurus Moon activities.

Gemini

This mutable air sign moves around so quickly that when the Moon is here we're a bit more restless than usual, and may find that we're suddenly in the mood for conversation, puzzles, riddles, and word games. We want two—at least two—of everything. Now is a great time for letter writing, phone calls, or short trips. It's when you'll find the best shortcuts, and when you'll need to take them, too. Watch for a tendency to become a bit scattered under this fun, fickle Moon.

Cancer

☽ ♋ The Moon in this cardinal water sign is at her most nurturing. Here the Moon's concerns turn to home, family, children, and mothers, and we respond by becoming more likely to express our emotions and to be sympathetic and understanding toward others. We often find ourselves in the mood to take care of someone, to cook for or cuddle our dear ones. During this time, feelings run high, so it's important to watch out for becoming overly sensitive, dependent, or needy. Now is a great time to putter around the house, have family over, and tend to domestic concerns.

Leo

☽ ♌ The Leo Moon loves drama with a capital *D*. This theatrical sign has long been known for its big entrances, love of display, and need for attention. When the Moon is in this sign, we're all feeling a need to be recognized, applauded, and appreciated. Now, all that excitement, pride, and emotion can turn into melodrama in the blink of an eye, so it's best to be careful of overreacting or being excessively vain during this period. It's a great time to take in a show (or star in one), be romantic, or express your feelings for someone in regal style.

Virgo

☽ ♍ The Moon is at her most discriminating and detail-oriented in Virgo, the sign most concerned with fixing and fussing. This Moon sign puts us in the mood to clean, scour, sort, troubleshoot, and help. Virgo, the most helpful of all the signs, is also more health conscious, work-oriented, and duty bound. Use this period to pay attention to your diet, hygiene, and daily schedules.

Libra

☽ ♎ The Libra Moon is most oriented toward relationships and partnerships. Since Libra's job is to restore balance, however, you may find yourself in situations of emotional imbalance that require a delicate tap of the scales to set them right. In general, this is a social, polite, and friendly time, when others will be cooperative and agree more easily to compromise. A Libra Moon prompts us to make our surroundings beautiful, or to put ourselves in situations where beauty is all around us. This is a great time to decorate, shop for the home, or visit places of elegant beauty.

Scorpio

☽ ♏ Scorpio is the most intense sign, and when the Moon is here, she feels everything to the nth degree—and needless to say, we do, too. Passion, joy, jealousy, betrayal, love, and desire can take center stage in our lives now, as our emotions deepen to the point of possible obsession. Be careful of a tendency to become secretive or suspicious, or to brood over an offense that was not intended. Now is a great time to investigate a mystery, do research, "dig"—both figuratively and literally—and allow ourselves to become intimate with someone.

Sagittarius

☽ ♐ The Moon is at her most optimistic and willing to let go of things in Sagittarius. Jupiter, the planet of long-distance travel and education of the higher mind, makes this a great time to take off for adventure or attend a seminar on a topic you've always been interested in—say, philosophy or religion. This is the sign with the gift of prophecy and wisdom. When the Moon is in this sign, spend time outdoors, be spontaneous, and laugh much too loudly; just watch for a tendency toward excess, waste, and overdoing.

Capricorn

☽ ♑ The Moon is at her most organized, practical, and businesslike in Capricorn. She brings out the dutiful, cautious, and pessimistic side of us. Our goals for the future become all-important. Now is the time to tend to the family business, act responsibly, take charge of something, organize any part of our lives that has become scattered or disrupted, set down rules and guidelines, or patiently listen and learn. Watch for the possibility of acting too businesslike at the expense of others' emotions.

Aquarius

☽ ♒ The Aquarius Moon brings out the rebel in us. This is a great time to break out of a rut, try something different, and make sure everyone sees us for the unique individuals we are.

This sign is ruled by Uranus, so personal freedom and individuality are more important than anything now. Our schedules become topsy-turvy, and our causes become urgent. Watch for a tendency to become fanatical, act deliberately rebellious without a reason, or break tradition just for the sake of breaking it.

Pisces

☽ ♓ When the Moon slips into this sign, sleep, meditation, prayer, drugs, or alcohol is often what we crave to induce a trance-like state that will allow us to escape from the harshness of reality. Now is when we're most susceptible to emotional assaults of any kind, when we're feeling dreamy, nostalgic, wistful, or impressionable. Now is also when we're at our most spiritual, when our boundaries are at their lowest, when we're compassionate, intuitive, and sensitive to those less fortunate. This is the time to attend a spiritual group or religious gathering.

2014 Eclipse Dates

Times are in Eastern Time and are rounded off to the nearest minute. The exact time of an eclipse generally differs from the exact time of a New or Full Moon. For solar eclipses, "greatest eclipse" represents the time (converted from Local Mean Time) of the Moon's maximum obscuration of the Sun as viewed from the earth in right ascension. For lunar eclipses, the time shown is when the Moon reaches the centermost point of its journey through the shadow cast by the earth passing between it and the Sun. Data is from *Astronomical Phenomena for the Year 2014,* prepared by the United States Naval Observatory and Her Majesty's Nautical Almanac Office (United Kingdom).

April 15

Total Lunar Eclipse at 3:46 AM EDT — 25° ♎ 16'

April 29

Annular Solar Eclipse at 2:04 AM EDT — 8° ♉ 51'

October 8

Total Lunar Eclipse at 6:55 AM EDT — 15° ♈ 07'

October 23

Partial Solar Eclipse at 5:45 PM EDT — 0° ♏ 15'

2014 Retrograde Planets

Planet	Begin	Eastern	Pacific	End	Eastern	Pacific
Jupiter	11/06/13		9:03 pm	03/06/14	5:42 am	2:42 am
Jupiter	11/07/13	12:03 am		03/06/14	5:42 am	2:42 am
Venus	12/21/13	4:53 pm	1:53 pm	01/31/14	3:49 pm	12:49 pm
Mercury	02/06/14	4:43 pm	1:43 pm	02/28/14	9:00 am	6:00 am
Mars	03/01/14	11:23 am	8:23 am	05/19/14	9:31 pm	6:31 pm
Saturn	03/02/14	11:20 am	8:20 am	07/20/14	4:35 pm	1:35 pm
Pluto	04/14/14	7:47 pm	4:47 pm	09/22/14	8:36 pm	5:36 pm
Mercury	06/07/14	7:56 am	4:56 am	07/01/14	8:50 am	5:50 am
Neptune	06/09/14	3:51 pm	12:51 pm	11/15/14		11:04 pm
Neptune	06/09/14	3:51 pm	12:51 pm	11/16/14	2:04 am	
Uranus	07/21/14	10:53 pm	7:53 pm	12/21/14	5:45 pm	2:45 pm
Mercury	10/04/14	1:02 pm	10:02 am	10/25/14	3:17 pm	12:17 pm
Jupiter	12/08/14	3:41 pm	12:41 pm	04/08/15	12:57 pm	9:57 am

Eastern Time in plain type, **Pacific Time in bold type**

32

2014 Planetary Phenomena

Information on Uranus and Neptune assumes the use of a telescope. Resource: *Astronomical Phenomena for the Year 2014*, prepared by the U.S. Naval Observatory and the Royal Greenwich Observatory. The dates are expressed in Universal Time and must be converted to your Local Mean Time. (See the World Map of Time Zones on page 193.)

Planets Visible in Morning and Evening

Planet	Morning	Evening
Mercury	Feb 22–April 18 June 29–Aug 1 Oct 23–Nov 22	Jan 13–Feb 9 May 4–June 10 Aug 18–Oct 11 Dec 25–31
Venus	Jan 17–Sept 17	Jan 1–5 Dec 5–31
Mars	Jan 1–April 8	April 8–Dec 31
Jupiter	Jan 1–5 Aug 8–Dec 31	Jan 5–July 11
Saturn	Jan 1–May 10 Dec 6–31	May 10–Nov 1

Mercury

Mercury can only be seen low in the east before sunrise or low in the west after sunset.

Venus

Venus is a brilliant object in the evening sky until the end of the first week of January, when it becomes too close to the Sun for observation. It reappears in the third week of January as a morning star and can be seen in the morning sky until mid-September, when it again becomes too close to the Sun for observation. From early December until the end of the year it is visible in the evening sky.

Mars

Mars rises around midnight at the beginning of the year. It is at opposition on April 8, when it is visible throughout the night as a bright, reddish object. Its eastern elongation gradually decreases, and from mid-July until the end of the year it is visible only in the evening sky.

Jupiter

Jupiter can be seen from the beginning of the year for most of the night. It is at opposition on January 5, when it can be seen throughout the night. From early April it can be seen only in the evening sky. In the second week of July it becomes too close to the Sun for observation until early August, when it reappears in the morning sky. From mid-November it can be seen for more than half the night.

Saturn

Saturn rises well after midnight at the beginning of the year. It is at opposition on May 10, when it can be seen throughout the night, and from early August until the start of November it is visible only in the evening sky. It then becomes too close to the Sun for observation until in early December it reappears, and it can be seen in the morning sky for the rest of the year.

Uranus

Uranus is visible at the beginning of the year in the evening sky. In the second week of March it becomes too close to the Sun for observation and reappears in the last week of April in the morning sky. Uranus is at opposition on October 7. Its eastward elongation gradually decreases, and Uranus can be seen for more than half the night.

Neptune

Neptune is visible at the beginning of the year in the evening sky. In early February it becomes too close to the Sun for observation and reappears in mid-March in the morning sky. Neptune is at opposition on August 29 and from late November can be seen only in the evening sky.

2014 Weekly Forecasts

by Pam Ciampi

Overview of 2014

By now everyone knows that the world didn't end in 2012, and that even though it's been tough, we also survived 2013. The big question on everyone's mind this year is whether the stars indicate that things are going to get better in 2014. The short answer is that while most of 2014 is going to be more of the same, there are a few bright lights on the horizon that provide hope for the future.

The "same old" part of the 2014 equation is the signature pattern of the disturbing Uranus/Pluto square that we've been dealing with for the past few years. This Uranus/Pluto conflict between the new order and the old guard is the astrological poster child for all the uneasy earth shifts, global conflicts, economic hardships, and social modifications the world has been going through since 2012. It comes to a head in April when Jupiter in Cancer and Mars in Libra move into the middle of this ongoing Pluto/Uranus conflict and all four planets square off at the 13th degree to form a super-charged pattern called a Grand Cross. Because the planets are all in cardinal signs, it is called a Cardinal Grand Cross. Although this formation isn't visible in the skies, its importance is monumental, with far-reaching consequences. Although Uranus and Pluto are on a cosmic schedule to do battle exactly seven times between 2012 and 2015, the one bit of good news is that with this Grand Cross, the battle will be more than halfway over.

Saturn also continues last year's story line as it remains in Scorpio until the end of the year, which means that dirty secrets that affect large portions of the population will continue to make headlines. But there's a mid-year shift when Jupiter moves from Cancer (where it smiles on real estate and the food industry) into Leo (where the focus of good luck moves to the entertainment industry and recreational centers).

The bright lights this year are a "last chance" trine between Saturn and Jupiter, two harmonious Solar Eclipses, and lots of feminine energy to help us make the transition from the old to the new. These are all indications of the positive steps that are being taken to move us into a new stage of civilization. The Saturn/Jupiter trine, one of the most powerful signs of this progress in balancing future growth with the old paradigms, is a last-chance opportunity because these two planets will not connect in a trine again until 2026.

Other happy sidebars are the positive connections that Jupiter, Neptune, and Pluto make to the Taurus Solar Eclipse in April and the gentle and healing influence that Neptune in Pisces exerts over the Scorpio Solar Eclipse in October. An additional favorable factoid is that 2014 is another year with a preponderance of planets in the water and earth signs (Cancer, Scorpio, Pisces, Capricorn). This is an indication that the earth will be experiencing a downtime, a time when it is possible to replenish as well as to make needed repairs. Because water and earth signs are fertile energies that provide the right environment for new beginnings, it's reasonable to assume that we will emerge from this downtime stronger than ever.

One of the big issues in 2014 may be how to protect our privacy, because Mercury, the communications guru of the zodiac, will be spending about a third of the year in water signs that are concerned with keeping things private, staying under the radar, and keeping secrets. If there is a breach in online privacy, it would negatively affect billions of people all over the world.

The actor Jeremy Irons once said: "We all have our time machines. Some take us back; they're called memories. Some take us forward; they're called dreams."

This is a year when, if we're willing to change, it's entirely possible that our memories and our dreams will become one and the same.

Hot Spots in 2014

February	Mercury retrograde (in Pisces/Aquarius)
April	Cardinal Grand Cross Taurus Solar Eclipse
May	Saturn/Jupiter trine
June	Mercury retrograde (in Cancer/Gemini)

July	Jupiter enters Leo
October	Mercury retrograde (in Scorpio/Libra)
	Scorpio Solar Eclipse
December	Saturn enters Sagittarius

January 1–5

New Moon warning. Venus retrograde. Jupiter retrograde.

At first glance, a New Moon on the first day of 2014 looks like an auspicious beginning. But when this Capricorn New Moon pairs up with Pluto, it sets off a conflict with Uranus that turns into more of a warning than something to celebrate. New Moons are lunar signals of a time of new beginnings, but the judgmental side of the Capricorn/Pluto combination issues a serious warning that we either change now or live to suffer the consequences. Another reason why this year looks like more of the same is that both Venus and Jupiter start off the year in retrograde motion, which is exactly how we left them at the end of 2013. In addition to the retrograde, Venus has another strike against it because it's uncomfortably placed in Capricorn. Saturn-ruled Capricorn is a sign that mirrors the seriousness of the New Moon by insisting on duty and responsibility first and pleasure second. This means that for the time being it looks like last year's austerity measures will remain in place. However, economic projections may begin to show some signs of life after Venus turns forward in a few weeks. Jupiter also starts out the year retrograde, which restricts travel and makes luck a little harder to come by. Because Jupiter retrograde can also be a test of faith, it's a time to look inside ourselves, rather than to the outer world, for the answers to the big questions about our social, political, and economic future.

January 6–12

Grand Water Trine. Sun/Moon trine. Jupiter/Sirius meetup. Mercury changes signs.

Two supportive trines and a sign change for Mercury brighten the atmosphere this week. Tuesday, January 7, is one of the days when the heavens give us a gift in the form of Jupiter by a time-honored technique known as the "translation of light" coming within orb of a Grand Water Trine with Saturn and the Pisces Moon. This triangle is a celestial reminder that when intuition and vision combine with good old-fashioned know-how, anything is possible. Another bit of good news arrives on Friday, January 10, when the Sun and Moon form a trine in practical Capricorn and Taurus. This combo gives extra points to anyone who finds a way to fuse the arts with money and worldly success. On the same day, lucky Jupiter pairs with Sirius, the brightest fixed star in the sky. Sirius is part of the Canis Major constellation, which is why is it also called the "Dog Star." Since Jupiter is in Cancer and Sirius brings success, this fortunate duo will shine a light on women and families, the food industry, and real estate values. Jupiter and Sirius have two meetups scheduled for this year, the first in January and the next in April. On Saturday, January 11, Mercury sprints out of Capricorn and into Aquarius. When Mercury moves into the thought-based vistas of Aquarius, the general style of thinking and communicating becomes less practical and more theoretical. During the next few weeks when Mercury is visiting Aquarius, those little gray cells will help you to think outside the box and come up with radical visions that offer solutions. Because Aquarius is a fixed sign, communications can be as stubborn as they are quirky. It may be harder to tell the difference between an exciting new take on things and something that is truly weird and bizarre.

January 13–19

Full Moon. Sun in Aquarius.

The Full Moon on Wednesday, January 15, lights up this week for the signs of Capricorn and Cancer, but everyone can relate to the inner/outer polarity between mother/home/family (Cancer) and father/career/success (Capricorn). Because boundary-loving Saturn is also a player in this Full Moon, January looks like a month where staying with the status quo will be your shortest road to success. But like January's namesake, the two-headed Roman god Janus who could see in both directions at once, this month gives a nod to the past as well as to the future, as we see on Sunday, January 19, when the old is left behind as the Sun moves out of Capricorn and into the futuristic sign of Aquarius. The four weeks of the year that the Sun spends in Aquarius are the best time for innovations and groundbreaking visions as well as for one-of-kind experiences. Besides bringing us one month closer to spring, this is a time to envision new ways to deal with things that are stale and past their sell-by date. Aquarius energy can go one of two ways; it can either completely make over a situation, or it can destroy it entirely, forcing you to start over from the beginning. It's your choice how you use the energy.

January 20–26

Moon/Venus trine. Sun/Moon air trine. Jupiter/Pluto face-off.
This week features two heavenly handouts to help you navigate the obstacles that a tough square throws in your way. The first perk comes at the beginning of the week on Monday, January 20, in the form of a practical trine between the Virgo Moon and Venus in Capricorn that makes it easy to manifest your heart's desires. The second is an air trine between the Aquarius Sun and the Libra Moon. This alignment, on Tuesday, January 21, favors all kinds of social gatherings, humanitarian pursuits, lovers, and friends. Between this week's Sun/Moon trine and the Jupiter/Sirius alignment earlier in the month, this should be a particularly auspicious time for folks with planets in Aquarius, Libra, and Cancer. The Jupiter/Pluto opposition on Sunday, January 26, is an indication that growth and expansion will not come without a power struggle. Because Jupiter is retrograde, this is a signal that greed or partisan politics could play a negative role in reaching successful outcomes. This conflict between Jupiter and Pluto will be in effect only for the next two weeks, but it will return for an encore (Cardinal Grand Cross) in April.

January 27–February 2

New Moon. Chinese New Year. Venus/Pluto meetup. Mercury changes signs.
Things really get going at the end of this week, which is also the end of the month, but they're going in a lot of different directions. After

the Aquarius New Moon kicks off Chinese New Year and it looks like the economy may be showing some signs of life, Mercury takes a turn by going off into an intuitive huddle. On Thursday, January 30, the Moon on its monthly trek meets up with the Sun in the sign of Aquarius. This alignment forms the Aquarius New Moon that signals new beginnings for the month ahead. If you follow the Chinese calendar, the Aquarius New Moon also marks the start of the Chinese New Year on Friday, January 31. In Chinese astrology, 2014 is the Year of the Wood Horse, which is said to be a strong year with positive energy because the wood element adds stability to the Horse's exuberant nature. Given what's been happening during the last two years of the Dragon and the Snake, it looks like the stable Wood Horse has galloped onto the scene just in time. On Friday, January 31, the same day as Chinese New Year, Venus ends her retrograde cycle and lands right in Pluto's lap, which can indicate a crisis or transformation for personal relationships and/or global economics. Then, as if Friday, January 31, weren't already busy enough, it's also the day Mercury leaves Aquarius and moves into Pisces. Get ready to be very flexible for the next three months, because Mercury will be moving back and forth between these two signs until April. Starting today, communications will favor right-brained, sensitive Pisces, but next week Mercury will turn retrograde and switch back to cool and detached, left-brained Aquarius. Then a few weeks later in March, things will get intuitive again when Mercury goes back to Pisces. With all these shifts, it's no wonder that Mercury is called "the trickster"!

February 3–9

First Mercury retrograde of the year. Sun/Moon air trine.
Mercury's retrograde is the headliner for this week, with an easy trine between the Sun and Moon as a sidebar. On Thursday, February 6, Mercury makes its first standstill of the year as it appears to turn backward (goes retrograde) until the end of the month. All the planets, except the Sun and Moon, go retrograde from time to time, but Mercury is the only one that does so three or four times a year. In 2014, Mercury will retrograde in February, June, and October. Mercury retrograde has become the one thing that most

non-astrologers know, and fear, about the astrological calendar, but few realize that the abbreviation for retrograde (R_x) comes from the Latin *recipe*, which means "to take." R_x is also said to be a corruption of the symbol for the planet Jupiter (♃), a symbol that was once found on prescriptions to invoke that god's blessings to help the patient recover. As the information specialist, Mercury needs a break sometimes, and so do you. If you persist in ignoring this celestial signal, your experiences could include some of the more negative potentials of this transit: annoying personal and business miscommunications, travel mix-ups or delays, and electronic or mechanical breakdowns. While Mercury is retrograde, it's time to relax (harder than you think). View it as a healing period when its okay to take time out to rest, recuperate, and rejuvenate your body, mind, and spirit. An easy trine between the Aquarius Sun and the Gemini Moon closes out the week. Because both planets are in signs that love the social networking scene, Sunday, February 9, would be a great day to have a conference call or just to meet up with friends.

February 10–16

Valentine's Day Full Moon. Mercury retrograde plays tricks.

Get ready for an unusual Valentine's Day where you could be looking for love in all the wrong places. Not only does this holiday for lovers fall on the same day as the Leo Full Moon, but this year Mercury retrograde (see February 3–9) is also in on the party. The kickoff is on Wednesday, February 12, when Mercury retrograde backs out of Pisces to finish up its second tour in Aquarius, which puts Mercury in the slot next to the Aquarius Sun. This retrograde could play the part of the bad fairy who casts a spell that ignites the drama-queen side of the Leo Full Moon on Friday, February 14. Because Leo is a fiery sign that loves excitement and everything that sparkles, this combination is sure to produce a big bang of a Valentine's Day. So whatever plans you make, be sure to lead with your heart. Mars, which is still in Libra, the sign of lovers, adds sparks to the flame of the Leo Full Moon. If you happen to find yourself alone on Valentine's Day, be sure to give yourself a special treat, and stay away from questionable online dating sites, where the Mercury retrograde might trick you into something quite different than what you bargained for.

February 17–23

Sun in Pisces. Sun/Moon water trine. Sun/Neptune meetup.

There are some big changes ahead in the celestial weather, but you'll find that out next week. This week is all sweetness and light. It's time to chill out and "go fishing" on Tuesday, February 18, because that's when the Sun moves out of the airy, intellectual sign of Aquarius and enters the watery emotional depths of Pisces the Fish. This movement shifts the energy into a gentle, more sensitive gear that operates under the radar. The next four weeks, when the Sun is traveling through Pisces, are a prime time of the year for using your imagination, being creative, and being of service to others. Some folks who regularly do such things include artists and musicians, doctors and healers, counselors and saints. The watchwords are "dream big but stay real." Since Pisces operates primarily through feelings and intuition, this overlay on the Jupiter/Uranus conflict could weave the next four weeks into your fondest fantasy or a spine-chilling nightmare. If you find yourself in a place where you're overwhelmed by your personal demons, the Pisces cure is to help out somebody in even worse shape. On Wednesday, February 19, the Moon moves into Scorpio and trines the Pisces Sun. Use this easy Sun/Moon combo to do things that call for secrecy or to dig for hidden treasure. Mercury remains retrograde (see February 3–9) for the rest of this week. There's an important once-a-year event on Sunday, February 23, when the Pisces Sun pairs with Neptune, and sensitivity levels are high and reality levels are low. Even though the Sun/Neptune pairing lasts for only a few days, it could still be a dangerous time for schemers as well as dreamers.

February 24–March 2

Jupiter/Uranus conflict. New Moon warning. Mars and Saturn turn retrograde.

"Due to turbulent conditions ahead, the captain asks that you fasten your seat belt." That's the news from the cockpit on Monday, February

24, which is launch time for a nine-week conflict between Jupiter and Uranus that will leave you either completely changed or still holding on for dear life to the past. Either way, Jupiter and Uranus will be battling it out until April, when they join the Cardinal Grand Cross that is the most important stellar crossroad of the year. But at the moment, this Jupiter/Uranus conflict is getting ready to reinvent the new normal, which will include things that shift you out of your conventional patterns, such as erratic twists and turns of fate, sudden opportunities, and unexpected surprises. Unstable conditions in times like these can make great heroes. If your head is in the right place, you could be one of them. Traffic on the celestial highway is also heavy at the end of this week, and you may find that you have to take a detour. Everything is quiet at the beginning of the week. On Friday, February 28, the Mercury retrograde ends and communications return to normal. Then things get interesting with the Pisces New Moon the next day, March 1. Although the Pisces New Moon usually marks a creative period of new beginnings when it seems like dreams really can come true, this year's Pisces New Moon is not like the others. The first reason it's different is that on the same day as the New Moon, March 1, Mars begins its three-month retrograde period. Any retrograde period is not favorable for starting new projects; it's a time to put the brakes on them—but with Mars it's especially so, because Mars is the initiator of the zodiac. If that wasn't a good enough reason not to initiate anything new this month, on the day after that, Sunday, March 2, Saturn follows suit by also turning retrograde for the next four months. Because these Mars and Saturn retrogrades completely upstage the Pisces New Moon, it looks like it might be better to take a step back and review your plan book than to try to get anything going this month. If life circumstances insist that you begin something new this month, take it nice and slow and use extreme caution.

March 3–9

Mardi Gras. Venus changes signs. Jupiter direct. Daylight Saving Time begins.
Although the slow-down effect of the Mars and Saturn retrogrades (see February 24–March 2) is still in force, there's also a lot of positive

energy available this week to take the edge off. The week starts off on a high note with the Sun making an easy sextile with the sensuous Taurus Moon on Mardi Gras (Fat Tuesday) on Tuesday, March 4, which should heighten the carnival atmosphere. Even though things come back down to earth the next day, Ash Wednesday, March 5, Venus takes to the skies as it finally ends its difficult four-month tour of Capricorn and enters Aquarius. During the next four weeks while Venus is visiting Aquarius, you can bet that the general attitude and ways of thinking about love and finance will be calm, cool, and collected but definitely out of the box. There's more good news the next day, Thursday, March 6, when lucky Jupiter starts moving forward again for the first time this year. Because Jupiter is traveling in the sign of Cancer, this movement could signal a positive surge in areas like the food industry or the real estate market or for women's issues. This is also the week when Daylight Saving Time (DST) goes into effect. Mark your calendar for Sunday, March 9, as the day to "spring ahead" by setting your clocks ahead one hour before you go to bed on Saturday.

March 10–16

Sun/Moon water trine. Sun/Saturn trine. Full Moon.

Continuing on last week's upbeat note, this week features a couple of sensitive water trines and a mysterious Full Moon at the end of the week. The first water trine, between the Pisces Sun and the Cancer Moon, on Tuesday, March 11, carries a sympathetic energy and the ability to delve deep into cosmic consciousness. This gentle but intense water trine makes it a good time to get involved in creative projects or to receive healing treatments. The danger of a Pisces/Cancer water trine is that it's so easy to get lost in time-wasting but harmless activities, like online gaming, as well as more dangerous activities, like yielding to addictions. This same theme is repeated with a slightly different variation on Thursday, March 13, when the Pisces Sun trines Saturn in Scorpio. Although Saturn is the most well-behaved planet in the solar system, a Pisces/Scorpio combo can add an element of too much and too deep to the mix, which under certain circumstances can also spell danger. Enjoy this trine, but keep your radar on high alert. These two trines are only appetizers to the final Full Moon of the winter season on Sunday, March 16. The Virgo Full Moon is your monthly signal to wind up projects, finish activities, and generally bring things to their natural conclusion. In the sign of perfectionist Virgo, this Full Moon also signals one of the easiest times of the year to release negative criticism and stop unhealthy habits. Virgo's love of details will also help you take the necessary steps to improve your health and/or your work as well as to help those who are less fortunate. Astrologer Isabel Hickey believed that the spiritual lesson of the Virgo/Pisces polarity was to "serve or suffer."

March 17–23

Mercury changes signs. Sun in Aries. Spring equinox. Sun/Moon fire trine. Mercury/Neptune meetup.

On Monday, March 17 (also St. Patrick's Day), Mercury celebrates by finally finishing up its extended seven-week tour in Aquarius and entering Pisces again for three more weeks. This switchback brings the curtain down on the Aquarius/Pisces/Aquarius/Pisces dance that Mercury's been doing since the beginning of the year. While that's a relief, the bad news is that Mercury is not at its best in Pisces, where emotions reign supreme and facts are often confused with feelings. The newsflash of this week comes on Thursday, March 20, with the announcement that winter is officially over. March 20 is the day that the Sun moves into Aries, which is also the first day of spring, or the vernal equinox. It is the first of the big four seasonal markers (spring, summer, fall, winter) in the Sun's journey through the sky. Because the vernal equinox is one of the two days a year when the hours of day and night are equal, it's a day for all of us to push the pause button and perform a self-check to see if our lives are in balance. Since the body, mind, and spirit are naturally reenergized in springtime, this is an easy week to get motivated and make plans for a brand-new beginning. These plans will get more help on the next day, Friday, March 21, when the newly minted Aries Sun makes a fire trine with the Sagittarius Moon and you may find yourself involved in an adventure. A lot of folks may be looking through rose-colored glasses on Saturday, March 22, when Mercury and Neptune pair up for their once-a-year event, so remember to keep it real. This Mercury/Neptune twosome doubles up on sensitivity, which can be a good as well as a bad thing.

March 24–30

Mercury/Jupiter trine. Moon/Jupiter/Saturn trine. Another New Moon warning. Jupiter/Uranus/Pluto T-square.

You can expect your emotional faucets to be turned on full force early this week with Mercury, Jupiter, Saturn, and the Moon all in water signs. But like all things, the emotional waterfall comes to an end with the Aries New Moon on Sunday, March 30. If Mercury in Pisces turned your brain to mush last week, you'll be happy to hear that on Wednesday, March 26, the messenger planet forms an engaging and sympathetic trine with Jupiter in Cancer. Although it's not less emotional, this Mercury/Jupiter trine should result in happier as well as more compassionate feelings. The therapeutic energy of Pisces and Cancer expands further when the Moon also moves into Pisces on Friday, March 28. Its first action is to form a two-day water trine with Jupiter in Cancer and then another trine with Saturn in Scorpio on Saturday, March 29. The healing energies of these water trines are particularly helpful if you use them to push back the continuing low-level frustrations of retrograde Mars and Saturn. The end of this week is a different kind of new beginning. Sunday, March 30, is the first New Moon of spring, the passionate Aries New Moon. Although every New Moon is the time of the month that's best for new beginnings, this year's Aries New Moon is paired with unpredictable Uranus, which means that this Aries New Moon runs right into the middle of the ongoing conflict between Uranus and Pluto that's been waging for the last few years. As a result, you might run into some trouble at this time if you try to start up your Aries engine. To make matters worse, Jupiter joins the Moon/Uranus/Pluto party to form a T-square. If you want to make a new beginning under this year's Aries New Moon, your task will be to find a way to preserve the good in the past before you can start to transition into the future.

March 31–April 6

Sun/Uranus meetup. Sign change for Venus.

You might want to hold your horses this week, because on Wednesday, April 2, the Aries Sun pairs up with Uranus for a once-a-year get-together that ushers in a time when taking chances could be risky business. While this Sun/Uranus combination brings possibilities for new insights or breakthroughs with authority figures, the downside can be violent eruptions or rebellions that destroy more than they create. The wise will also see the Sun/Uranus merger as a warning of the Cardinal Grand Cross later this month. Mars still retrograde and Venus in Pisces are both good indicators of the possibilities of softening any surprises from the Sun/Uranus pairing. The chances of the ongoing Uranus/Pluto/Jupiter conflict erupting into full-fledged chaos are also lessened because with the retrograde in nonconfrontational Libra, Mars's full fighting force isn't up to speed. On Saturday, April 5, when Venus moves into Pisces, this gentle combo will add bits of compassion and a desire for peace to the mix.

April 7–13

Mercury changes signs. Sun/Mars face-off. Sun/Moon trine. Venus/Neptune meetup.

Fire signs light up the sky this week when another planet enters Aries and the Sun and Mars have a face-off. But there's a harmonizing aspect between Venus and Neptune that keeps things on the down low and counteracts the volatile effects. The week starts off with a bang on Monday, April 7, when Mercury exits Pisces and steps into Aries for the shortest (two-week) tour of the year. During this time, all communications will shift from the intuitive, right-brained Pisces style to the Aries straight-talk mode of making snap decisions that are flavored with wild enthusiasm and a burning need to make things happen now. Although this swift and direct style of communication appeals to some, there's no worry if it gets annoying and overbearing because it will all be over before you know it. The fire gets even hotter the next day, Tuesday, April 8, when retrograde Mars rises at sunset to face its once-a-year opposition with the Sun. Even though powerful Mars is weakened from its retrograde motion and its detriment in

Libra, it is still a force to be reckoned with. A Sun/Mars opposition is a once-a-year face-off when confrontations tend to reach their climax. The firepower triples on Wednesday, April 9, when the Aries Sun trines the Leo Moon. Hopefully the diplomatic side of Mars in Libra will prevail, and local and global problems will be solved with words, not guns. Venus throws some water on the fire on Friday, April 11, when it pairs with Neptune in Pisces. The positive side of this mushy Venus/Neptune alignment is compassion and service to others; the negative side includes seductions, addictions, and denial.

April 14–20

Pluto retrograde. Full Moon. Total Lunar Eclipse. Passover. Mercury/Uranus meetup. Sun in Taurus. Easter. Jupiter/Pluto face-off. Get ready to rock and roll, because this is one of those weeks when the music never stops. It starts off with a major directional change for Pluto on the same day that Mercury and Uranus decide to stir the pot, then moves right into the spring eclipse season with the first Lunar Eclipse of the year. The grand finale is a sign change for the Sun that ushers in a late Easter. It all begins on Monday, April 14, when Pluto begins its five-month retrograde period. Pluto retrogrades can be times of private upheavals that lead to complete transformations in your outer life. During the next five months, it's important to remember that although you may not always be able to control the circumstances of a Pluto retrograde, you are always in control of how you choose to respond or react to them. Mental sparks begin to fly on that same day, April 14, because that's when Mercury/Uranus have their once-a-year meetup that floods the mind with exciting new information and encourages out-of-the-box types of thinking and communications. As usual, the 15th of April is Tax Day, but this year it is also the same day as Passover and is also home to the Libra Full Moon/Total Lunar Eclipse. The eclipse on April 15 is the first total eclipse in almost four years and the first to be visible in its entirety from North America since 2011. It is scheduled to last for one hour and eighteen minutes, and if we use the ancient formula that says that the effects of a lunar eclipse will be felt for as many *months* as the eclipse lasts in *hours*, then this eclipse could spark a surge of protests, outbursts, and explosions over the next five weeks. During this time (which includes the Cardinal Grand Cross next week), it might be a good idea to stay calm, have patience, and try to keep things on the down low. An eclipse will influence you on a personal level if it falls on the same degree as a personal planet in your natal chart. The beat moves on Saturday, April 19, when the Sun leaves forceful Aries in the dust and lumbers into Taurus. Like the symbol for Taurus, the Bull, the month that the Sun is in Taurus can a very powerful and creative time when it is easy to make steady progress if you stay on task. Because Taurus is a slow-moving energy that loves and appreciates the status quo, the next four weeks are not a time when abrupt changes of direction will be welcome. On Sunday, April 20, Jupiter makes a second opposition with Pluto (the first was in January), but this one is different because this time Jupiter is direct, which means its benevolent influence is stronger. The Jupiter/Pluto opposition joins the Lunar Eclipse as a preview of next week's Cardinal Grand Cross. The Christian holiday (holy day) of Easter on Sunday, April 20, celebrates the theme of resurrection, which is a yearly reminder that life comes out of death and that light follows darkness. Easter Sunday is considered to be late this year, because although Easter is always on a "Sun" day, it falls on the Sunday after the first Full Moon following the first day of spring, and this year the first Full Moon was on Tuesday, April 15.

April 21–27

Cardinal Grand Cross. Second Jupiter/Sirius meetup. Moon/Jupiter/Saturn trine.

After last week you might feel like you need a nap, but there's no rest in sight. On Wednesday, April 23, Mars retrogrades to the 13th degree of Libra, which sets up the fourth point of the Cardinal Grand Cross—the major crossroad of 2014. The four players on the pivotal points of this Grand Cross are all at the 13th degree of cardinal signs: Uranus in Aries, Jupiter in Cancer, Mars in Libra, and Pluto in Capricorn. Symbolically, a cross is a universal symbol of death and rebirth. Astrologically, a Grand Cross is a pattern made up of four points that create six difficult and challenging aspects (four squares and two oppositions). The exact alignment of these four planets meeting at the crossroad of cardinal signs is considered by some to be a symbol of the transition from the end of the Age of Pisces to the beginning of the Age of Aquarius. It's also considered to be a call that it's time for the world to change (Uranus), to expand its horizons (Jupiter), to mobilize its forces (Mars), and to transform its institutions (Pluto). If this energy is not used for positive purposes, the picture could get ugly in the form of earthquakes and tidal waves (Uranus), things getting blown out of proportion (Jupiter), wars and bloodshed (Mars), and social, political, or economic disasters (Pluto). On a lighter note, on the same day as the 13th degree Cardinal Grand Cross, April 23, Mercury exits Aries to take a second trip through Taurus that will slow down communications for the next two weeks. Although we are still under the shadow of the Grand Cross, there are two celestial lights that send a promise of hope for the future. Jupiter pairs for the final time this year with fixed star Sirius on Friday, April 25 (see January 6–12). This happy alignment between Jupiter and Sirius will have the greatest effect on women and children and real estate values. On the same day, April 25, there will also a calming three-way trine between the Pisces Moon, Jupiter in Cancer, and Saturn in Scorpio.

April 28–May 4

New Moon. Solar Eclipse. Venus changes signs. Moon/Jupiter meetup. Moon/Saturn trine.

It's still eclipse season and this next one will be one to remember. There's also a tricky sign change on tap for Venus, as well as a variation on last week's Jupiter/Saturn/Moon water trine that could bring a lucky pot of gold into the mix. Depending on your time zone, the Taurus New Moon ushers in the Annular Solar Eclipse late on Monday, April 28, or early on Tuesday, April 29. Although this partial eclipse is not as dramatic as the Total Lunar Eclipse two weeks earlier, because it will only be visible from parts of Antarctica and Australia, the influence of a Solar Eclipse is stronger, and this one is much more positive because the patterns of the eclipse include good connections to the Sun and Moon from Neptune and Jupiter as well as a trine from Pluto that mark it as both a hopeful and an upbeat sign of future progress. Things shift on Friday, May 2, when Venus enters Aries, and for the next four weeks the ultimate feminine planet will be traveling uncomfortably through the ultimate male sign. Some relationships may tank during this time, because when Venus is in Aries, passions run hot and the ability to cooperate is at an all-time low. But it's not all bad, because Venus also rules finance, where an over-infusion of aggressive Aries energy could drive an upward spike in the economy. Even though Saturn is still retrograde, long-range Saturnian goals get a boost on Sunday, May 4, when the Cancer Moon pairs with expansive Jupiter and they form a double trine to Saturn. Success is yours if you are patient and employ a disciplined approach.

May 5–11

Mercury sign change. Sun/Saturn face-off. Moon/Mars meetup.
High-speed Mercury is finally heading toward home base for a well-deserved rest. After zipping through Aries and Taurus in a record two weeks for each sign, Mercury slides into Gemini on Wednesday, May 7, where it enjoys status as a favorite son. With Mercury in Gemini, sales, marketing, and social networking will be brimming with new ways to connect that have never been thought of before. Retrograde Saturn faces off against the Taurus Sun on Saturday, May 10, which makes it the kind of day when you have to deal with obstacles. Whenever a planet opposes the Sun, it is always closest to the earth and in retrograde motion. Even though Taurus is known for never giving up and Scorpio is famous for taking no prisoners, the secret of this Sun/Saturn face-off is that deep down the Taurus Sun really wants change and behind its nasty façade Saturn in Scorpio really wants to be loved. Mother's Day, on Sunday, May 11, may be marred when a lovely Libra Moon is unfortunately paired with Mars, creating a combination that could reignite the fireworks of last month's Cardinal Grand Cross.

May 12–18

Full Moon. Venus/Uranus meetup.

The Scorpio Full Moon is the bright light in this fairly quiet week. The Full Moon on Wednesday, May 14, is a time of completion, when it's best to wrap up projects and finalize deals. It's also a good time to find the sweet spot between whatever you need to let go of (Scorpio Moon) while holding tight to your security blanket (Taurus Sun). Because this Moon is paired with sensible Saturn and also makes a trine to idealistic Jupiter, this is a week to work hard (Saturn) and make your dreams (Jupiter) come true. The next day, Thursday, May 15, Venus has its once-a-year meetup with Uranus as it makes its way through Aries. Because this Venus/Uranus alignment can bring surprises about love and/or money, there's a possibility of love (or lust) at first sight or for going on a spending spree. If a Venus/Uranus paring hits a sensitive spot in your natal chart, the consequences can last a lifetime. This is a good week to keep a tight grip on your heart as well as your wallet. It's also time to start thinking about how to start up your internal engine again, because this is the final week of the three-month Mars retrograde.

May 19–25

Mars direct. Sun in Gemini. Jupiter/Saturn trine.

All is clear on the horizon this week, because we've got three positive energy shifts on standby. Monday, May 19, is a red-letter day to take positive action, because that's when Mars takes off the handcuffs it's been wearing since turning retrograde last March. By getting into gear and moving forward again, Mars sends out the signal that it's time for us to power up our engines and get ready to charge. The next day, May 20, the Sun mirrors this lead from Mars when it exits slow-moving Taurus and enters fast-paced and anything-goes-as-long-as-it's-not-boring Gemini for the next four weeks. During the month that the Sun spends in Gemini, there's a restless, curious feeling in the air that can increase communications and social networking (web, mobile, face to face) or just be a collective energy that craves something new and wants to mix things up. On Saturday, May 24, a powerful trine between Jupiter in Cancer and Saturn in Scorpio marks the third (and final) time in the last two years that a Jupiter/Saturn trine has signaled growth toward a brighter future. When their energies are in this positive combination, Jupiter and Saturn offer a unique chance to offset and stabilize the unrest pictured by the Uranus/Pluto squares. Jupiter has the enthusiasm and optimism that Saturn lacks, and Saturn gives the structure and practical application that Jupiter needs. Don't waste this unique opportunity, because this Saturn/Jupiter gift won't come our way again until 2026!

May 26–June 1

New Moon. Neptune square. Venus and Mercury change signs.
The forecast from Skywatch Central for this week is mostly sunny with a few light clouds. A sociable New Moon and an easy sign change for Venus balance out a tricky sign change for Mercury. The highlight of the week is the Gemini New Moon on Wednesday, May 28, which forms an easygoing air trine with Mars in Libra that makes all forms of communications and social activities a breeze. This New Moon provides the right set of circumstances to start off on a new footing in areas like sales and marketing, in learning some new technique or skill, or with siblings, neighbors, and/or roommates. With Libra in the picture, any kind of gathering, including a wedding, is sure to be a stellar event. The bad fairy of this New Moon is the square between Neptune and the Sun/Moon, but this doesn't look like a major stumbling block since the Sun/Moon and Neptune are all in flexible signs. Because your head is in the clouds, it's important to remember to keep your feet on terra firma. And speaking of earth, Venus goes back to the ground on Wednesday, May 28, when it moves into its earthy home sign of Taurus. This is a signal that the status quo will reign over love and money for the next three weeks. Enjoy the fruits of your labors and don't make any big changes. On Thursday, May 29, when Mercury moves into Cancer and travels there for the next few weeks, communications and messaging can get a little tricky. Look out for verbal zings that are wearing camouflage. When Mercury is in the sensitive and emotional sign of the Crab, feelings can get easily hurt and communications can be emotional at best and defensive at worst.

June 2–8

Mercury retrograde. Sun/Moon trine. Venus/Pluto trine.

Things are shifting fast in the sky this week. There's a major change of direction in how we communicate, a trine in air signs that grease the social network to keep things rolling, and another trine in practical earth signs to keep us grounded. On Saturday, June 7, Mercury begins its second retrograde of the year (see February 3–9). Mercury retrograde seems to be the one thing that most non-astrologers know, and fear, about the astrological calendar. But as the hardworking communications expert of the zodiac, Mercury deserves a break sometimes, too. If you ignore this celestial signal that it's time to back off and do things that begin with "re," such as relax and rejuvenate, then your experiences might include some of the more negative potentials of this transit: annoying personal and business miscommunications, travel mix-ups or delays, and electronic or mechanical breakdowns. Since Mercury just entered Cancer last week, this retrograde has a slightly different twist. This year, Mercury's tour of Cancer is longer than usual and is split up into three weeks in May/June and three weeks in July. This extended tour puts the spotlight for a longer time than usual on Cancer-type matters, such as the housing market, women, and the plight of people who are homeless. But for the next ten days when Mercury is retrograde in Cancer, any progress in these areas may be stalled. Take this as a clue to relax (harder than you think) and view it as a healing period when it's okay to back off and take time to rest and recuperate. The Gemini Sun trine the Libra Moon on Sunday, June 8, looks like the best day of the week for any kind of social get-together or conference. Earthy Venus in trine with Pluto on the same day favors working on any deep changes that need to be made in the areas of finance or relationships.

June 9–15

Neptune retrograde. Full Moon. Moon/Pluto meetup. Moon/Pluto/Mars conflict.

This week starts and ends with a whimper, but there's a big bang in the middle. On Monday, June 9, Neptune, the planet that loves to operate under the radar, retreats even further into its mysterious fog when it turns retrograde for the next five months. Neptune's change of direction brings this month's total number of retrograde planets to four: Mercury, Saturn, Pluto, and Neptune. Because the Sun and Moon never go retrograde, this means that as of this week, fifty percent of the planets are moving backward, which is not the best sign for the economic recovery everyone is looking for. Things get a momentary boost from the adventurous Sagittarius Full Moon on lucky Friday, June 13, a signal that it's the time of the month to complete projects, finish deals, and make ends meet. This is especially important in the Sagittarian areas of sports, travel, higher education, and anything where risk-taking is a must. Things go south later that same day, June 13, when the Moon turns an Indiana Jones–type adventure into the *Vampire Diaries* when it moves into Capricorn and meets up with Pluto. Together they get into a brawl with Mars and a standoff with Jupiter, forming a T-square that spells trouble with a capital *T*. Prepare yourself to get ready for a major fight or to simply stay on the down low. Sunday, June 15, is Father's Day, and this year it strikes a nostalgic note because Saturn, the planet that represents the father principle, is retrograde. Whether your father is in the here and now or in the hereafter, this could be the time to balance the scales with him.

June 16–22

Mercury changes signs. Sun/Moon air trine. Sun in Cancer. Summer solstice.

The feature presentation at the celestial picture show this week is the first day of summer. The previews include a rerun starring Mercury and a short but sweet romance between the Sun and Moon. If you had the misfortune to develop foot-in-the-mouth disease during the last two weeks of May when Mercury was in Gemini, you'll get a chance to redeem yourself starting on Tuesday, June 17, when retrograde Mercury leaves Cancer and backs up for another Gemini tour. This U-turn extends Mercury's tour in Gemini to four weeks and keeps the focus on the information highway and social networking until the middle of July. That same day is also good for meetings, webinars, or conference calls, because that's when the socially aware Aquarius Moon forms a congenial trine with the Gemini Sun (keep it "lite"). Saturday, June 21, is the second season-turning of the year, as the Sun passes into Cancer and marks the first day of summer, or the summer solstice, as the longest day of the year. The long days and short nights on the summer solstice, June 21, make it an easy time for everything to prosper and grow. During the month the Sun is in Cancer, the focus is on women and children, the food industry, real estate, and personal security.

June 23–29

Venus changes signs. New Moon. Sun/Moon/Neptune/Saturn water trine.

Attitudes about love and the things we value shift this week when Venus makes a sign change, and a New Moon highlights new horizons for women and family matters, the food industry, and real estate. On Monday, June 23, Venus exchanges the creativity and comforts of Taurus for a four-week stint in Gemini, which shifts the focus away from the arts and material security to being more curious about what's new and hot in the world around us. This next month, while Venus is in Gemini, is a prime time for anyone who relies on charm to get their message across, including actors, writers, teachers, salespeople, and advertising execs. The Cancer New Moon on Friday, June 27, makes a trine first with Neptune and then with Saturn (both retrograde), which is another of those magical gifts that keep happening in the sky this year. The Moon aligned with Neptune and Saturn in water signs is a time when technical engineering (Saturn) can magically (Neptune) come up with new solutions to the world's problems. Mercury, Saturn, Neptune, and Pluto remain retrograde, which emphasizes that the need is still there to go inside and dig deep for answers.

June 30–July 6

Mercury direct. Sun/Pluto face-off.

There's a play-action pass at the beginning of the week when Mercury shifts into forward gear, but it's blocked when the Sun has a standoff with Pluto. The three-week Mercury retrograde ends on Tuesday, July 1, and travel and information exchanges will begin to return to normal. Mercury's forward motion is a prompt to make up for any misdirection or miscommunications that happened over the last few months. The celestial signature on this 4th of July indicates that there could be some fireworks in the next few weeks for the United States. There's a red flag over this Friday, July 4, because that's the one day this year that Pluto stands opposite the Sun in the sky. Even though Pluto is retrograde and its powers are hidden, it is not disabled. At first glance it might seem like this isn't significant because it lasts for only a day. But because July 4 is also the U.S. birthday, this means that Pluto is also opposing the U.S. Sun, which could be a setup for a potential landmine that poses a threat to large corporations, economic giants like the Federal Reserve, and an unstable government. If you were born on the 4th of July, this is a year to avoid going up against large organizations (the government/insurance companies) and authority figures (police/military/boss).

July 7–13

Sun/Moon trine. Full Moon. Sun/Uranus conflict. Mercury changes signs.

This week has a few ups and one down. It starts off with a gentle trine between the Sun in Cancer and the Moon in Scorpio on Monday, July 7, that increases sensitivity in ways that can be both good and not so good. On the plus side, there's an infusion of loving generosity for those in crisis situations, but on the minus side, jealousy and fear of loss could lead to manipulation. Either way, it's a week to apply a lot of tender loving care to yourself and to everyone around you. It's always wise to be prepared, so on Tuesday, July 8, when the Sun and Uranus square off, get ready for things to come unglued and expect the unexpected. All this is a lead-up to the high point of the week, the Capricorn Full Moon on Saturday, July 12. Every Full Moon is a stopping point in the four-week lunar cycle that lets you know it's time to get ready for the next cycle by winding things down, finishing projects, completing journeys, or ending bad habits. Full Moon emotions (and tides) are expected to be bigger than usual this month because Jupiter is involved in this Full Moon, which means that it is easier than usual for things to get blown out of proportion. Depending on your time zone, either later that same night, July 12, or early the next day, July 13, Mercury bids its final farewell to Gemini as it ends its seven-week split tour that began in May. Mercury's second tour in Cancer will last for most of July. Since Cancer focuses on the home and is said to rule the stomach, Mercury will emphasize increased communications about issues such as additives in our food, organics versus fast food, GMOs (genetically modified organisms), and the national problem of obesity.

July 14–20

Jupiter changes signs. Sun/Moon water trine. Sun/Mars conflict. Saturn direct.

If you have any big plans for this week, there are lots of interesting changes in the celestial sphere that you should be aware of. Lucky Jupiter starts off the show on Wednesday, July 16, when it ends its one-year journey in Cancer, the sign of women, real estate, and the food industry, and moves into Leo, where the accent is on entertainment, recreation, and children. This is a lucky break for those with birthdays in the sign of the Lion that will last for the next twelve months. Warm and fuzzy feelings flow easily later that same day, July 16, because the Pisces Moon is on track to trine the Cancer Sun. When Venus exchanges the sign of Gemini for Cancer on Friday, July 18, affections become softer and gentler even though there is also a chance that folks will become a bit more defensive about the home and family. Because Cancer is centered on food, home, and family, this is a great week to plan the menu for a summer family get-together. The word on the street for Saturday, July 19, is to stay cool. That's when Mars and the Sun square each other and things in general can take a nasty turn. This busy week closes out with one final shift when Saturn ends its four-month retrograde on Sunday, July 20. This forward motion brings long-term goals out of our inner caves, where they've been stewing since last March. Although your circumstances may remain in a fixed slowdown until Saturn leaves Scorpio for good next year, Saturn's direct movement is a sign of forward progress.

July 21–27

Uranus retrograde. Sun in Leo. Sun/Jupiter meetup. Mars changes signs. New Moon.

The featured players in the cosmos this week are the signs of Leo and Scorpio and the planet Uranus. The story line is that it's time for a break from all the chaos. It starts off on Monday, July 21, when Uranus turns retrograde and goes offline for the next five months. Uranus's backward motion gives us a little breathing space, because the urge to change at all costs, even if it means crashing and burning, is now on the back burner until December. The Sun moves into Leo the next day, Tuesday, July 22, and the focus for the next month shifts from Cancer to Leo and the heart center. For the next four weeks, the celestial directive is warm, loving, and creative and about having fun for its own sake, even if it means being dramatic about it. The reason Leo loves children so much is because Leos exude a childlike enthusiasm for life that is innocent at heart as well as infectious. On Thursday, July 24, the Sun makes its once-a-year connection with Jupiter, bringing even more optimism and enthusiasm and a positive outlook to the table. At the end of the week on Friday, July 25, Mars finally trades the uncomfortable sign of Libra, where it has spent the last two years, for Scorpio, where all of its natural characteristics, good and bad, are stronger. Scorpio is a much better fit for the planet of war. Mars's aggressive energies are more intense, more passionate, more loyal, more stubborn, crueler, more secretive, more manipulative, more jealous, and (surprise!) more sensitive here than in any other sign. Mars in Scorpio is a combo that holds its cards close to the chest, but when push comes to shove, this combination is willing to fight to the end. Then on Saturday, July 26, the Sun and Moon pair up to form the Leo New Moon. All of Leo's characteristics are increased when on the same day, July 26, a Jupiter meetup turns the New Moon into a lucky Leo trio. Anything that's passionate or dramatic is best when it begins under the powerful Leo New Moon. Shine on, but don't try to fly too high. The downside of Leo is that, like the Greek god Icarus, Leo has a ton of pride. If you fly too close to the sun, the heat can burn up your wings, which will cause your downfall. Leo is one of the fixed signs, and the gift of the Leo New Moon is the power to endure. Be careful what you start during this New Moon, because whatever it is, it will have a very long shelf life.

July 28–August 3

Mercury changes signs. Mercury/Jupiter/Mars conflict.
The three outermost planets—Uranus, Neptune, and Pluto—are still on their retrograde breaks this week, and it's not a bad idea for you to consider doing the same. There's not too much on the celestial calendar, but on Thursday, July 31, Mercury finally ends its five-week tour of Cancer and moves on for a short two-week tour in Leo, where it meets up with newly minted Jupiter. With this Mercury/Jupiter pair in Leo, any drama or event will spread like wildfire over web-based platforms, including blogs, vlogs, wall postings, e-mail, instant messaging, music sharing, and tweeting. On Saturday, August 2, Mercury/Jupiter get involved in a conflict with Mars in Scorpio. The danger comes from the fact that on the Mercury/Jupiter side, things could get blown totally out of proportion, and in the Mars corner, there could be bullying and a yearning for revenge.

August 4–10

Sun/Moon fire trine. Mars/Neptune trine. Sun/Mercury meetup. Full Moon.
As usual, this week is a mixed bag of some days when everything goes right and a couple when it would be better to stay in bed. There's not a cloud in sight on Wednesday, August 6, when the lucky Sagittarius Moon makes a trine with the Leo Sun. It's a day when you may feel like something is lighting a match under your creative fire, and you might be more restless than usual and need to get outside and do something that gets your heart rate going. The energy is still high but in a calmer way on Thursday, August 7, when Mars in secretive Scorpio forms a trine with Neptune in sensitive Pisces. Even though it's a trine, this potent combination can also be dangerous because it has the power to take you for a walk on the wild side. All Mars/Neptune connections should come with a label that reads, "May have dangerous side effects—use with caution." The next day,

August 8, when the Sun takes a meeting with Mercury, mental powers will be buzzing and it's a good day to brainstorm. The Aquarius Full Moon closes out this interesting week on Sunday, August 10. While every Full Moon is the emotional high tide of the month and the best time to complete projects and resolve relationship issues, the special gift of the Aquarius Full Moon is to explore new and different ways to balance your personal ego against the good of your community. Unfortunately, this month's Full Moon is involved in a difficult T-square pattern with Saturn, which is an indication that it will be harder to achieve balance. But at best, a difficult Saturn square never denies success; it just slows things down and means you have to work harder to get it. In any difficult Saturn situation, staying power and commitment are the keys to success.

August 11–17

Venus and Mercury change signs. Sun/Moon fire trine.
It looks like it's going to be pretty easy to navigate the stars this week. Tuesday, August 12, is a day to get out of the house, because that's when Venus switches from Cancer to Leo. It's time to get into some high heels and be somewhere noisy, happy, and full of life where you can shine a bright light on your relationships and your finances. Because Venus in Leo carries a definite star power, you can count on an extra helping of charisma and charm to be on your plate for the next month. It's time to strike while the iron is hot on Thursday, August 14, when the Aries Moon trines the Leo Sun. The next day, Mercury gets home-field advantage when it crosses into conscientious Virgo on Friday, August 15. This placement encourages all left-brain activities, including practical discussions, detailed analyses, critiques, and fine-tuning things with employees, the details in your healthcare plan, and your diet.

August 18–24

Venus/Jupiter meetup. Moon/Mars/Saturn trine. Sun in Virgo.
Things are still quiet at Skywatch Central, and hopefully you're enjoying this summer break in the midst of a pretty challenging year. You'll be happy to hear that all the items on this week's agenda

make this look like a piece of cake. Flattery will get you everywhere on Monday, August 18, when Venus pairs with Jupiter in Leo and too much of a good thing can never be enough. On Thursday, August 21, the Cancer Moon will make two trines to planets in Scorpio. First there's Moon trine Mars and then Moon trine Saturn. This gentle influence will take the edge off some of the intense frustrations, annoyances, and spikes of anger that can be expected from this Mars/Saturn pairing next week. Depending on your time zone, the Sun will enter Virgo on either Friday, August 22, or Saturday, August 23. The month when the Sun is traveling through Virgo is the best time of the year to fine-tune any existing course of action as well as to refine your techniques in areas that Virgo loves, such as health and treatment plans, dietary concerns, work, employees, and mastering new systems or strategies. The Virgo umbrella also extends over pets of all makes and sizes.

August 25–31

New Moon warning. Mars/Saturn meetup. Sun/Neptune face-off.
Hope you enjoyed the time-out last week, because this week the stars are back in business with a New Moon, two difficult planets that gang up in Scorpio, and a Sun/Neptune opposition that muddies the waters. The gift of this month's Virgo New Moon on Monday, August 25, is that it offers a purity of purpose that can both heal and be of service to others. The challenge with Virgo is that you never feel good enough (or pure enough, or thin enough, or rich enough, or smart enough, or pretty enough) for anything. While every New Moon is a time of peace and tranquility in the lunar cycle and is usually a good moment in the month to set your intentions to bring something new into your life, the energy of this year's Virgo New Moon is seriously compromised, because on the same day, August 25, two planetary bullies, Mars and Saturn, pair up in Scorpio for the next two weeks. The result of this Mars/Saturn combination is frustration, like you have one foot on the gas (Mars) and the other on the brakes (Saturn). Mars in Scorpio has the edge over Saturn, because Scorpio is Mars's home sign. This is good news, because it means it's possible to break through Saturn's bondage if

you apply Mars's laser-like energy. Under the negative influence of this Mars/Saturn pair, this month's Virgo New Moon is not its usual self and unfortunately does not signal a time to start anything new. On Friday, August 29, retrograde Neptune rises at sunset to make its once-a-year opposition to the Sun. As with most other Neptune connections, things can get very fuzzy and it can be hard to figure out which road to take. On Sunday, August 31, the Scorpio Moon twists the complicated Mars/Saturn duo into a trio with scorpion-like stingers. Although this influence will be in effect only over the next few days, it's another warning of dangerous times, and the wise will avoid playing with things that have predatory intentions. The best use of this Moon/Mars/Saturn triple threat is to clean out and get rid of your extra baggage (physical, mental, emotional), and make an attempt to forgive everyone for everything.

September 1–7

Sign changes for Mercury and Venus. Sun/Moon earth trine.
In general, this is a pretty low-key week with an emphasis on planets in quiet earth signs. Mercury changes signs on Labor Day, September 1. As Mercury moves into Libra for the next four weeks, the accent is on marriage, legal documents and balance sheets, and business partnerships and mergers. A calm earth trine between the Virgo Sun and Capricorn Moon on Thursday, September 4, reduces the chances of violent geophysical changes and adds a veneer of temporary stability. Venus also makes a sign change on Friday, September 5, as it leaves Leo and moves into earthy Virgo until the end of the month. When Venus is in Virgo, it's time to be of service to others and to remember that the devil's in the details by fine-tuning Venus-ruled areas like relationships and finances. You may also want to look over the small print in any contract you've signed, whether it deals with business or pleasure. Mercury and Venus are in mutual reception for the next three weeks. *Mutual reception* is a term for a situation where Mercury is in the sign ruled by Venus (Libra) at the same time that Venus is in the sign ruled by Mercury (Virgo). In short, this means that for the rest of September, communications will be the key to relationships and relationship will be the key to communications. Uranus

and Neptune are retrograde for all of September, but you can look forward to Pluto turning direct in a few weeks.

September 8–14

Full Moon. Sun/Moon earth trine. Venus/Pluto trine. Mars changes signs.

If last week was calm and quiet, this week's night sky is making up for it with a Full Moon, a T-square, a sign change for Mars, two interesting connections for Venus, and a Sun/Moon trine all on standby. The week begins with a bang on Monday, September 8, with the Full Moon. Like all Full Moons, this Pisces Full Moon signals the emotional high tide for the month. While every Full Moon is a time to complete unfinished projects and find resolutions to relationship issues or anything else left hanging in the balance, the mysterious Pisces Full Moon is a time when hidden dreams come out of the closet and can appear as either your favorite fantasy or your darkest nightmare. Venus doubles the Pisces Full Moon effect on Wednesday, September 10, with an opposition to Neptune in Pisces. But the Virgo Sun and Taurus Moon bring things back down to earth when they form an earth trine on Saturday, September 13. On that same day, Mercury (still in Libra) makes a short but difficult foray into the middle of the ongoing Uranus/Pluto conflict. Hopefully Mercury can introduce bits of rational thinking and diplomacy into solving some of the conflicts this square represents. Then, on Sunday, September 14, Venus applies the same practical energy as the Sun/Moon trine when it forms its own earth trine with Pluto. The excitement level goes up on Saturday, September 13, when Mars moves into the fire sign of Sagittarius, one of its most active placements. With this Mars/Sagittarius combination, you can expect that for the next six weeks things will be more spontaneous than usual. Travel, business adventures, and athletic competitions are a few examples of the "places you'll go" under this wide-open combo.

September 15–21

Moon/Mars/Neptune T-square.

All is quiet on the celestial front with the three outermost planets—Uranus, Neptune, and Pluto—still retrograde and offline. But there's one major headline on the sky calendar this week that's definitely worthy of notice, and that's a T-square pattern that involves Moon/Mars/Neptune on Sunday, September 21. Mars is playing center as it squares both Moon and Neptune, who stand opposite each other. The good news is that all three players are in signs that change easily (mutable signs), which means that the conflicts are not set in stone and can be easily solved with a change of attitude. The other part of this T-square is Neptune's tendency to choose to ignore boundaries or any form of limitation. While the Virgo Moon gives you a good head on your shoulders, Neptune and Mars will overrule any rational objections that might be raised. If you remember to apply a large dose of common sense to any dreams or schemes, this could be a great week to experience some amazing adventures. If you don't, you'll be kicking yourself because you bit off more than you could chew.

September 22–28

Sun in Libra. Fall equinox. Pluto direct. Jupiter/Uranus trine. Mercury changes signs.

Summer is officially over on Monday, September 22, when the Sun moves into Libra to mark the first day of fall, or the autumnal equinox. The fall equinox marks the halfway point in the Sun's yearly journey around the zodiac. Monday, September 22, is one of the two days a year (the other is the spring equinox on March 20) when the hours of day and night are equal. This is a signal that it's time to push the pause button and see if your life is in a state of balance. If last spring marked a time to make a new beginning, then the fall equinox is a time to reap the harvest of what you began. The fall equinox gets some additional balancing power from the Libra New Moon on Wednesday, September 24. The Libra New Moon puts the focus on new beginnings in partnerships, the arts, or legal affairs. On Monday, September 22, Pluto ends its five-month retrograde. With Pluto back in the game, there is a return to active duty for the planet of crisis transformation, which we will feel in our social lives, political movements, and the economy. On Thursday, September 25, Uranus gets a much-needed boost in the form of a trine from Jupiter that reminds us that one of the best parts about being human is the ability to see humor even in the most desperate situations. On Saturday, September 27, Mercury enters Scorpio, which ends Mercury's three-week mutual reception/love fest with Venus and intensifies communications. With Mercury in Scorpio for the next two weeks, you can expect to have the conversation that starts with four of the most dreaded words in the English language: "We have to talk." Because *intense* is also a polite term for *passive-aggressive*, watch out for stingers that come in the form of biting sarcasm, veiled mocking, or hidden ridicule. On the plus side, Mercury in Scorpio is a terrific asset for reorganizations, research projects, or implementing secret strategies.

September 29–October 5

Venus changes signs. Sun/Moon air trine. Final Mercury retrograde of the year. Mars/Uranus trine.

Life is a mixed bag this week with a positive move for Venus, two trines, and the third (and last) Mercury retrograde of the year. Venus starts things off by exchanging Virgo for Libra on Monday, September 29. Libra is home base for Venus, so partnerships, social networking, and legal affairs move to the top of the list for the next three weeks. The social agenda continues with a compatible air trine between the Libra Sun and the humanitarian Aquarius Moon on Friday, October 3. On Saturday, October 4, Mercury turns retrograde, which is something that many folks have come to dread about the astrological calendar. But as the hard-working communications expert of the solar system, Mercury deserves a break, and so do you. If you ignore this celestial signal that it's time to back off, your experiences might include some of the more negative potentials of this transit, such as annoying personal and business miscommunications, travel mix-ups or delays, and electronic or mechanical breakdowns. There's a high-risk alert in the form of a firepower trine between Mars in Sagittarius and Uranus in Aries late Saturday, October 4 (West Coast), or early Sunday, October 5 (East Coast). If you think of Mars as the match to Uranus's fire, you get an idea of what a volatile combo this is. This trine is one of those dangerous connections where the ease of a trine can be more of a liability than an asset. The upside of this trine can include a strong desire for adventure combined with extreme physical courage or the announcement of some new invention or technological innovation.

October 6–12

Sun/Uranus face-off. Full Moon. Total Lunar Eclipse. Mercury changes signs.

This week marks the beginning of the fall eclipse season with the Aries Full Moon, a once-a-year Uranus/Sun opposition, and a Mercury replay. On Tuesday, October 7, Uranus in Aries is on its closest approach to the earth to make a 180-degree opposition to the Libra Sun. This face-off indicates a restless duel between trying to change the status quo and simultaneously trying to keep things in balance. Whenever Uranus is involved, there's a possibility of losing something in order to gain something more important. Although this Sun/Uranus face-off happens once a year, it can have far-reaching consequences. It's the appetizer to the main event of the week on Wednesday, October 8, which is when the Aries Full Moon lines up for a Total Lunar Eclipse that will be visible over east Australia, the Pacific, and the Americas. Because this eclipse is involved in the ongoing Uranus/Pluto conflict as well as trines with Jupiter and Mars, it can be a major positive influence on national or global power struggles. On a personal level, this eclipse also indicates a watermark year for those celebrating birthdays today, October 8, or on April 8. Because this super-charged eclipse signifies the end of a cycle, this is a week of completion rather than initiation. There's a Mercury replay on Friday, October 10, when this planet retrogrades into another four-week tour in Libra. This is yet another reminder to keep minding your manners no matter how tough the going gets.

October 13–19

Sun/Moon air trine. Mercury/Venus meetup. Moon/Uranus conflict. Moon/Saturn conflict.

Things are a bit calmer this week with an easy air trine between the Sun and Moon, a pairing between Mercury/Venus, and a couple of short scuffles between Moon/Uranus and Moon/Saturn. On Monday, October 13, the Libra Sun makes an interesting trine with the Gemini Moon that makes it easy to fuse what's trendy with what's conventional while remaining cool, objective, and somewhat detached from it all. The next day, Tuesday, October 14, the Cancer Moon squares Uranus and sets off another battle between the past and the future. Retrograde Mercury pairs with Venus on Friday, October 17, which is a handy if short-lived gift of a golden tongue that will benefit those who earn their living through words, including writers, teachers, and marketing and sales people. On Saturday, October 18, the Leo Moon gets into a conflict with Saturn. If you find yourself up against an immovable force, the best thing is do is accept the inevitable and quit while you're still ahead.

October 20–26

New Moon/Solar Eclipse. Sun in Scorpio. Venus changes signs. Sun/Venus meetup. Mars changes signs. Mercury direct.
After you pencil in the New Moon/Solar Eclipse for this week, be sure to leave room for three planets that will change signs as well as the one that will change direction. With all this going on, you might find yourself changing your mind several different times as well. The fun starts with the entry of both the Sun and Venus into Scorpio. That happens on the same day, Thursday, October 23, when Sun/Venus form a three-way meetup with the Scorpio Moon. Later that same day, Venus makes an uncomfortable addition to the Scorpio New Moon/Solar Eclipse because the darker Scorpio side of Venus introduces jealousy and other possessive behaviors into the mix. With the Sun/Moon already in Scorpio, the general atmosphere of this eclipse is a mix of a laser-like intensity and considerable emotional depth. This eclipse is expected to be influential in the United States because it will be visible across most of North America. This widespread visibility over the United States can indicate that compassionate actions such as charitable contributions may be required on the part of the "haves" toward the "have-nots." Taking precautions is wise, because with five planets in water signs, it could also be an indication of dangerous high tides and flash floods, and with

this eclipse in a trine to Neptune, there's a tendency to deny reality. Saturday, October 25, is the final day of the last Mercury retrograde period of the year. This marks the time when travel and communications will return to normal and documents can now be signed without fear of misunderstandings. The final shift of the busy week comes on Sunday, October 26, when fiery Mars slides into cool Capricorn. Because Capricorn is one of Mars's favorite zodiac hangouts, the upside of this combination is a strong drive to succeed as well as the ability to put your plan into action. The downside is a tendency to be a control freak. Because Mars will be in Capricorn until December, this is an important time to establish long-term goals and to go for the gold.

October 27–November 2

Halloween. Sun/Neptune trine. Sun/Moon water trine. Daylight Saving Time ends.

This is a week to eat, drink, and be scary. On Tuesday, October 28, the Scorpio Sun sets the mood for trick-or-treating on the weekend with a trine to Neptune. Because Scorpio enjoys being scared and loves anything dark and forbidden and Neptune is the master of disguise, there might be more tricks than treats this week. The far-out Aquarius Moon may increase the number of aliens and ghostly creatures coming to your door on Halloween, Friday, October 31. Daylight Saving Time comes to an end on Sunday, November 2, at 2:00 AM local time. Remember to "fall back" by setting your clocks one hour earlier before you go to sleep on Saturday night. Because a supersensitive trine between the Scorpio Sun and the Pisces Moon on that same day, November 2, is likely to bring up old fears and tears, it might be a good idea to have some extra tissues on hand.

November 3–9

Full Moon. Mercury changes signs.

Thursday, November 6, is host to the Taurus Full Moon, which is the emotional high tide for November. The Full Moon is the time of the month to complete unfinished projects and resolve relationship issues or anything else left hanging in the balance. But this Full

Moon is complicated, because the Taurus/Scorpio polarity is passively stubborn, loyal, and intensely sensual and can shine its light on undercover feelings you have about your relationship or secret attitudes you're hiding about money. Because Taurus rules the throat, this is also a time to ask if there's anything about those two areas that you're having a hard time swallowing. Communications go underground on Saturday, November 8, when Mercury plunges into Scorpio for the next three weeks and the style of communications is pointed, secretive, and manipulative and the green-eyed monster (jealousy) comes out to play. This Mercury-in-Scorpio combo is one of the best times of the year to file for bankruptcy or a foreclosure as well as to check to see that your insurance coverage is adequate and up-to-date.

November 10–16

Mars/Pluto meetup. Sun/Moon water trine. Venus/Saturn meetup. Neptune direct. Venus changes signs.

The week starts out with a dangerous pairing between Mars/Pluto on Monday, November 10. Because power struggles and control issues play a big role in any Mars/Pluto meeting, it's vital to find a way to handle the extra wattage of this meetup in a constructive way so you don't self-destruct. The combination of the god of war (Mars) with the planetary version of Darth Vader (Pluto) can be an obsessive-compulsive force that sends feelings of rage to center stage, or it can make you overworked and stressed-out. An important and well-timed trine between the Scorpio Sun and the Cancer Moon on Tuesday, November 11, will help cool things down. Things get even more serious the next day, Wednesday, November 12, when Venus pairs with Saturn. Venus/Saturn is not going to kick the fun meter up very far, because it's oriented toward commitment and emphasizes the responsible side of love. It also reminds us to be accountable for our choices and for how we spend and save our money. There's another shift when Neptune comes back online on Saturday, November 15, and ends its five-month retrograde period. Although Neptune back in the game makes it harder to stick with reality, it will also be easier for us to express our idealism, compassion, and imagination. But serious commitments become a thing of the past on Sunday, November 16, when Venus leaves Saturn and leaps into adventurous and optimistic Sagittarius for the next month. In Sagittarius, Venus is known more for its fun-loving flexibility than for its ability to be faithful.

November 17–23

Sun/Saturn meetup. Sun in Sagittarius. New Moon. Sun/Moon/ Neptune conflict.

It's time for your once-a-year reality check-up. Tuesday, November 18, is the day, because that's when Saturn and the Sun have their annual meetup. Since this short (one-day) Sun/Saturn pairing can have long-term results, this is a day to get down to business and take a good hard look at your commitments and responsibilities. Don't let this opportunity pass you by, because this is the last business the Sun has in Scorpio. It moves into Sagittarius on Saturday, November 22, where things get a lot brighter and more cheerful for the next month. When the Sun is in Sagittarius, the key issue is the quest for new horizons. Whether your journey is in sports, business, foreign travel, graduate studies, religion, or any type of adventure, the energy is restless, hot-blooded, independent, enthusiastic, and optimistic. The downside of Sagittarius is that because it favors exaggeration (so much more fun!) over truth, it can get you into a lot of trouble. The Sagittarius New Moon doubles this carefree attitude on the same day, November 22. Because the New Moon is the emotional low tide in the lunar cycle and is a time of tranquility, this is the perfect time to plant the seeds of a big, new adventure. While you're making those big plans, keep the Sun/Saturn reality check in mind. This New Moon is also squared by Neptune, which carries a warning that your dreams might get a little bit bigger than you can handle.

November 24–30

Mercury/Saturn meetup. Thanksgiving—"In everything give thanks." Mercury changes signs.

It might feel like the weight of the world is on your shoulders on Tuesday, November 25, when Mercury meets up with Saturn in Scorpio, so it's important to keep two things in mind. The first is that this influence has a short shelf life, and the second is that the depressive nature of this combination will shift into a happier place by Thanksgiving, on Thursday, November 27, when Mercury moves into Sagittarius. It's easy to be thankful for all our blessings when this naturally enthusiastic combination assures us that there's a lucky opportunity around the next corner. Even though it's filled with good cheer, this Mercury/Sagittarius placement still has its dark side, which includes a tendency to talk too much or too loudly to exaggerate a point or to skip over the facts in favor of the fun factor. As annoying as this can be, especially to critical Virgo types, the intent is innocent and lasts only for the next three weeks.

December 1–7

Sun/Moon fire trine. Mars changes signs. Full Moon.

This week is filled with planets in fire and air, which means that the emphasis will be on the head, not the heart. It starts out with a powerful, upbeat trine on Monday, December 1, between the two brightest lights in the sky, the Sun in Sagittarius and the Moon in Aries. That trine sets the power base for the shift on Thursday, December 4, when Mars ends its journey in Capricorn and moves into the open-ended landscape of Aquarius. Because Aquarius believes in open sources of information and in innovation that takes place through the collective effort of the many, all modes of communication, including social networking platforms, are energized and electrified when Mars is traveling through this sign. On Saturday, December 6, the Gemini Full Moon brings us to the emotional high tide for December. Like all Full Moons, this is a reminder to complete unfinished projects and find resolutions to relationship issues or anything else left hanging in the balance. This Gemini Full Moon connects to Mars in Aquarius because it makes two positive connections with Uranus, the ruler of Aquarius. Uranus trine to the Sun and sextile to the Moon increases the likelihood of coming up with cutting-edge technologies and mindsets that will make information more transparent and available to everyone.

December 8–14

Jupiter retrograde. Venus changes signs. Sun/Moon fire trine.

With Jupiter turning retrograde on Monday, December 8, it's beginning to look as though 2014 will end up the same the way it began. But there is one important difference. Jupiter began the year retrograde in Cancer, but when it goes retrograde this week, it will be in Leo. When Jupiter is in Cancer, it puts things like real estate and the food industry on a temporary hold, but those areas will now be in forward motion. On Monday, December 8, when Jupiter turns retrograde in Leo, it signals an enforced timeout for the entertainment industry, recreational activities, and things that have to do with children. Jupiter's pause in Leo can also mean travel restrictions that will put the emphasis on more home-based entertainment like staycations for the next four months. The fun meter drops on Wednesday, December 10, when Venus switches signs and moves into practical Capricorn. Venus in Capricorn understands the value of a good deal, whether in business or pleasure, which is why it's a sign of an arranged marriage rather than a love match. Enthusiasm will heat up again on Thursday, December 11, under a Sun/Moon fire trine.

December 15–21

Mercury changes signs. Venus/Pluto meetup. Sun in Capricorn. Winter solstice. Uranus direct.

"The day is done, and darkness falls from the wings of night." This quote from Longfellow is a perfect description of the celestial weather for the end of fall and the beginning of winter. The previews leading up to the first day of winter, which is also the darkest day and longest night of the year, are Mercury's move into Capricorn and a Venus meetup with Pluto. The feature presentation is the winter solstice, which coincides with the end of the Uranus retrograde as well as the New Moon. Although Mercury sets a somber and serious tone on Tuesday, December 16, when it shifts into Capricorn, it's important to remember that this combo also possesses some of the driest humor in the zodiac, which is a great source of comic relief. Later that week, Venus and Pluto meet up for a short but intense once-a-year get-together. Although this passionate duo can have a transformative effect on love or money, its shadow side can also produce strong feelings of jealousy and possessiveness. On Sunday, December 21, the Sun moves into Capricorn and marks the first day of winter, which is also called the winter solstice. This is the Sun's final turning point in the four seasons and the darkest day of the year. The winter solstice is always a special moment in the astrological calendar, but this year it is supercharged because it occurs in tandem with the Capricorn New Moon as well as the end of the five-month Uranus retrograde period. This surprise triple whammy makes the end of 2014 seem more like a new beginning. As we navigate our way among the many transformations taking place in our lives, it's important to remember that these changes are all necessary steps in a much larger plan on the path to the future. From this day forth, the light of the Sun will begin to grow longer every day, which is why on the winter solstice, the darkest day of the year, we celebrate the return of the light.

December 22–28

Saturn changes signs. Christmas week. Mercury/Pluto meetup.

Here comes the Sun… On Tuesday, December 23, Saturn takes a temporary leave from its tour of Scorpio and moves into Sagittarius until next June (2015), when it will make a U-turn for one final visit to the last degree of Scorpio until the following September. Until then, planets in Scorpio will get a break as the torch of Saturn's judgmental eye is passed to those in the early degrees of Sagittarius. Christmas falls on Thursday, December 25, a fairly quiet day for the planets that can be spent chilling out, enjoying yourself, and not making any decisions bigger than if you should have another piece of pie. Although Christians celebrate the birth of Christ on this day, December 25, it was originally the day of a major Pagan festival called Saturnalia, named after the Roman god Saturn, who ruled over agriculture, liberation, and time. The festival included traditions that have morphed into Christian tradition, such as drinking, gift giving, bonfires, candles, going naked and singing house to house (this has been preserved as caroling minus the naked part), and sometimes sacrifices (transformed into eating human-shaped biscuits, like gingerbread men). Mercury/Pluto is another variation on the Saturnalia theme when the two planets pair up in Saturn-ruled Capricorn either late on Christmas Eve, December 24, or early on Christmas Day, December 25. Even though it is only a few days past the winter solstice, the light is increasing by many seconds every day.

December 29–31

Sun/Moon earth trine.

This year ends as it began, with Jupiter, the planet of abundance, moving backward. Jupiter retrograde is a sign that the return to peace and prosperity that we all desire is nearby but still in our future. But as we say our farewells, it is important to note that the other nine planets are in direct motion, which is a good sign that things will soon be moving forward. On Tuesday, December 30, the Capricorn Sun dances in a trine with the Taurus Moon, a connection that speaks to the power of love. If planets could talk, they might be saying something like this:

> *We look forward to the time*
> *When the power of love will*
> *Replace the love of power.*
> *Then will our world know the*
> *Blessings of peace.*

Thanks for coming along on our 2014 journey through the stars, and best wishes to all for a happy and healthy New Year!

About the Astrologer

Pam Ciampi is a Certified Professional Astrologer (ISAR) who has practiced astrology since 1975. She is the past president of the San Diego Astrological Society and president emeritus of the San Diego chapter of NCGR. Pam has been writing the weekly forecasts for the *Daily Planetary Guide* since 2007. She is also the author of several astrological almanacs on gardening by the Moon and has contributed articles to national astrology publications. She maintains a full-time astrological practice for clients all over the United States and also teaches astrology and tarot classes in Southern California. Pam's other interests include astronomy, art history, cooking, music, and gardening. Contact her at www.pciampi-astrology.com or pamciampi @gmail.com.

Finding Opportunity Periods

by Jim Shawvan

There are times when the most useful things you can do are ordinary tasks such as laundry, cooking, listening to music, reading, learning, or meditating. There are other times when the universe opens the gates of opportunity. Meetings, decisions, or commitments during these "Opportunity Periods" can lead to new and positive developments in your life. Most people are unaware of these subtle changes in the energies, so they wind up doing laundry when they could be signing an important contract, or they go out to try to meet a new sweetheart when the energies for such a thing are totally blocked.

I developed the Opportunity Periods system over more than thirty years, as I tested first one hypothesis and then another in real life. In about 1998, when I studied classical astrology with Lee Lehman, the system got some added zing, including William Lilly's idea that the Moon when void-of-course in the signs of the Moon and Jupiter "performeth somewhat." The signs of the Moon and Jupiter are Taurus, Cancer, Sagittarius, and Pisces. For those who want to understand the details of the system, they are explained here. If you simply want to use the system, all the information you need is on the calendar pages (you don't need to learn the technicalities).

An Opportunity Period (OP) is a period in which the aspects of the transiting Moon to other transiting planets show no interference with the free flow of decision and action.

Opportunity Periods apply to everyone in the world all at once; although, if the astrological influences on your own chart are putting blocks in your path, you may not be able to use every OP to the fullest. Nevertheless, you are always better off taking important actions and making crucial decisions during an Opportunity Period.

Signs of the Moon and Jupiter

- Taurus: the Moon's exaltation
- Cancer: the Moon's domicile and Jupiter's exaltation
- Sagittarius: Jupiter's fiery domicile
- Pisces: Jupiter's watery domicile

Steps to Find Your Opportunity Periods

Under Sun's Beams

Step 1: Determine whether the Moon is "under Sun's beams"; that is, less than 17 degrees from the Sun. If it is, go to step 7. If not, continue to step 2.

Moon Void-of-Course

Step 2: Determine when the Moon goes void-of-course (v/c). The Moon is said to be void-of-course from the time it makes the last Ptolemaic aspect (conjunction, sextile, square, trine, or opposition) in a sign until it enters the next sign.

In eight of the twelve signs of the zodiac, Moon-void periods are NOT Opportunity Periods. In the other four signs, however, they are! According to seventeenth-century astrologer William Lilly, the Moon in the signs of the Moon and Jupiter "performeth somewhat." Lee Lehman says that she has taken this to the bank many times—and so have I.

Stressful or Easy Aspect

Step 3: Determine whether the aspect on which the Moon goes void is a stressful or an easy aspect. Every square is stressful, and every trine and every sextile is easy. Conjunctions and oppositions require judgment according to the nature of the planet the Moon is aspecting, and according to your individual ability to cope with the energies of that planet. For example, the Moon applying to a conjunction of Jupiter, Venus, or Mercury is easy, whereas, for most purposes, the Moon applying to a conjunction of Saturn, Mars, Neptune, Pluto, or Uranus is stressful. However, if you are a person for whom Uranus or Pluto is a familiar and more or less comfortable energy, you may find that the period before the Moon's conjunction to that planet is an Opportunity Period for you. (Since this is true for relatively few people, such periods are not marked as OPs in this book.)

Oppositions can work if the Moon is applying to an opposition of Jupiter, Venus, Mercury, or the Sun (just before the Full Moon). The Moon applying to a conjunction with the Sun (New Moon) presents a whole set of issues on its own. See step 7.

Easy Equals Opportunity

Step 4: If the aspect on which the Moon goes void is an easy aspect, there is an Opportunity Period before the void period. If the aspect on which the Moon goes void is a stressful aspect, there is no Opportunity Period preceding the void period in that sign. To determine the beginning of the Opportunity Period, find the last stressful aspect the Moon makes in the sign. The Opportunity Period runs from the last stressful aspect to the last aspect (assuming that the last aspect is an easy one). If the Moon makes no stressful aspects at all while in the sign, then the Opportunity Period begins as soon as the Moon enters the sign, and ends at the last aspect.

When Is an Aspect Over?

Step 5: When is an aspect over? There are three different answers to this question, and I recommend observation to decide. I also recommend caution.

- An aspect is over (in electional astrology) as soon as it is no longer exact. For example, if the Moon's last stressful aspect in a sign is a square to Saturn at 1:51 P.M., the Opportunity Period (if there is one) would be considered to begin immediately. This is the way the Opportunity Periods are shown in this book.

- Lee Lehman says an aspect is effective (for electional purposes) until it is no longer partile. An aspect is said to be partile if the two planets are in the same degree numerically. For example, a planet at 0° Aries 00' 00" is in partile trine to a planet at 0° Leo 59' 59", but it is not in partile conjunction to a planet at 29° Pisces 59' 59", even though the orb of the conjunction is only one second of arc ($\frac{1}{3,600}$) of a degree.

- An aspect is effective until the Moon has separated from the exact aspect by a full degree, which takes about two hours. This is the most cautious viewpoint. If you have doubts about the wisdom of signing a major contract while the Moon is still within one degree of a nasty aspect, then for your own peace of mind you should give it two hours, to get the one-degree separating orb.

Translating Light and Translating Darkness

Step 6: One should avoid starting important matters when the Moon is translating light from a stressful aspect with a malefic planet to an ostensibly easy aspect with another malefic planet—or even a series of such aspects uninterrupted by any aspects to benefic planets. I refer to this as "translating darkness." Translation of light is a concept used primarily in horary astrology, and it is discussed in great detail in books and on websites on that subject. For example, the Moon's last difficult aspect is a square to Saturn, and there is an apparent Opportunity Period because the Moon's next aspect is a trine to Mars, on which the Moon goes void-of-course. The problem is this: the Moon is translating light from one malefic to another, and this vitiates what would otherwise be an Opportunity Period. The same would be true if the sequence were, for example, Moon square Saturn, then Moon trine Mars, then Moon sextile Neptune—an unbroken series of malefics.

For the purpose of this system, we may regard all of the following planets as malefics: Mars, Saturn, Uranus, Neptune, and Pluto. I can almost hear the howls of protest from the folks who believe there is no such thing as a malefic planet or a bad aspect. On the level of spiritual growth, that is doubtless true, but this book is meant to be used to make your everyday life easier. Anyone who urges others to suffer more than absolutely necessary in the name of spirituality is indulging in great spiritual arrogance themselves.

New Moon, Balsamic Phase, and Cazimi Notes

Step 7: Here are some notes on the period around the New Moon: waxing, waning, Balsamic, under beams, combust, and Cazimi.

As it separates from conjunction with the Sun (New Moon) and moves towards opposition (Full Moon), the Moon is said to be waxing, or increasing in light. Traditionally the period of the waxing Moon is considered favorable for electional purposes.

Then after the Full Moon, as the Moon applies to a conjunction with the Sun, the Moon is said to be waning, or decreasing in light. Traditionally this period is regarded as a poor choice for electional purposes, and the closer the Moon gets to the Sun, the worse it is said to be. In practice, I find that problems seem to occur only as the Moon gets very close to the Sun.

When the Moon is applying to a conjunction with the Sun (New Moon) and is less than 45 degrees away from the Sun, the Moon is said to be in its Balsamic phase. This phase is associated with giving things up and is considered especially unfavorable for starting things you wish to increase.

Any planet within 17 degrees of the Sun is said to be under Sun's beams. Traditionally this weakens the planet, particularly for electional and horary purposes.

Any planet within 8 degrees of the Sun is said to be combust. Traditionally this weakens the planet even more, particularly in electional and horary work.

Any planet whose center is within 17 minutes of arc of the center of the Sun in celestial longitude is said to be Cazimi. Oddly, this is considered the highest form of accidental dignity. In other words, a planet is thought to be weak when under Sun's beams, weaker still when combust, but—surprisingly—very powerful and benefic when Cazimi!

The average speed of the Moon is such that it remains Cazimi for about an hour; that is, half an hour before and half an hour after the exact conjunction with the Sun (New Moon). Other things being equal, you can use the Cazimi Moon to start something if you really want it to succeed.

However, please do not attempt to use the Cazimi Moon at the time of a Solar Eclipse, nor if the Moon is moving from the Cazimi into a stressful aspect. Cazimi is powerful, but it cannot override the difficulties shown by a Solar Eclipse, nor those shown by, say, the Moon's application to a square of Saturn.

If you really need to start something around the time of the New Moon, and you cannot use the Cazimi, it is a good idea to wait until the first Opportunity Period after the Moon has begun waxing. Even if the Moon is still under Sun's beams at that time, it is better than starting the new project while the Moon is still waning. However, if you can reasonably do so, it is best to wait for the first Opportunity Period after the Moon is no longer under Sun's beams;

that is, after the Moon has separated from the Sun by at least 17 degrees. For the principles to use at that time, see step 2.

About the Astrologer

Jim Shawvan developed the system of Opportunity Periods over a period of three decades, out of his interest in electional astrology —the art of picking times for important actions such as getting married, opening a business, or incorporating a company (or even matters of only medium importance). Jim began the study of astrology in 1969; he teaches classes in predictive astrology and has lectured numerous times to the San Diego Astrological Society and other astrological groups and conferences.

Jim's articles have appeared in the *Mountain Astrologer* and other publications, a number of which are linked at his website, www.jshawvan.homestead.com. He predicted the delay in the results of the U.S. presidential election of 2000; and in early 2001, he predicted that, in response to anti-American terrorism, the United States would be at war in Afghanistan in the first two years of George W. Bush's presidency.

Jim studied cultural anthropology and structural linguistics at Cornell University, and later became a computer programmer and systems analyst. From 1989 to 1997, he was the technical astrologer at Neil Michelsen's Astro Communications Services, handling the most difficult questions and orders. He holds the Certified Astrological Professional certificate issued by the International Society for Astrological Research (ISAR).

Jim offers consultations in the areas of electional, horary, karmic, natal, predictive, relationship, relocation, and travel astrology. Consultations are done by phone or in person, and are taped. The client receives both the cassette and the charts.

Contact Jim Shawvan and Right Place Consulting at jshawvan@ yahoo.com or www.jshawvan.homestead.com.

Business Guide

Collections

Try to make collections on days when your Sun is well aspected. Avoid days when Mars or Saturn are aspected. If possible, the Moon should be in a cardinal sign: Aries, Cancer, Libra, or Capricorn. It is more difficult to collect when the Moon is in Taurus or Scorpio.

Employment, Promotion

Choose a day when your Sun is favorably aspected or the Moon is in your tenth house. Good aspects of Venus or Jupiter are beneficial.

Loans

Moon in the first and second quarters favors the lender; in the third and fourth it favors the borrower. Good aspects of Jupiter or Venus to the Moon are favorable to both, as is Moon in Leo, Sagittarius, Aquarius, or Pisces.

New Ventures

Things usually get off to a better start during the increase of the Moon. If there is impatience, anxiety, or deadlock, it can often be broken at the Full Moon. Agreements can be reached then.

Partnerships

Agreements and partnerships should be made on a day that is favorable to both parties. Mars, Neptune, Pluto, and Saturn should not be square or opposite the Moon. It is best to make an agreement or partnership when the Moon is in a mutable sign, especially Gemini or Virgo. The other signs are not favorable, with the possible exception of Leo or Capricorn. Begin partnerships when the Moon is increasing in light, as this is a favorable time for starting new ventures.

Public Relations

The Moon rules the public, so this must be well aspected, particularly by the Sun, Mercury, Uranus, or Neptune.

Selling

Selling is favored by good aspects of Venus, Jupiter, or Mercury to the Moon. Avoid aspects to Saturn. Try to get the planetary ruler of your product well aspected by Venus, Jupiter, or the Moon.

Signing Important Papers

Sign contracts or agreements when the Moon is increasing in a fruitful sign. Avoid days when Mars, Saturn, Neptune, or Pluto are afflicting the Moon. Don't sign anything if your Sun is badly afflicted.

Calendar Pages
How to Use Your *Daily Planetary Guide*

Both Eastern and Pacific times are given in the datebook. The Eastern times are listed in the left-hand column. The Pacific times are in the right-hand column in bold typeface. Note that adjustments have been made for Daylight Saving Time. The void-of-course Moon is listed to the right of the daily aspect at the exact time it occurs. It is indicated by "☽ v/c." On days when it occurs for only one time zone and not the other, it is indicated next to the appropriate column and then repeated on the next day for the other time zone. Note that the monthly ephemerides in the back of the book are shown for midnight, Greenwich Mean Time (GMT). Opportunity Periods are designated by the letters "OP." See page 77 for a detailed discussion on how to use Opportunity Periods.

Symbol Key

Planets/	⊙	Sun	♃	Jupiter
Asteroids	☽	Moon	♄	Saturn
	☿	Mercury	♅	Uranus
	♀	Venus	♆	Neptune
	♂	Mars	♇	Pluto
	⚷	Chiron		

Signs	♈	Aries	♎	Libra
	♉	Taurus	♏	Scorpio
	♊	Gemini	♐	Sagittarius
	♋	Cancer	♑	Capricorn
	♌	Leo	♒	Aquarius
	♍	Virgo	♓	Pisces

Aspects	♂	Conjunction (0°)	△	Trine (120°)
	✶	Sextile (60°)	⚻	Quincunx (150°)
	□	Square (90°)	☍	Opposition (180°)

Motion	℞	Retrograde	D	Direct

Moon Phase	●	New Moon	◑	Second Quarter
	○	Full Moon	◐	Fourth Quarter

30 Mon
4th ♐
OP: After Moon sextiles Mars today until Moon enters Capricorn on Tuesday. Take care of business during this break between holidays, but be aware that the Moon becomes Balsamic this afternoon.

☉♑□ ♅♈	12:05 am	
☽♐△ ♅♈	2:51 am	
☽♐□ ♋♓	4:53 am	**1:53 am**
☽♐ ⚹ ♂♎	6:36 am	**3:36 am** ☽ v/c
☿♑ ⚹ ♋♓	10:47 am	**7:47 am**
☽♐ ⚻ ♃♋	3:10 pm	**12:10 pm**
♂♎□ ♇♑	8:22 pm	**5:22 pm**

31 Tue
4th ♐
New Year's Eve

☿♑ ☌ ♇♑	6:26 am	**3:26 am**
☉♑⚹ ♋♓	6:36 am	**3:36 am**
☿♑□ ♂♎	9:59 am	**6:59 am**
☽ enters ♑	1:01 pm	**10:01 am**
☽♑ ⚹ ♆♓	6:06 pm	**3:06 pm**
☽♑□ ♅♈		**11:40 pm**

1 Wed
4th ♑
● New Moon 10 ♑ 57
New Year's Day
Kwanzaa ends

☽♑□ ♅♈	2:40 am	
☽♑ ⚹ ♋♓	4:43 am	**1:43 am**
☽♑ ☌ ☉♑	6:14 am	**3:14 am**
☽♑ ☌ ♀♑	6:44 am	**3:44 am**
☽♑□ ♂♎	7:41 am	**4:41 am**
☽♑ ☌ ☿♑	9:32 am	**6:32 am**
☉♑☌ ♀♑	1:57 pm	**10:57 am**
☽♑ ☍ ♃♋	2:09 pm	**11:09 am**
☽♑ ⚹ ♄♏	9:06 pm	**6:06 pm**

2 Thu
1st ♑

☽♑ ☌ ♀♑	6:12 am	**3:12 am** ☽ v/c
☽ enters ≈	12:03 pm	**9:03 am**
☉♑□♂♎	7:14 pm	**4:14 pm**
☽≈ ⚹ ♅♈		**10:46 pm**
☿♑ ☍ ♃♋		**11:11 pm**

☽≈ ⚹ ♅♈	1:46 am		**Fri**	**3**
☿♑ ☍ ♃⊗	2:11 am			1st ≈
☽≈ △ ♂♎	8:12 am	**5:12 am**		
☽≈ ⚻ ♃⊗	12:57 pm	**9:57 am**		
☽≈ □ ♄♏	8:47 pm	**5:47 pm** ☽ v/c		

☽ enters ♓	11:58 am	**8:58 am**	**Sat**	**4**
☽♓ ☌ ♆♓	5:26 pm	**2:26 pm**		1st ≈

OP: **After Moon conjoins Neptune today until Moon enters Aries on Monday.** Good for artistic matters, meditation, and helping others.

☽♓ ☌ ⚸♓	4:45 am	**1:45 am**	**Sun**	**5**
☽♓ ⚹ ♀♑	6:52 am	**3:52 am**		1st ♓
☽♓ ⚻ ♂♎	10:40 am	**7:40 am**		
☽♓ ⚹ ☉♑	1:30 pm	**10:30 am**		
☽♓ △ ♃⊗	1:43 pm	**10:43 am**		
☉♑ ☍ ♃⊗	4:11 pm	**1:11 pm**		
☽♓ ⚹ ☿♑	10:10 pm	**7:10 pm**		
☽♓ △ ♄♏	10:49 pm	**7:49 pm**		

Eastern Time plain / **Pacific Time bold**

DECEMBER 2013						
S	M	T	W	T	F	S
1	2	3	4	5	6	7
8	9	10	11	12	13	14
15	16	17	18	19	20	21
22	23	24	25	26	27	28
29	30	31				

JANUARY						
S	M	T	W	T	F	S
			1	2	3	4
5	6	7	8	9	10	11
12	13	14	15	16	17	18
19	20	21	22	23	24	25
26	27	28	29	30	31	

FEBRUARY						
S	M	T	W	T	F	S
						1
2	3	4	5	6	7	8
9	10	11	12	13	14	15
16	17	18	19	20	21	22
23	24	25	26	27	28	

6 Mon

1st ♓︎

OP continues until Moon enters Aries today. Good for artistic matters, meditation, and helping others. (Pisces is one of four signs in which the v/c Moon is a good thing. See page 77.)

☿♑ ⚹ ♄♏	3:51 am	**12:51 am**
☽♓ ⚹ ♀♑	4:44 am	**1:44 am** ☽ v/c
☽ enters ♈	2:45 pm	**11:45 am**

7 Tue

1st ♈

◗ 17 ♈ 46

☽♈ ☌ ♅♈	6:20 am	**3:20 am**
☽♈ □ ♀♑	11:13 am	**8:13 am**
☽♈ ☍ ♂♎	4:54 pm	**1:54 pm**
☿♑ ☌ ♀♑	5:02 pm	**2:02 pm**
☽♈ □ ♃♋	5:55 pm	**2:55 pm**
☽♈ □ ☉♑	10:39 pm	**7:39 pm**

8 Wed

2nd ♈

☽♈ ⚻ ♄♏	4:36 am	**1:36 am**
☽♈ □ ♀♑	8:19 am	**5:19 am**
☽♈ □ ☿♑	11:22 am	**8:22 am** ☽ v/c
♂♎ □ ♃♋	5:36 pm	**2:36 pm**
☽ enters ♉	9:24 pm	**6:24 pm**

9 Thu

2nd ♉

☽♉ ⚹ ♆♓	3:56 am	**12:56 am**
☽♉ ⚹ ♆♓	5:05 pm	**2:05 pm**
☽♉ △ ♀♑	7:27 pm	**4:27 pm**
☽♉ ⚹ ♃♋		**10:48 pm**

☽♉ ⚹ ♃♋	1:48 am	
☽♉ ⊼ ♂♎	3:16 am **12:16 am**	
☽♉ △ ⊙♑	12:34 pm **9:34 am**	
☽♉ ☍ ♄♏	2:07 pm **11:07 am**	
☽♉ △ ♀♑	2:57 pm **11:57 am**	

Fri 10
2nd ♉

OP: After Moon opposes Saturn today until Moon enters Gemini on Saturday. You can get a lot done now and enjoy yourself afterwards. (Taurus is one of the four signs in which the v/c Moon is a good thing. See page 77.)

♀♑ ⚹ ♄♏	5:44 am **2:44 am**	
☽♉ △ ☿♑	5:58 am **2:58 am** ☽ v/c	
⊙♑♂ ♀♑	7:24 am **4:24 am**	
☽ enters ♊	7:26 am **4:26 am**	
⊙♑⚹ ♄♏	8:39 am **5:39 am**	
☽♊ □ ♆♓	2:25 pm **11:25 am**	
☿ enters ♒	4:35 pm **1:35 pm**	
☽♊ ⚹ ♅♈	**10:02 pm**	

Sat 11
2nd ♉

OP: After Moon squares Neptune today until v/c Moon on Sunday. Good for either work or play.

☽♊ ⚹ ♅♈	1:02 am	
☽♊ □ ♂♓	4:12 am **1:12 am**	
☽♊ ⊼ ♀♑	6:36 am **3:36 am**	
☽♊ △ ♂♎	4:33 pm **1:33 pm** ☽ v/c	
☽♊ ⊼ ♀♑	11:39 pm **8:39 pm**	
☽♊ ⊼ ♄♏	**11:05 pm**	

Sun 12
2nd ♊

Eastern Time plain / **Pacific Time bold**

DECEMBER 2013								JANUARY								FEBRUARY					
S	M	T	W	T	F	S		S	M	T	W	T	F	S		S	M	T	W	T	F	S
1	2	3	4	5	6	7					1	2	3	4								1
8	9	10	11	12	13	14		5	6	7	8	9	10	11		2	3	4	5	6	7	8
15	16	17	18	19	20	21		12	13	14	15	16	17	18		9	10	11	12	13	14	15
22	23	24	25	26	27	28		19	20	21	22	23	24	25		16	17	18	19	20	21	22
29	30	31						26	27	28	29	30	31			23	24	25	26	27	28

January

13 Mon
2nd ♊

☽♊ ⚻ ♄♏	2:05 am	
☽♊ ⚻ ☉♑	5:39 am	**2:39 am**
☽ enters ♋	7:25 pm	**4:25 pm**
☽♋ △ ♆♓		**11:41 pm**

14 Tue
2nd ♋

☽♋ △ ♆♓	2:41 am	
☽♋ ⚻ ☿≈	3:44 am	**12:44 am**
☽♋ □ ♅♈	1:25 pm	**10:25 am**
☽♋ △ ⚷♓	4:46 pm	**1:46 pm**
☽♋ ☍ ♀♑	7:07 pm	**4:07 pm**
☽♋ ♂ ♃♋		**9:06 pm**

15 Wed
2nd ♋

○ Full Moon 25 ♋ 58

OP: After Moon squares Mars today until Moon enters Leo on Thursday. The Full Moon brings our emotions to the fore. Allow yourself to play tonight. (Cancer is one of the four signs in which the v/c Moon is a good thing. See page 77.)

☽♋ ♂ ♃♋	12:06 am	
☽♋ □ ♂♎	7:03 am	**4:03 am**
☽♋ ☍ ♀♑	9:16 am	**6:16 am**
☽♋ △ ♄♏	2:59 pm	**11:59 am**
☽♋ ☍ ☉♑	11:52 pm	**8:52 pm** ☽ v/c

16 Thu
3rd ♋

☽ enters ♌	8:00 am	**5:00 am**
♀♑ □ ♂♎	12:13 pm	**9:13 am**
☽♌ ⚻ ♆♓	3:27 pm	**12:27 pm**
☿≈ ✶ ♅♈		**10:25 pm**
☽♌ △ ♅♈		**11:09 pm**
☽♌ ☍ ☿≈		**11:16 pm**

☿≈ ✶ ♅♈ 1:25 am
☽♌ △ ♅♈ 2:09 am
☽♌ ☍ ☿≈ 2:16 am
☽♌ ⚻ ♗♓ 5:37 am **2:37 am**
☽♌ ⚻ ♇♑ 7:53 am **4:53 am**
☽♌ ⚻ ♀♑ 7:07 pm **4:07 pm**
☽♌ ✶ ♂♎ 9:34 pm **6:34 pm**

Fri 17
3rd ♌

☽♌ □ ♄♏ 3:51 am **12:51 am** ☽ v/c
☽♌ ⚻ ☉♑ 5:56 am **2:56 pm**
☽ enters ♍ 8:23 pm **5:23 pm**

Sat 18
3rd ♌

☽♍ ☍ ♆♓ 3:55 am **12:55 am**
☽♍ ⚻ ♅♈ 2:28 pm **11:28 am**
☽♍ ☍ ♗♓ 5:59 pm **2:59 pm**
☿≈ ⚻ ♃♋ 8:03 pm **5:03 pm**
☽♍ △ ♀♑ 8:09 pm **5:09 pm**
☉ enters ≈ 10:51 pm **7:51 pm**
☽♍ ✶ ♃♋ 11:26 pm **8:26 pm**
☽♍ ⚻ ☿≈ **9:01 pm**

Sun 19
3rd ♍

Sun enters Aquarius
OP: After Moon opposes Neptune today until v/c Moon on Monday. Even though it's Sunday, this is actually a very good time to get a lot of work done.

Eastern Time plain / **Pacific Time bold**

DECEMBER 2013						
S	M	T	W	T	F	S
1	2	3	4	5	6	7
8	9	10	11	12	13	14
15	16	17	18	19	20	21
22	23	24	25	26	27	28
29	30	31				

JANUARY						
S	M	T	W	T	F	S
			1	2	3	4
5	6	7	8	9	10	11
12	13	14	15	16	17	18
19	20	21	22	23	24	25
26	27	28	29	30	31	

FEBRUARY						
S	M	T	W	T	F	S
						1
2	3	4	5	6	7	8
9	10	11	12	13	14	15
16	17	18	19	20	21	22
23	24	25	26	27	28	

20 Mon
3rd ♍
Birthday of Martin Luther King, Jr. (observed)

☽♍ ☌ ☿≈ 12:01 am
☽♍ △ ♀♑ 4:42 am **1:42 am**
☽♍ ⚹ ♄♏ 3:55 pm **12:55 pm** ☽ v/c

21 Tue
3rd ♍

☽ enters ♎ 7:43 am **4:43 am**
☽♎ △ ☉≈ 10:41 am **7:41 am**
☽♎ ☌ ♆♓ 3:12 pm **12:12 pm**
☽♎ ☌ ♅♈ **10:22 pm**

22 Wed
3rd ♎

☽♎ ☌ ♅♈ 1:22 am
☽♎ ☌ ♀♓ 4:53 am **1:53 am**
☽♎ □ ♀♑ 6:53 am **3:53 am**
☽♎ □ ♃♋ 9:20 am **6:20 am**
☽♎ □ ♀♑ 1:06 pm **10:06 am**
☽♎ △ ☿≈ 7:00 pm **4:00 pm**
☽♎ ☌ ♂♎ 10:50 pm **7:50 pm** ☽ v/c

23 Thu
3rd ♎
◖ 4 ♏ 08 (Pacific)

☽ enters ♏ 4:43 pm **1:43 pm**
☽♏ △ ♆♓ 11:56 pm **8:56 pm**
☽♏ □ ☉≈ **9:19 pm**

☽♏□☉≈	12:19 am		**FRI 24**
☽♏⊼♅♈	9:32 am	**6:32 am**	3rd ♏
☿≈△♂♎	9:57 am	**6:57 am**	◑ 4 ♏ 08 (Eastern)
☽♏△⚷♓	12:56 pm	**9:56 am**	
☽♏⚹♇♑	2:43 pm	**11:43 am**	
☽♏△♃♋	4:23 pm	**1:23 pm**	
☽♏⚹♀♑	7:06 pm	**4:06 pm**	

☿≈□♄♏	6:56 am	**3:56 am**	**SAT 25**
☽♏☌♄♏	8:42 am	**5:42 am**	4th ♏
☽♏□☿≈	8:55 am	**5:55 am** ☽ v/c	
☽ enters ♐	10:13 pm	**7:13 pm**	

☽♐□♆♓	5:03 am	**2:03 am**	**SUN 26**
☽♐⚹☉≈	9:23 am	**6:23 am**	4th ♐
☽♐△♅♈	1:58 pm	**10:58 am**	
☽♐□⚷♓	5:13 pm	**2:13 pm**	
☽♐⊼♃♋	7:49 pm	**4:49 pm**	

OP: After Moon squares Neptune today until Moon enters Capricorn on Monday/Tuesday. Good for both physical and mental work. (Sagittarius is one of the four signs in which the v/c Moon is a good thing. See page 77.)

Eastern Time plain / **Pacific Time bold**

DECEMBER 2013

S	M	T	W	T	F	S
1	2	3	4	5	6	7
8	9	10	11	12	13	14
15	16	17	18	19	20	21
22	23	24	25	26	27	28
29	30	31				

JANUARY

S	M	T	W	T	F	S
			1	2	3	4
5	6	7	8	9	10	11
12	13	14	15	16	17	18
19	20	21	22	23	24	25
26	27	28	29	30	31	

FEBRUARY

S	M	T	W	T	F	S
						1
2	3	4	5	6	7	8
9	10	11	12	13	14	15
16	17	18	19	20	21	22
23	24	25	26	27	28	

January

27 Mon
4th ♐

☽♐ ⚹ ♂︎♎	10:52 am	**7:52 am**	
☽♐ ⚹ ☿♒	5:02 pm	**2:02 pm**	☽ v/c
☽ enters ♑		**9:04 pm**	

28 Tue
4th ♐

☽ enters ♑	12:04 am		
☽♑ ⚹ ♆♓	6:37 am	**3:37 am**	
☽♑ □ ♅♈	3:01 pm	**12:01 pm**	
☽♑ ⚹ ♀♓	6:09 pm	**3:09 pm**	
☽♑ ☌ ♀♑	7:35 pm	**4:35 pm**	
☽♑ ☍ ♃♋	8:06 pm	**5:06 pm**	
☽♑ ☌ ♀♑	9:57 pm	**6:57 pm**	

29 Wed
4th ♑

☉♒ ⚹ ♅♈	3:33 am	**12:33 am**	
☽♑ ⚹ ♄♏	11:43 am	**8:43 am**	
☽♑ □ ♂︎♎	11:47 am	**8:47 am**	☽ v/c
☽ enters ♒	11:33 pm	**8:33 pm**	

30 Thu
4th ♒
● New Moon 10 ♒ 55

☽♒ ⚹ ♅♈	2:16 pm	**11:16 am**	
☽♒ ☌ ☉♒	4:39 pm	**1:39 pm**	
☽♒ ⚻ ♃♋	6:51 pm	**3:51 pm**	

Mercury Note: Mercury enters its Storm (moving less than 40 minutes of arc per day) on Sunday, as it slows down before going retrograde. The Storm acts like the retrograde. Don't start any new projects now—just follow through with the items that are already on your plate. Write down new ideas with date and time they occurred.

Fri 31

1st ♒

Chinese New Year (horse)

♃♋ ☍ ♇♑	4:16 am	**1:16 am**
☿ enters ♓	9:29 am	**6:29 am**
☽♒ □ ♄♏	10:56 am	**7:56 am**
☽♒ △ ♂♎	11:45 am	**8:45 am** ☽ v/c
♀ D	3:49 pm	**12:49 pm**
☽ enters ♓	10:45 pm	**7:45 pm**
☉♒ ⚻ ♃♋	11:05 pm	**8:05 pm**
☽♓ ☌ ☿♓	11:38 pm	**8:38 pm**

Sat 1

1st ♓

☽♓ ☌ ♆♓	5:29 am	**2:29 am**
☽♓ ☌ ⚷♓	5:18 pm	**2:18 pm**
☽♓ △ ♃♋	6:16 pm	**3:16 pm**
☽♓ ⚹ ♇♑	6:37 pm	**3:37 pm**
☽♓ ⚹ ♀♑	8:38 pm	**5:38 pm**

OP: After Moon conjoins Neptune today until Moon enters Aries on Sunday. Good for artistic matters, meditation, and helping others. (Pisces is another of the four signs in which the v/c Moon is a good thing. See page 77.)

Sun 2

1st ♓

Groundhog Day

Imbolc

☽♓ △ ♄♏	11:35 am	**8:35 am** ☽ v/c
☽♓ ⚻ ♂♎	1:13 pm	**10:13 am**
☽ enters ♈	11:55 pm	**8:55 pm**

Eastern Time plain / **Pacific Time bold**

JANUARY

S	M	T	W	T	F	S
			1	2	3	4
5	6	7	8	9	10	11
12	13	14	15	16	17	18
19	20	21	22	23	24	25
26	27	28	29	30	31	

FEBRUARY

S	M	T	W	T	F	S
						1
2	3	4	5	6	7	8
9	10	11	12	13	14	15
16	17	18	19	20	21	22
23	24	25	26	27	28	

MARCH

S	M	T	W	T	F	S
						1
2	3	4	5	6	7	8
9	10	11	12	13	14	15
16	17	18	19	20	21	22
23	24	25	26	27	28	29
30	31					

February

3 Mon
1st ♈

☽♈ ☌ ♅♈	4:17 pm	**1:17 pm**	
☽♈ ☐ ♃♋	8:26 pm	**5:26 pm**	
☽♈ ☐ ♀♑	9:16 pm	**6:16 pm**	
☽♈ ☐ ♀♑	11:40 pm	**8:40 pm**	
☽♈ ⚹ ☉♒		**11:31 pm**	

4 Tue
1st ♈

☽♈ ⚹ ☉♒	2:31 am		
☽♈ ⚻ ♄♏	3:37 pm	**12:37 pm**	
☽♈ ☍ ♂♎	6:14 pm	**3:14 pm**	☽ v/c

5 Wed
1st ♈

☽ enters ♉	4:47 am	**1:47 am**	
☽♉ ⚹ ☿♓	10:39 am	**7:39 am**	
☽♉ ⚹ ♆♓	12:50 pm	**9:50 am**	
♃♋ △ ♅♓	2:53 pm	**11:53 am**	
☽♉ ⚹ ♃♋		**11:35 pm**	
☽♉ ⚹ ♅♓		**11:43 pm**	

6 Thu
1st ♉
☽ 17 ♉ 56

☽♉ ⚹ ♃♋	2:35 am		
☽♉ ⚹ ♅♓	2:43 am		
☽♉ △ ♀♑	4:00 am	**1:00 am**	
☽♉ △ ♀♑	7:13 am	**4:13 am**	
☽♉ ☐ ☉♒	2:22 pm	**11:22 am**	
☿ ℞	4:43 pm	**1:43 pm**	
☽♉ ☍ ♄♏	11:49 pm	**8:49 pm**	☽ v/c

96

Mercury Note: Mercury goes retrograde on Thursday and remains so until February 28, after which it will still be in its Storm until March 8. Projects begun during this entire period may not work out as planned. It's best to use this time for review, editing, escrows, and so forth.

Fri 7
2nd ♉

☽♉ ⚻ ♂♎ 3:34 am **12:34 am**
☽ enters ♊ 1:44 pm **10:44 am**
☽♊ □ ☿♓ 8:03 pm **5:03 pm**
☽♊ □ ♆♓ 10:29 pm **7:29 pm**

OP: After Moon squares Neptune today until v/c Moon on Sunday. Good for either work or play.

Sat 8
2nd ♊

☽♊ ⚹ ♅♈ 8:56 am **5:56 am**
☽♊ □ ⚷♓ 1:18 pm **10:18 am**
☽♊ ⚻ ♇♑ 2:31 pm **11:31 am**
☽♊ ⚻ ♀♑ 7:02 pm **4:02 pm**

Sun 9
2nd ♊

☽♊ △ ☉♒ 6:42 am **3:42 am**
☽♊ ⚻ ♄♏ 11:19 am **8:19 am**
☽♊ △ ♂♎ 4:08 pm **1:08 pm** ☽ v/c
☽ enters ♋ **10:33 pm**

Eastern Time plain / **Pacific Time bold**

JANUARY

S	M	T	W	T	F	S
			1	2	3	4
5	6	7	8	9	10	11
12	13	14	15	16	17	18
19	20	21	22	23	24	25
26	27	28	29	30	31	

FEBRUARY

S	M	T	W	T	F	S
						1
2	3	4	5	6	7	8
9	10	11	12	13	14	15
16	17	18	19	20	21	22
23	24	25	26	27	28	

MARCH

S	M	T	W	T	F	S
						1
2	3	4	5	6	7	8
9	10	11	12	13	14	15
16	17	18	19	20	21	22
23	24	25	26	27	28	29
30	31					

February

10 Mon
2nd ♊

☽ enter ♋	1:33 am	
☽♋ △ ☿ ♓	5:59 am	**2:59 am**
☽♋ △ ♆ ♓	10:44 am	**7:44 am**
☽♋ □ ♅ ♈	9:27 pm	**6:27 pm**
☽♋ ♂ ♃ ♋		**9:27 pm**
☽♋ △ ♄ ♓		**11:00 pm**

11 Tue
2nd ♋

☽♋ ♂ ♃ ♋	12:27 am	
☽♋ △ ♄ ♓	2:00 am	
☽♋ ♂ ♀ ♑	3:05 am	**12:05 am**
☽♋ ♂ ♀ ♑	9:20 am	**6:20 am**
☉≈ □ ♄ ♏	2:57 pm	**11:57 am**
☽♋ △ ♄ ♏		**9:09 pm**
☽♋ ⊼ ☉≈		**9:59 pm**

12 Wed
2nd ♋

☽♋ △ ♄ ♏	12:09 am	
☽♋ ⊼ ☉≈	12:59 am	
☽♋ □ ♂ ♎	5:51 am	**2:51 am** ☽ v/c
☽ enters ♌	2:15 pm	**11:15 am**
☽♌ ⊼ ☿ ♓	2:52 pm	**11:52 am**
☿ enters ≈	10:30 pm	**7:30 pm**
☽♌ ⊼ ♆ ♓	11:38 pm	**8:38 pm**

13 Thu
2nd ♌

☽♌ △ ♅ ♈	10:19 am	**7:19 am**
☽♌ ⊼ ♄ ♓	2:56 pm	**11:56 am**
☽♌ ⊼ ♀ ♑	3:50 pm	**12:50 pm**
☽♌ ⊼ ♀ ♑		**9:05 pm**

☽♌ ⚻ ♀♑ 12:05 am
☽♌ □ ♄♏ 12:41 pm **9:41 am**
☽♌ ☌ ☉≈ 6:53 pm **3:53 pm**
☽♌ ✳ ♂♎ 7:02 pm **4:02 pm**
☉≈ △ ♂♎ 9:05 pm **6:05 pm**
☽♌ ☍ ☿≈ 10:13 pm **7:13 pm** ☽ v/c
☽ enters ♍ **11:26 pm**

FRI 14
2nd ♌
○ Full Moon 26 ♌ 13
VALENTINE'S DAY
OP: After Moon squares Saturn until v/c Moon. Keep busy with projects that you already began before January 31.

☽ enters ♍ 2:26 am
☽♍ ☍ ♆♓ 11:50 am **8:50 am**
☉≈ ☌ ☿≈ 3:22 am **12:22 pm**
☽♍ ⚻ ♅♈ 10:22 pm **7:22 pm**
☽♍ ✳ ♃♋ **9:11 pm**
☽♍ ☍ ♇♓ **11:58 pm**

SAT 15
3rd ♌
OP: After Moon opposes Neptune today until v/c Moon on Sunday/Monday. Potentially a highly productive time.

☽♍ ✳ ♃♋ 12:11 am
☽♍ ☍ ♇♓ 2:58 am
☿≈ △ ♂♎ 3:19 am **12:19 am**
☽♍ △ ♆♑ 3:41 am **12:41 am**
☽♍ △ ♀♑ 2:08 pm **11:08 am**
☽♍ ✳ ♄♏ **9:04 pm** ☽ v/c

SUN 16
3rd ♍

Eastern Time plain / **Pacific Time bold**

JANUARY						
S	M	T	W	T	F	S
			1	2	3	4
5	6	7	8	9	10	11
12	13	14	15	16	17	18
19	20	21	22	23	24	25
26	27	28	29	30	31	

FEBRUARY						
S	M	T	W	T	F	S
						1
2	3	4	5	6	7	8
9	10	11	12	13	14	15
16	17	18	19	20	21	22
23	24	25	26	27	28	

MARCH						
S	M	T	W	T	F	S
						1
2	3	4	5	6	7	8
9	10	11	12	13	14	15
16	17	18	19	20	21	22
23	24	25	26	27	28	29
30	31					

February

17 Mon
3rd ♍

☽♍ ⚹ ♄♏	12:04 am	☽ v/c
☽♍ ⚻ ☿≈	4:15 am	**1:15 am**
☽♍ ⚻ ☉≈	11:17 am	**8:17 am**
☽ enters ♎	1:23 pm	**10:23 am**
☽♎ ⚻ ♆♓	10:43 pm	**7:43 pm**

18 Tue
3rd ♎
Sun enters Pisces

☽♎ ☍ ♅♈	9:00 am	**6:00 am**
☽♎ □ ♃♋	10:18 am	**7:18 am**
☉ enters ♓	12:59 pm	**9:59 am**
☽♎ ⚻ ♀♓	1:33 pm	**10:33 am**
☽♎ □ ♇♑	2:04 pm	**11:04 am**
☿≈ □ ♄♏		**11:11 pm**
☽♎ □ ♀♑		**11:45 pm**

19 Wed
3rd ♎

☿≈ □ ♄♏	2:11 am	
☽♎ □ ♀♑	2:45 am	
☽♎ △ ☿≈	9:14 am	**6:14 am**
☽♎ ☌ ♂♎	4:52 pm	**1:52 pm** ☽ v/c
☽ enters ♏	10:33 pm	**7:33 pm**
☽♏ △ ☉♓		**10:24 pm**

20 Thu
3rd ♏

☽♏ △ ☉♓	1:24 am	
☽♏ △ ♆♓	7:42 am	**4:42 am**
☽♏ ⚻ ♅♈	5:37 pm	**2:37 pm**
☽♏ △ ♃♋	6:27 pm	**3:27 pm**
☽♏ △ ♀♓	10:02 pm	**7:02 pm**
☽♏ ⚹ ♇♑	10:22 pm	**7:22 pm**

)♏ □ ☿ ≈ 12:58 pm **9:58 am**
)♏ ⚹ ♀ ♑ 1:04 pm **10:04 am**
)♏ ☌ ♄♏ 5:10 pm **2:10 pm**) v/c

) enters ♐ 5:12 am **2:12 am**
)♐ □ ⊙⋇ 12:15 pm **9:15 am**
)♐ □ ♆⋇ 2:02 pm **11:02 am**
)♐ △ ♅♈ 11:26 pm **8:26 pm**
)♐ ⚻ ♃⊙ 11:52 pm **8:52 pm**

OP: After Moon squares Neptune today until Moon enters Capricorn on Monday. As the Sun conjoins Neptune, this is a good time to meditate, help others, or put your energy into artistic creativity. (Sagittarius is one of the four signs in which the v/c Moon is a good thing. See page 77.)

)♐ □ ♅⋇ 3:40 am **12:40 am**
⊙⋇ ☌ ♆⋇ 1:11 pm **10:11 am**
)♐ ⚹ ☿ ≈ 3:04 pm **12:04 pm**

Eastern Time plain / **Pacific Time bold**

		JANUARY								FEBRUARY								MARCH				
S	M	T	W	T	F	S		S	M	T	W	T	F	S		S	M	T	W	T	F	S
			1	2	3	4								1								1
5	6	7	8	9	10	11		2	3	4	5	6	7	8		2	3	4	5	6	7	8
12	13	14	15	16	17	18		9	10	11	12	13	14	15		9	10	11	12	13	14	15
19	20	21	22	23	24	25		16	17	18	19	20	21	22		16	17	18	19	20	21	22
26	27	28	29	30	31			23	24	25	26	27	28			23	24	25	26	27	28	29
																30	31					

February

24 Mon
4th ♐

☽♐ ⚹ ♂︎♎	4:25 am	**1:25 am**	☽ v/c
☽ enters ♑	8:50 am	**5:50 am**	
☽♑ ⚹ ♆♓	5:19 pm	**2:19 pm**	
☽♑ ⚹ ☉♓	7:20 pm	**4:20 pm**	
♀♑ ⚹ ♄♏	11:50 pm	**8:50 pm**	
☽♑ □ ♅♈		**11:15 pm**	
☽♑ ☌ ♃♋		**11:23 pm**	

25 Tue
4th ♑

☽♑ □ ♅♈	2:15 am	
☽♑ ☌ ♃♋	2:23 am	
☽♑ ⚹ ♀♓	6:19 am	**3:19 am**
☽♑ ☌ ♀♑	6:20 am	**3:20 am**
♀♑ ⚹ ♀♓	5:34 pm	**2:34 pm**
☽♑ ⚹ ♄♏	11:08 pm	**8:08 pm**
☽♑ ☌ ♀♑		**9:17 pm**
♃♋ □ ♅♈		**11:29 pm**

26 Wed
4th ♑

☽♑ ☌ ♀♑	12:17 am		
♃♋ □ ♅♈	2:29 am		
☽♑ □ ♂︎♎	5:51 am	**2:51 am**	☽ v/c
☽ enters ♒	9:55 am	**6:55 am**	
☽♒ ☌ ♃♋		**11:47 pm**	
☽♒ ⚹ ♅♈		**11:54 pm**	

27 Thu
4th ♒

☽♒ ☌ ♃♋	2:47 am	
☽♒ ⚹ ♅♈	2:54 am	
☽♒ ☌ ☿♒	3:01 pm	**12:01 pm**
☽♒ □ ♄♏	11:11 pm	**8:11 pm**

Mercury Note: Mercury goes direct on Friday but remains in its Storm, moving slowly until March 8. Until then, it is not yet time for new ideas to be workable.

Fri 28

4th ♒

☽♒ △ ♂♎	5:55 am	**2:55 am**	☽ v/c
☿ D	9:00 am	**6:00 am**	
☽ enters ♓	9:53 am	**6:53 am**	
☽♓ ☌ ♆♓	6:17 pm	**3:17 pm**	
☉♓ △ ♃♋	11:05 pm	**8:05 pm**	
☽♓ △ ♃♋		**11:44 pm**	

Sat 1

4th ♓

● New Moon 10 ♓ 39

☽♓ △ ♃♋	2:44 am		
☽♓ ☌ ☉♓	3:00 am	**12:00 am**	
☽♓ ⚹ ♇♑	6:55 am	**3:55 am**	
☽♓ ☌ ⚷♓	7:10 am	**4:10 am**	
♂℞	11:23 am	**8:23 am**	
☽♓ △ ♄♏	11:37 pm	**8:37 pm**	

OP: This Cazimi Moon is usable ½ hour before and ½ hour after the Sun-Moon conjunction. If you have something important to start around now that is part of a project already begun before January 31, this is a great time to do it.

Sun 2

1st ♓

☽♓ ⚹ ♀♑	6:04 am	**3:04 am**	☽ v/c
☽♓ ⚻ ♂♎	6:34 am	**3:34 am**	
☽ enters ♈	10:40 am	**7:40 am**	
♄℞	11:20 am	**8:20 am**	
♀♑ □ ♂♎	3:03 pm	**12:03 pm**	

Eastern Time plain / **Pacific Time bold**

FEBRUARY

S	M	T	W	T	F	S
						1
2	3	4	5	6	7	8
9	10	11	12	13	14	15
16	17	18	19	20	21	22
23	24	25	26	27	28	

MARCH

S	M	T	W	T	F	S
						1
2	3	4	5	6	7	8
9	10	11	12	13	14	15
16	17	18	19	20	21	22
23	24	25	26	27	28	29
30	31					

APRIL

S	M	T	W	T	F	S
		1	2	3	4	5
6	7	8	9	10	11	12
13	14	15	16	17	18	19
20	21	22	23	24	25	26
27	28	29	30			

MARCH

3 **Mon**
1st ♈

☽♈□ ♃⊙	4:14 am	**1:14 am**	
☽♈♂ ♅♈	4:50 am	**1:50 am**	
☽♈□ ♀♑	8:47 am	**5:47 am**	
☉♓⚹ ♀♑	2:16 pm	**11:16 am**	
☽♈⚹ ☿≈	6:28 pm	**3:28 pm**	
☉♓♂ ⚷♓	8:26 pm	**5:26 pm**	
☽♈⚻ ♄♏		**11:24 pm**	

4 **Tue**
1st ♈
Mardi Gras (Fat Tuesday)

☽♈⚻ ♄♏	2:24 am		
☽♈♂ ♂♎	9:44 am	**6:44 am**	
☽♈□ ♀♑	12:31 pm	**9:31 am**	☽ v/c
☽ enters ♉	2:12 pm	**11:12 am**	
☽♉⚹ ♆♓	11:53 pm	**8:53 pm**	

5 **Wed**
1st ♉
Ash Wednesday

☽♉⚹ ♃⊙	9:02 am	**6:02 am**	
☽♉△ ♀♑	2:02 pm	**11:02 am**	
☽♉⚹ ⚷♓	2:38 pm	**11:38 am**	
♀ enters ≈	4:03 pm	**1:03 pm**	
☽♉⚹ ☉♓	5:57 pm	**2:57 pm**	
☽♉□ ☿≈		**11:17 pm**	

6 **Thu**
1st ♉

OP: After Moon opposes Saturn until Moon enters Gemini.
Good for either work or play. (Taurus is one of the four signs in
which the v/c Moon is a good thing. See page 77.)

☽♉□ ☿≈	2:17 am		
♃ D	5:42 am	**2:42 am**	
☽♉♂ ♄♏	8:55 am	**5:55 am**	☽ v/c
☽♉⚻ ♂♎	4:36 pm	**1:36 pm**	
☽ enters ♊	9:37 pm	**6:37 pm**	
☽♊△ ♀≈	11:45 pm	**8:45 pm**	

☽Ⅱ □ ♅♓ 8:11 am **5:11 am**
☽Ⅱ ✶ ♅♈ 7:00 pm **4:00 pm**
☽Ⅱ ⊼ ♀♑ 11:14 pm **8:14 pm**
☽Ⅱ □ ⛢♓ **9:05 pm**

FRI 7
1st Ⅱ

☽Ⅱ □ ⛢♓ 12:05 am
☽Ⅱ □ ☉♓ 8:27 am **5:27 am**
☽Ⅱ △ ☿♒ 3:19 pm **12:19 pm**
☽Ⅱ ⊼ ♄♏ 7:08 pm **4:08 pm**
☽Ⅱ △ ♂♎ **11:53 pm** ☽ v/c

SAT 8
1st Ⅱ
◗ 17 Ⅱ 54

OP: After Moon squares Sun today until v/c Moon today/Sunday. Now and during the next few OPs, look at the notes you made about new ideas that occurred to you while Mercury was retrograde and/or slow. How do those ideas look now?

☽Ⅱ △ ♂♎ 3:53 am ☽ v/c
☽ enters ♋ 9:33 am **6:33 am**
☽♋ ⊼ ♀♒ 4:23 pm **1:23 pm**
☽♋ △ ♅♓ 8:46 pm **5:46 pm**

SUN 9
2nd Ⅱ
DAYLIGHT SAVING TIME BEGINS AT 2:00 AM

Eastern Time plain / **Pacific Time bold**

FEBRUARY								MARCH								APRIL					
S	M	T	W	T	F	S		S	M	T	W	T	F	S		S	M	T	W	T	F	S
						1								1				1	2	3	4	5
2	3	4	5	6	7	8		2	3	4	5	6	7	8		6	7	8	9	10	11	12
9	10	11	12	13	14	15		9	10	11	12	13	14	15		13	14	15	16	17	18	19
16	17	18	19	20	21	22		16	17	18	19	20	21	22		20	21	22	23	24	25	26
23	24	25	26	27	28			23	24	25	26	27	28	29		27	28	29	30			
								30	31													

10 Mon
2nd ⊚

☽⊚ ♂ ♃⊚	6:37 am	**3:37 am**	
☽⊚ □ ♅♈	8:05 am	**5:05 am**	
☽⊚ ♂ ♀♑	12:16 pm	**9:16 am**	
☽⊚ △ ⚷♓	1:22 pm	**10:22 am**	
☿≈ □ ♄♏		**11:14 pm**	

11 Tue
2nd ⊚

☿≈ □ ♄♏	2:14 am		
☽⊚ △ ☉♓	3:11 am	**12:11 am**	
☽⊚ △ ♄♏	8:29 am	**5:29 am**	
☽⊚ ⊼ ☿≈	8:59 am	**5:59 am**	
☽⊚ □ ♂♎	3:50 pm	**12:50 pm**	☽ v/c
☽ enters ♌	10:09 pm	**7:09 pm**	

12 Wed
2nd ♌

☽♌ ⊼ ♆♓	9:37 am	**6:37 am**	
☽♌ ♂ ♀≈	9:57 am	**6:57 am**	
☽♌ △ ♅♈	9:00 pm	**6:00 pm**	
☽♌ ⊼ ♀♑		**9:58 pm**	
☽♌ ⊼ ⚷♓		**11:18 pm**	

13 Thu
2nd ♌
OP: After Moon squares Saturn today until v/c Moon on Friday. Good for night owls.

☽♌ ⊼ ♀♑	12:58 am		
☽♌ ⊼ ⚷♓	2:18 am		
☉♓ △ ♄♏	5:15 pm	**2:15 pm**	
☽♌ □ ♄♏	8:48 pm	**5:48 pm**	
☽♌ ⊼ ☉♓	9:07 pm	**6:07 pm**	
☽♌ ♂ ☿≈		**11:27 pm**	

☽♌ ☌ ☿≈ 2:27 am
☽♌ ⚹ ♂♎ 3:24 am **12:24 am** ☽ v/c
☽ enters ♍ 10:17 am **7:17 am**
☿≈ △ ♂♎ 12:17 pm **9:17 am**
☽♍ ☌ ♆♓ 9:41 pm **6:41 pm**
☽♍ ⊼ ♀≈ **11:42 pm**

FRI 14
2nd ♌

OP: After Moon opposes Neptune today until v/c Moon on Sunday. A lot can be accomplished on Saturday especially. This is the next-to-last long OP in an earth sign before the tax deadline of April 15, so make good use of it.

☽♍ ⊼ ♀≈ 2:42 am
☽♍ ⚹ ♃⊗ 7:07 am **4:07 am**
☽♍ ⊼ ♅♈ 8:52 am **5:52 am**
☽♍ △ ♀♑ 12:33 pm **9:33 am**
☽♍ ☌ ⚷♓ 2:04 pm **11:04 am**

SAT 15
2nd ♍

☽♍ ⚹ ♄♏ 7:36 am **4:36 am**
☽♍ ☌ ☉♓ 1:08 pm **10:08 am** ☽ v/c
☉♓ ⊼ ♂♎ 2:38 pm **11:38 am**
☽♍ ⊼ ☿≈ 6:37 pm **3:37 pm**
☽ enters ♎ 8:46 pm **5:46 pm**

SUN 16
2nd ♍
○ Full Moon 26 ♍ 02
PURIM

Eastern Time plain / **Pacific Time bold**

FEBRUARY							MARCH							APRIL					
S	M	T	W	T	F	S	S	M	T	W	T	F	S	S	M	T	W	T	F	S
						1							1			1	2	3	4	5
2	3	4	5	6	7	8	2	3	4	5	6	7	8	6	7	8	9	10	11	12
9	10	11	12	13	14	15	9	10	11	12	13	14	15	13	14	15	16	17	18	19
16	17	18	19	20	21	22	16	17	18	19	20	21	22	20	21	22	23	24	25	26
23	24	25	26	27	28		23	24	25	26	27	28	29	27	28	29	30			
							30	31												

March

17 Mon
3rd ♎
St. Patrick's Day

☽♎ ⚻ ♆♓	7:57 am	**4:57 am**
♀♒ ⚻ ♃♋	2:01 pm	**11:01 am**
☽♎ □ ♃♋	5:03 pm	**2:03 pm**
☽♎ △ ♀♒	5:17 pm	**2:17 pm**
☿ enters ♓	6:24 pm	**3:24 pm**
☽♎ ☍ ♅♈	6:50 pm	**3:50 pm**
☽♎ □ ♇♑	10:12 pm	**7:12 pm**
☽♎ ⚻ ⚷♓	11:53 pm	**8:53 pm**

18 Tue
3rd ♎

♀♒ ⚹ ♅♈	3:00 pm	**12:00 pm**
☽♎ ☌ ♂♎	9:07 pm	**6:07 pm** ☽ v/c
☽♎ ⚻ ☉♓		**11:35 pm**

19 Wed
3rd ♎

☽♎ ⚻ ☉♓	2:35 am	
☽ enters ♏	5:13 am	**2:13 am**
☽♏ △ ☿♓	8:41 am	**5:41 am**
☽♏ △ ♆♓	4:10 pm	**1:10 pm**
☽♏ △ ♃♋		**9:57 pm**
☽♏ ⚻ ♅♈		**11:44 pm**

20 Thu
3rd ♏
Spring Equinox
Ostara
International Astrology Day
Sun enters Aries

☽♏ △ ♃♋	12:57 am	
☽♏ ⚻ ♅♈	2:44 am	
☽♏ □ ♀♒	5:24 am	**2:24 am**
☽♏ ⚹ ♇♑	5:48 am	**2:48 am**
☽♏ △ ⚷♓	7:38 am	**4:38 am**
☉ enters ♈	12:57 pm	**9:57 am**
☽♏ ☌ ♄♏	11:12 pm	**8:12 pm** ☽ v/c

Fri 21
3rd ♏

☽ enters ♐ 11:39 am **8:39 am**
☽♐ △ ☉♈ 1:27 pm **10:27 am**
☽♐ □ ☿♓ 8:29 pm **5:29 pm**
☽♐ □ ♆♓ 10:20 pm **7:20 pm**

OP: After Moon squares Neptune today until Moon enters Capricorn on Sunday. As Mercury conjoins Neptune, this is a good time to meditate, help others, or put your energy into artistic creativity. (Sagittarius is one of the four signs in which the v/c Moon is a good thing. See page 77.)

Sat 22
3rd ♐

☽♐ ⚻ ♃♋ 6:50 am **3:50 am**
☽♐ △ ♅♈ 8:36 am **5:36 am**
☽♐ □ ⚷♓ 1:19 pm **10:19 am**
☽♐ ⚹ ♀♒ 3:03 pm **12:03 pm**
☿♓ ☌ ♆♓ 4:16 pm **1:16 pm**

Sun 23
3rd ♐
◑ 3 ♑ 21

☽♐ ⚹ ♂♎ 6:40 am **3:40 am** ☽ v/c
☽ enters ♑ 4:03 pm **1:03 pm**
☽♑ □ ☉♈ 9:46 pm **6:46 pm**
☽♑ ⚹ ♆♓ **11:28 pm**

Eastern Time plain / **Pacific Time bold**

FEBRUARY

S	M	T	W	T	F	S
						1
2	3	4	5	6	7	8
9	10	11	12	13	14	15
16	17	18	19	20	21	22
23	24	25	26	27	28	

MARCH

S	M	T	W	T	F	S
						1
2	3	4	5	6	7	8
9	10	11	12	13	14	15
16	17	18	19	20	21	22
23	24	25	26	27	28	29
30	31					

APRIL

S	M	T	W	T	F	S
		1	2	3	4	5
6	7	8	9	10	11	12
13	14	15	16	17	18	19
20	21	22	23	24	25	26
27	28	29	30			

March

24 Mon
4th ♑

☽♑ ⚹ ♆♓	2:28 am	
☽♑ ⚹ ☿♓	5:56 am	**2:56 am**
☽♑ ☍ ♃♋	10:44 am	**7:44 am**
☽♑ □ ♅♈	12:26 pm	**9:26 am**
☽♑ ☌ ♀♑	2:57 pm	**11:57 am**
☽♑ ⚹ ⚷♓	5:01 pm	**2:01 pm**

25 Tue
4th ♑

☽♑ ⚹ ♄♏	6:47 am	**3:47 am**
☽♑ □ ♂♎	8:35 am	**5:35 am** ☽ v/c
☽ enters ♒	6:39 pm	**3:39 pm**

26 Wed
4th ♒

☽♒ ⚹ ☉♈	3:54 am	**12:54 am**
☿♓ △ ♃♋	9:11 am	**6:11 am**
☽♒ ⚻ ♃♋	1:02 pm	**10:02 am**
☽♒ ⚹ ♅♈	2:41 pm	**11:41 am**

27 Thu
4th ♒

☽♒ ☌ ♀♒	3:52 am	**12:52 am**
☽♒ □ ♄♏	8:20 am	**5:20 am**
☽♒ △ ♂♎	9:13 am	**6:13 am** ☽ v/c
☽ enters ♓	8:10 pm	**5:10 pm**
☿♓ ⚹ ♀♑		**10:32 pm**

☿♓ ⚹ ♀♑	1:32 am			
☽♓ ♂ ♆♓	6:27 am	**3:27 am**		
☽♓ △ ♃♋	2:42 pm	**11:42 am**		
☽♓ ⚹ ♀♑	6:27 pm	**3:27 pm**		
☽♓ ♂ ☿♓	8:20 pm	**5:20 pm**		
☽♓ ♂ ♅♓	8:48 pm	**5:48 pm**		
☿♓ ♂ ♅♓		**10:08 pm**		

FRI 28
4th ♓

OP: After Moon conjoins Neptune today until Moon enters Aries on Saturday. Good for artistic matters, meditation, and helping others. (Pisces is another of the four signs in which the v/c Moon is a good thing. See page 77.)

☿♓ ♂ ♅♓	1:08 am		
☽♓ ⚼ ♂♎	9:41 am	**6:41 am**	
☽♓ △ ♄♏	9:44 am	**6:44 am** ☽ v/c	
♀≈ △ ♂♎	3:05 pm	**12:05 pm**	
♀≈ □ ♄♏	5:14 pm	**2:14 pm**	
☽ enters ♈	9:54 pm	**6:54 pm**	

SAT 29
4th ♓

☽♈ ♂ ☉♈	2:45 pm	**11:45 am**
☽♈ □ ♃♋	5:08 pm	**2:08 pm**
☽♈ ♂ ♅♈	6:45 pm	**3:45 pm**
☽♈ □ ♀♑	8:47 pm	**5:47 pm**

SUN 30
4th ♈
● New Moon 9 ♈ 59

Eastern Time plain / **Pacific Time bold**

	FEBRUARY							MARCH							APRIL					
S	M	T	W	T	F	S	S	M	T	W	T	F	S	S	M	T	W	T	F	S
						1							1			1	2	3	4	5
2	3	4	5	6	7	8	2	3	4	5	6	7	8	6	7	8	9	10	11	12
9	10	11	12	13	14	15	9	10	11	12	13	14	15	13	14	15	16	17	18	19
16	17	18	19	20	21	22	16	17	18	19	20	21	22	20	21	22	23	24	25	26
23	24	25	26	27	28		23	24	25	26	27	28	29	27	28	29	30			
							30	31												

111

31 Mon
1st ♈

☽♈ ☍ ♂︎♎	11:21 am	**8:21 am**
☽♈ ⚻ ♄♏	12:27 am	**9:27 am**
☽♈ ⚹ ♀≈	4:07 pm	**1:07 pm** ☽ v/c
☽ enters ♉		**10:20 pm**

1 Tue
1st ♈
April Fools' Day

☽ enters ♉	1:20 am	
☉♈ □ ♃♋	3:39 am	**12:39 am**
☽♉ ⚹ ♆♓	12:38 pm	**9:38 am**
☽♉ ⚹ ♃♋	9:55 pm	**6:55 pm**
☽♉ △ ♀♑		**10:29 pm**

2 Wed
1st ♉

☽♉ △ ♀♑	1:29 am	
☉♈ ☌ ♅♈	3:09 am	**12:09 am**
☽♉ ⚹ ⚷♓	4:28 am	**1:28 am**
☿♓ ⚻ ♂︎♎	5:44 am	**2:44 am**
☽♉ ⚻ ♂︎♎	3:30 pm	**12:30 pm**
☽♉ ⚹ ☿♓	5:09 pm	**2:09 pm**
☽♉ ☍ ♄♏	5:54 pm	**2:54 pm**
☿♓ △ ♄♏	11:03 pm	**8:03 pm**
☽♉ □ ♀≈		**11:43 pm** ☽ v/c

3 Thu
1st ♉

OP: After Moon squares Venus on Wednesday/today until Moon enters Gemini today. Short; good for night owls. (Taurus is one of the four signs in which the v/c Moon is a good thing. See page 77.)

☽♉ □ ♀≈	2:43 am	☽ v/c
☉♈ □ ♀♑	5:22 am	**2:22 am**
☽ enters ♊	7:48 am	**4:48 am**
☽♊ □ ♆♓	7:58 pm	**4:58 pm**

☽Ⅱ	⚹	♅♈	7:42 am	**4:42 am**
☽Ⅱ	⊼	♀♑	9:33 am	**6:33 am**
☽Ⅱ	⚹	☉♈	11:57 am	**8:57 am**
☽Ⅱ	□	♅♓	12:57 pm	**9:57 am**
☽Ⅱ	△	♂♎	10:45 pm	**7:45 pm**
☽Ⅱ	⊼	♄♏		**11:43 pm**

FRI 4
1st Ⅱ

☽Ⅱ	⊼	♄♏	2:43 am	
☽Ⅱ	□	☿♓	10:55 am	**7:55 am** ☽ v/c
♀ enters ♓			4:31 pm	**1:31 pm**
☽ enters ♋			5:40 pm	**2:40 pm**
☽♋	△	♀♓	5:46 pm	**2:46 pm**

SAT 5
1st Ⅱ

☽♋	△	♆♓	6:37 am	**3:37 am**
☽♋	♂	♃♋	5:33 pm	**2:33 pm**
☽♋	□	♅♈	7:02 pm	**4:02 pm**
☽♋	☍	♀♑	8:42 pm	**5:42 pm**
☽♋	△	♅♓		**9:30 pm**

SUN 6
1st ♋

Eastern Time plain / **Pacific Time bold**

MARCH						
S	M	T	W	T	F	S
						1
2	3	4	5	6	7	8
9	10	11	12	13	14	15
16	17	18	19	20	21	22
23	24	25	26	27	28	29
30	31					

APRIL						
S	M	T	W	T	F	S
		1	2	3	4	5
6	7	8	9	10	11	12
13	14	15	16	17	18	19
20	21	22	23	24	25	26
27	28	29	30			

MAY						
S	M	T	W	T	F	S
				1	2	3
4	5	6	7	8	9	10
11	12	13	14	15	16	17
18	19	20	21	22	23	24
25	26	27	28	29	30	31

April

7 Mon

1st ♋

◐ 17 ♋ 27

OP: After Moon trines Saturn today (see "Translating Darkness" on page 80) until Moon enters Leo on Tuesday. (Cancer is one of the four signs in which the v/c Moon is a good thing. See page 77.)

☽♋ △ ⚷♓	12:30 am		
☽♋ □ ☉♈	4:31 am	**1:31 am**	
☽♋ □ ♂♎	8:34 am	**5:34 am**	
☿ enters ♈	11:35 am	**8:35 am**	
☽♋ △ ♄♏	2:14 pm	**11:14 am**	☽ v/c

8 Tue

2nd ♋

☽ enters ♌	5:50 am	**2:50 am**	
☽♌ △ ☿♈	8:56 am	**5:56 am**	
☽♌ ⊼ ♀♓	11:53 am	**8:53 am**	
☉♈ ☍ ♂♎	5:04 pm	**2:04 pm**	
☽♌ ⊼ ♆♓	7:11 pm	**4:11 pm**	

9 Wed

2nd ♌

☽♌ △ ♅♈	7:50 am	**4:50 am**	
☽♌ ⊼ ♇♑	9:14 am	**6:14 am**	
☽♌ ⊼ ⚷♓	1:19 pm	**10:19 am**	
☽♌ ✶ ♂♎	7:12 pm	**4:12 pm**	
☽♌ △ ☉♈	10:28 pm	**7:28 pm**	
☽♌ □ ♄♏		**11:26 pm**	☽ v/c

10 Thu

2nd ♌

☽♌ □ ♄♏	2:26 am		☽ v/c
☽ enters ♍	6:08 pm	**3:08 pm**	

☽♍ ☍ ♀♓	5:55 am	**2:55 am**	
☽♍ ☍ ♆♓	7:21 am	**4:21 am**	
☽♍ ⊼ ☿♈	7:26 am	**4:26 am**	
☽♍ ✶ ♃♋	6:47 pm	**3:47 pm**	
☽♍ ⊼ ♅♈	7:47 pm	**4:47 pm**	
☉♈⊼ ♄♏	8:23 pm	**5:23 pm**	
☽♍ △ ♀♑	8:53 pm	**5:53 pm**	
♀♓ ♂ ♆♓	10:23 pm	**7:23 pm**	
☽♍ ☍ ♅♓		**10:05 pm**	

Fri 11
2nd ♍

OP: After Moon opposes Neptune today until v/c Moon on Saturday. With the Moon in Virgo, this can be an excellent time to finish preparing your tax returns. However, as Venus conjoins Neptune, this is also a good time to meditate, help others, or put your energy into artistic creativity.

☽♍ ☍ ♅♓	1:05 am		
☽♍ ✶ ♄♏	1:12 pm	**10:12 am** ☽ v/c	
☽♍ ⊼ ☉♈	2:43 pm	**11:43 am**	

Sat 12
2nd ♍

☽ enters ♎	4:33 am	**1:33 am**	
☽♎⊼ ♆♓	5:20 pm	**2:20 pm**	
☽♎⊼ ♀♓	9:14 pm	**6:14 pm**	

Sun 13
2nd ♍
Palm Sunday

Eastern Time plain / **Pacific Time bold**

	MARCH								APRIL								MAY					
S	M	T	W	T	F	S		S	M	T	W	T	F	S		S	M	T	W	T	F	S
						1				1	2	3	4	5						1	2	3
2	3	4	5	6	7	8		6	7	8	9	10	11	12		4	5	6	7	8	9	10
9	10	11	12	13	14	15		13	14	15	16	17	18	19		11	12	13	14	15	16	17
16	17	18	19	20	21	22		20	21	22	23	24	25	26		18	19	20	21	22	23	24
23	24	25	26	27	28	29		27	28	29	30					25	26	27	28	29	30	31
30	31																					

14 Mon
2nd ♎

☽♎☍ ☿♈	3:01 am	**12:01 am**	
☽♎□ ♃⊛	4:37 am	**1:37 am**	
☽♎☍ ♅♈	5:20 am	**2:20 am**	
☽♎□ ♀♑	6:08 am	**3:08 am**	
☽♎⚻ ⚷♓	10:22 am	**7:22 am**	
☽♎☌ ♂♎	12:00 pm	**9:00 am**	
☿♈□ ♃⊛	2:32 pm	**11:32 am**	
☿♈☌ ♅♈	7:15 pm	**4:15 pm**	
♀℞	7:47 pm	**4:47 pm**	
☿♈□ ♀♑		**9:13 pm**	

15 Tue
2nd ♎
Total Lunar Eclipse | ◯ Full Moon 25 ♎ 16
PASSOVER BEGINS

☿♈□ ♀♑	12:13 am		
☽♎☍ ☉♈	3:42 am	**12:42 am**	☽ v/c
☽ enters ♏	12:20 pm	**9:20 am**	
☽♏△ ♆♓		**9:39 pm**	

16 Wed
3rd ♏

☽♏△ ♆♓	12:39 am		
☿♈☍ ♂♎	7:15 am	**4:15 am**	
☽♏△ ♀♓	9:08 am	**6:08 am**	
☽♏△ ♃⊛	11:47 am	**8:47 am**	
☽♏⚻ ♅♈	12:14 pm	**9:14 am**	
☽♏⚹ ♀♑	12:46 pm	**9:46 am**	
♂♎⚻ ⚷♓	1:04 pm	**10:04 am**	
☽♏△ ⚷♓	5:01 pm	**2:01 pm**	
☽♏⚻ ☿♈	6:50 pm	**3:50 pm**	

17 Thu
3rd ♏

☽♏☌ ♄♏	3:09 am	**12:09 am**	☽ v/c
☽♏⚻ ☉♈	1:34 am	**10:34 am**	
☽ enters ♐	5:44 pm	**2:44 pm**	
♀♓△ ♃⊛	9:19 pm	**6:19 pm**	

♀♓ ⚹ ♀♑	5:26 am	**2:26 am**	
☽♐ □ ♆♓	5:42 am	**2:42 am**	
☽♐ ☊ ♃♋	4:50 pm	**1:50 pm**	
☽♐ △ ♅♈	5:00 pm	**2:00 pm**	
☽♐ □ ♀♓	6:19 pm	**3:19 pm**	
☽♐ ⚹ ♂♎	7:59 pm	**4:59 pm**	
☽♐ □ ♄♓	9:38 pm	**6:38 pm**	
☿♈ ☊ ♄♏		**11:31 pm**	

FRI 18
3rd ♐
GOOD FRIDAY
ORTHODOX GOOD FRIDAY
OP: After Moon squares Venus today until Moon enters Capricorn on Saturday. Probably best for enjoying ourselves. (Sagittarius is one of the four signs in which the v/c Moon is a good thing. See page 77.)

☿♈ ☊ ♄♏	2:31 am		
☽♐ △ ☿♈	7:48 am	**4:48 am**	
♀♓ ☊ ♂♎	10:31 am	**7:31 am**	
☽♐ △ ☉♈	9:17 am	**6:17 pm**	☽ v/c
☽ enters ♑	9:28 pm	**6:28 pm**	
☉ enters ♉	11:56 pm	**8:56 pm**	

SAT 19
3rd ♐
SUN ENTERS TAURUS

♃♋ □ ♅♈	3:29 am	**12:29 am**	
☽♑ ⚹ ♆♓	9:15 am	**6:15 am**	
♀♓ ☌ ♄♓	1:40 pm	**10:40 am**	
♃♋ ☍ ♀♑	7:26 pm	**4:26 pm**	
☽♑ □ ♅♈	8:27 pm	**5:27 pm**	
☽♑ ☌ ♀♑	8:32 pm	**5:32 pm**	
☽♑ ☍ ♃♋	8:32 pm	**5:32 pm**	
☽♑ □ ♂♎	9:56 pm	**6:56 pm**	
☽♑ ⚹ ♄♓		**9:58 pm**	
☽♑ ⚹ ♀♓		**10:53 pm**	

SUN 20
3rd ♑
EASTER
ORTHODOX EASTER

Eastern Time plain / **Pacific Time bold**

MARCH								APRIL								MAY						
S	M	T	W	T	F	S		S	M	T	W	T	F	S		S	M	T	W	T	F	S
						1				1	2	3	4	5						1	2	3
2	3	4	5	6	7	8		6	7	8	9	10	11	12		4	5	6	7	8	9	10
9	10	11	12	13	14	15		13	14	15	16	17	18	19		11	12	13	14	15	16	17
16	17	18	19	20	21	22		20	21	22	23	24	25	26		18	19	20	21	22	23	24
23	24	25	26	27	28	29		27	28	29	30					25	26	27	28	29	30	31
30	31																					

APRIL

Uranus-Pluto Note: These two slow outer planets make the fifth exact square of their current series on Monday. They will make seven exact squares in all from June 24, 2012, to March 16, 2015. Think of the 1930s and the 1960s all over again, with the appropriate changes. "History doesn't repeat itself, but it does rhyme."

21 MON
3rd ♑

☽♑ ⚹ ♅♓	12:58 am		
☽♑ ⚹ ♀♓	1:53 am		
☽♑ ⚹ ♄♏	9:48 am	**6:48 am**	
♅♈ □ ♀♑	3:21 pm	**12:21 pm**	
☽♑ □ ☿♈	7:21 pm	**4:21 pm**	☽ v/c
☽ enters ♒		**9:18 pm**	

22 TUE
3rd ♑
🌓 2 ♒ 07
EARTH DAY
PASSOVER ENDS

☽ enters ♒	12:18 am	
☽♒ □ ☉♉	3:52 am	**12:52 am**
♂♎ □ ♃♋	3:28 pm	**12:28 pm**
☽♒ ⚹ ♅♈	11:18 pm	**8:18 pm**
☽♒ △ ♂♎	11:24 pm	**8:24 pm**
☽♒ ⚻ ♃♋	11:40 pm	**8:40 pm**

23 WED
4th ♒

♂♎ ☍ ♅♈	3:08 am	**12:08 am**	
☿ enters ♉	5:16 am	**2:16 am**	
♂♎ □ ♀♑	9:38 am	**6:38 am**	
☽♒ □ ♄♏	12:10 pm	**9:10 am**	☽ v/c
☽ enters ♓		**11:55 pm**	

24 THU
4th ♒

OP: After Moon conjoins Neptune today until Moon enters Aries on Saturday. Good for artistic matters, meditation, and helping others. (Pisces is another of the four signs in which the v/c Moon is a good thing. See page 77.)

☽ enters ♓	2:55 am	
☽♓ ⚹ ☿♉	6:41 am	**3:41 am**
☽♓ ⚹ ☉♉	10:14 am	**7:14 am**
☽♓ ☌ ♆♓	2:49 pm	**11:49 am**
☽♓ ⚻ ♂♎		**10:01 pm**
♀♓ △ ♄♏		**10:15 pm**
☽♓ ⚹ ♀♑		**10:54 pm**
☽♓ △ ♃♋		**11:54 pm**

FRI 25
4th ♓

☽♓ ⚻ ♂︎♎	1:01 am	
♀♓ △ ♄♏	1:15 am	
☽♓ ✶ ♀♑	1:54 am	
☽♓ △ ♃♋	2:54 am	
☽♓ ☌ ♅♓	6:44 am	**3:44 am**
☽♓ △ ♄♏	2:48 pm	**11:48 am**
☽♓ ☌ ♀♓	4:03 pm	**1:03 pm** ☽ v/c
☉♉ ☌ ☿♉	11:27 am	**8:27 pm**

SAT 26
4th ♓

☽ enters ♈	6:01 am	**3:01 am**
☿♉ ✶ ♆♓	1:27 pm	**10:27 am**

SUN 27
4th ♈

☽♈ ☍ ♂︎♎	3:28 am	**12:28 am**
☽♈ □ ♀♑	5:27 am	**2:27 am**
☽♈ ☌ ♅♈	6:01 am	**3:01 am**
☉♉ ✶ ♆♓	6:34 am	**3:34 am**
☽♈ □ ♃♋	7:02 am	**4:02 am** ☽ v/c
☽♈ ⚻ ♄♏	6:26 pm	**3:26 pm**

Eastern Time plain / **Pacific Time bold**

	MARCH					
S	M	T	W	T	F	S
						1
2	3	4	5	6	7	8
9	10	11	12	13	14	15
16	17	18	19	20	21	22
23	24	25	26	27	28	29
30	31					

	APRIL					
S	M	T	W	T	F	S
		1	2	3	4	5
6	7	8	9	10	11	12
13	14	15	16	17	18	19
20	21	22	23	24	25	26
27	28	29	30			

	MAY					
S	M	T	W	T	F	S
				1	2	3
4	5	6	7	8	9	10
11	12	13	14	15	16	17
18	19	20	21	22	23	24
25	26	27	28	29	30	31

28 Mon
4th ♈︎

Annular Solar Eclipse | ● New Moon 8 ♉︎ 51 (Pacific)

☽ enters ♉︎	10:23 am	**7:23 am**
☿♉︎ ⚼ ♂︎♎︎	7:44 pm	**4:44 pm**
☽♉︎ ✶ ♆♓︎	11:07 pm	**8:07 pm**
☽♉︎ ☌ ☉♉︎		**11:14 pm**

29 Tue
4th ♉︎

Annular Solar Eclipse | ● New Moon 8 ♉︎ 51 (Eastern)

☽♉︎ ☌ ☉♉︎	2:14 am	
☽♉︎ ⚼ ♂︎♎︎	7:32 am	**4:32 am**
☽♉︎ ☌ ☿♉︎	10:07 am	**7:07 am**
☽♉︎ △ ♀︎♑︎	10:40 am	**7:40 am**
☽♉︎ ✶ ♃⊗	12:56 pm	**9:56 am**
☿♉︎ △ ♀︎♑︎	1:30 pm	**10:30 am**
☽♉︎ ✶ ⚷♓︎	4:14 pm	**1:14 pm**
☽♉︎ ☍ ♄♏︎	11:56 pm	**8:56 pm**

30 Wed
1st ♉︎

☿♉︎ ✶ ♃⊗	4:32 am	**1:32 am**	
☽♉︎ ✶ ♀︎♓︎	11:53 am	**8:53 am** ☽ v/c
☽ enters ♊︎	4:56 pm	**1:56 pm**	
☿♉︎ ✶ ⚷♓︎		**9:22 pm**	

1 Thu
1st ♊︎

Beltane

☿♉︎ ✶ ⚷♓︎	12:22 am		
☽♊︎ □ ♆♓︎	6:23 am	**3:23 am**	
☉♉︎ ⚼ ♂︎♎︎	12:55 pm	**9:55 am**	
☽♊︎ △ ♂︎♎︎	2:02 pm	**11:02 am**	
☽♊︎ ⚼ ♀︎♑︎	6:22 pm	**3:22 pm**	
☽♊︎ ✶ ♅♈︎	7:32 pm	**4:32 pm** ☽ v/c
☽♊︎ □ ⚷♓︎		**9:27 pm**	

☽♊ □ ♅♓	12:27 am	
☽♊ ⚻ ♄♏	8:02 am	**5:02 am**
☿♉ ⚼ ♄♏	8:56 pm	**5:56 pm**
♀ enters ♈	9:21 pm	**6:21 pm**
☽ enters ♋		**11:13 pm**
☽♋ □ ♀♈		**11:43 pm**

FRI 2
1st ♊

☽ enters ♋	2:13 am	
☽♋ □ ♀♈	2:43 am	
☽♋ △ ♆♓	4:25 pm	**1:25 pm**
☉♉ △ ♀♑	8:37 pm	**5:37 pm**
☽♋ □ ♂♎	11:16 pm	**8:16 pm**

SAT 3
1st ♊

☽♋ ⚼ ♀♑	4:50 am	**1:50 am**
☽♋ ⚹ ☉♉	5:33 am	**2:33 am**
☽♋ □ ♅♈	6:20 am	**3:20 am**
☽♋ ☌ ♃♋	8:51 am	**5:51 am**
☽♋ △ ♅♓	11:24 am	**8:24 am**
☽♋ △ ♄♏	6:44 pm	**3:44 pm**

SUN 4
1st ♋

OP: After Moon squares Uranus today until Moon enters Leo on Monday. Today is good for practical matters. (Cancer is one of the four signs in which the v/c Moon is a good thing. See page 77.)

Eastern Time plain / **Pacific Time bold**

APRIL						
S	M	T	W	T	F	S
		1	2	3	4	5
6	7	8	9	10	11	12
13	14	15	16	17	18	19
20	21	22	23	24	25	26
27	28	29	30			

MAY						
S	M	T	W	T	F	S
				1	2	3
4	5	6	7	8	9	10
11	12	13	14	15	16	17
18	19	20	21	22	23	24
25	26	27	28	29	30	31

JUNE						
S	M	T	W	T	F	S
1	2	3	4	5	6	7
8	9	10	11	12	13	14
15	16	17	18	19	20	21
22	23	24	25	26	27	28
29	30					

MAY

5 MON
1st ♋
CINCO DE MAYO

☽♋ ✶ ☿♉	4:46 am	**1:46 am**	☽ v/c
☽ enters ♌	1:55 pm	**10:55 am**	
☽♌ △ ♀♈	8:45 pm	**5:45 pm**	

6 TUE
1st ♌
◐ 16 ♌ 30

☽♌ ⊼ ♆♓	4:36 am	**1:36 am**
☉♉ ✶ ♃♋	5:54 am	**2:54 am**
☽♌ ✶ ♂♎	10:33 am	**7:33 am**
☽♌ ⊼ ♀♑	5:06 pm	**2:06 pm**
☽♌ △ ♅♈	6:56 pm	**3:56 pm**
☽♌ □ ☉♉	11:15 pm	**8:15 pm**
☽♌ ⊼ ⚷♓		**9:01 pm**

7 WED
2nd ♌

☽♌ ⊼ ⚷♓	12:01 am		
☽♌ □ ♄♏	6:50 am	**3:50 am**	☽ v/c
☉♉ ✶ ⚷♓	9:03 am	**6:03 am**	
☿ enters ♊	10:57 am	**7:57 am**	
☽ enters ♍		**11:24 pm**	

8 THU
2nd ♌

☽ enters ♍	2:24 am	
☽♍ □ ☿♊	5:25 am	**2:25 am**
☽♍ ⊼ ♀♈	3:29 pm	**12:29 pm**
☽♍ ☍ ♆♓	5:00 pm	**2:00 pm**

☽♍ △ ♀♑	5:06 am	**2:06 am**
☽♍ ⊼ ♅♈	7:12 am	**4:12 am**
☽♍ ✶ ♃⊛	10:47 am	**7:47 am**
☽♍ ☍ ⚷♓	12:04 pm	**9:04 am**
☽♍ △ ☉♉	4:16 pm	**1:16 pm**
☽♍ ✶ ♄♏	6:08 pm	**3:08 pm** ☽ v/c

FRI 9
2nd ♍

OP: After Moon trines Pluto (see "Translating Darkness" on page 80) until v/c Moon. A very productive day.

☽ enters ♎	1:19 pm	**10:19 am**
☉♉ ☍ ♄♏	2:28 pm	**11:28 am**
☽♎ △ ☿♊		**11:28 pm**

SAT 10
2nd ♍

☽♎ △ ☿♊	2:28 am	
☽♎ ⊼ ♆♓	3:19 am	**12:19 am**
♀♈ ☍ ♂♎	5:27 am	**2:27 am**
☽♎ ☌ ♂♎	7:22 am	**4:22 am**
☽♎ ☍ ♀♈	7:34 am	**4:34 am**
☿♊ □ ♆♓	8:34 am	**5:34 am**
☽♎ □ ♀♑	2:40 pm	**11:40 am**
☽♎ ☍ ♅♈	4:56 pm	**1:56 pm**
☽♎ □ ♃⊛	8:51 pm	**5:51 pm** ☽ v/c
☽♎ ⊼ ⚷♓	9:28 pm	**6:28 pm**

SUN 11
2nd ♎
MOTHER'S DAY

Eastern Time plain / **Pacific Time bold**

		APRIL				
S	M	T	W	T	F	S
		1	2	3	4	5
6	7	8	9	10	11	12
13	14	15	16	17	18	19
20	21	22	23	24	25	26
27	28	29	30			

		MAY				
S	M	T	W	T	F	S
				1	2	3
4	5	6	7	8	9	10
11	12	13	14	15	16	17
18	19	20	21	22	23	24
25	26	27	28	29	30	31

		JUNE				
S	M	T	W	T	F	S
1	2	3	4	5	6	7
8	9	10	11	12	13	14
15	16	17	18	19	20	21
22	23	24	25	26	27	28
29	30					

MAY

12 MON
2nd ♎︎

☽ ♎︎ ⊼ ☉ ♉︎	5:50 am	**2:50 am**	
☿ ♊︎ △ ♂ ♎︎	12:02 pm	**9:02 am**	
☽ enters ♏︎	9:07 pm	**6:07 pm**	

13 TUE
2nd ♏︎

☽ ♏︎ △ ♆ ♓︎	10:21 am	**7:21 am**	
☽ ♏︎ ⊼ ☿ ♊︎	5:34 pm	**2:34 pm**	
☽ ♏︎ ⊼ ♀ ♈︎	7:21 pm	**4:21 pm**	
☽ ♏︎ ✶ ♀ ♑︎	8:55 pm	**5:55 pm**	
☽ ♏︎ ⊼ ♅ ♈︎	11:17 pm	**8:17 pm**	

14 WED
2nd ♏︎
○ Full Moon 23 ♏︎ 55
OP: **After Moon conjoins Saturn until v/c Moon.** A short but potentially very helpful period.

☽ ♏︎ △ ♃ ♋︎	3:28 am	**12:28 am**	
☽ ♏︎ △ ♅ ♓︎	3:30 am	**12:30 am**	
♃ ♋︎ △ ♅ ♓︎	7:35 am	**4:35 am**	
☽ ♏︎ ♂ ♄ ♏︎	8:02 am	**5:02 am**	
♀ ♈︎ □ ♀ ♑︎	1:50 pm	**10:50 am**	
☽ ♏︎ ☌ ☉ ♉︎	3:16 pm	**12:16 pm**	☽ v/c
☿ ♊︎ ⊼ ♀ ♑︎	9:18 pm	**6:18 pm**	
☽ enters ♐︎		**10:44 pm**	

15 THU
3rd ♏︎
OP: **After Moon squares Neptune today until Moon enters Capricorn on Saturday.** Tonight is an especially great time to meet new people. (Sagittarius is another of the four signs in which the v/c Moon is a good thing. See page 77.)

☽ enters ♐︎	1:44 am		
☽ ♐︎ □ ♆ ♓︎	2:22 pm	**11:22 am**	
☽ ♐︎ ✶ ♂ ♎︎	5:16 pm	**2:16 pm**	
☿ ♊︎ ✶ ♀ ♈︎	5:54 pm	**2:54 pm**	
☿ ♊︎ ✶ ♅ ♈︎	7:22 pm	**4:22 pm**	
♀ ♈︎ ☌ ♅ ♈︎	7:54 pm	**4:54 pm**	
☽ ♐︎ △ ♅ ♈︎		**11:51 pm**	

124

☽♐ △ ♅♈	2:51 am	
☽♐ △ ♀♈	3:26 am	**12:26 am**
☽♐ ☍ ☿♊	3:43 am	**12:43 am** ☽ v/c
☽♐ □ ♆♓	6:50 am	**3:50 am**
☽♐ ⊼ ♃♋	7:19 am	**4:19 am**
☽♐ ⊼ ☉♉	9:42 pm	**6:42 pm**

FRI 16
3rd ♐

☽ enters ♑	4:12 am	**1:12 am**
☿♊ □ ♆♓	10:14 am	**7:14 am**
☽♑ ⚹ ♆♓	4:34 pm	**1:34 pm**
☽♑ □ ♂♎	7:13 pm	**4:13 pm**
☽♑ ☌ ♀♑		**11:17 pm**

SAT 17
3rd ♐

☽♑ ☌ ♀♑	2:17 am	
☽♑ □ ♅♈	4:57 am	**1:57 am**
☽♑ ⚹ ♆♓	8:50 am	**5:50 am**
☽♑ □ ♀♈	9:42 am	**6:42 am**
☽♑ ☍ ♃♋	9:49 am	**6:49 am**
☽♑ ⊼ ☿♊	11:15 am	**8:15 am**
♀♈ □ ♃♋	11:31 am	**8:31 am**
☽♑ ⚹ ♄♏	12:25 pm	**9:25 am**
☿♊ ⊼ ♄♏	10:58 pm	**7:58 pm**

SUN 18
3rd ♑

OP: After Moon squares Venus today until v/c Moon on Monday.
Venus square Jupiter brings a great feeling of optimism now.

Eastern Time plain / **Pacific Time bold**

APRIL						
S	M	T	W	T	F	S
		1	2	3	4	5
6	7	8	9	10	11	12
13	14	15	16	17	18	19
20	21	22	23	24	25	26
27	28	29	30			

MAY						
S	M	T	W	T	F	S
				1	2	3
4	5	6	7	8	9	10
11	12	13	14	15	16	17
18	19	20	21	22	23	24
25	26	27	28	29	30	31

JUNE						
S	M	T	W	T	F	S
1	2	3	4	5	6	7
8	9	10	11	12	13	14
15	16	17	18	19	20	21
22	23	24	25	26	27	28
29	30					

May

19 Mon
3rd ♏

☽♑ △ ☉♉	3:02 am	**12:02 am**	☽ v/c
☽ enters ♒	5:58 am	**2:58 am**	
♀♈ ⊼ ♄♏	5:50 pm	**2:50 pm**	
☽♒ △ ♂♎	9:00 pm	**6:00 pm**	
♂ D	9:31 pm	**6:31 pm**	

20 Tue
3rd ♒

SUN ENTERS GEMINI

OP: **After Moon squares Saturn until v/c Moon.** Short but usable for whatever purpose you have in mind.

☽♒ ⚹ ♅♈	7:01 am	**4:01 am**	
☽♒ ⊼ ♃♋	12:26 pm	**9:26 am**	
☽♒ □ ♄♏	2:11 pm	**11:11 am**	
☽♒ ⚹ ♀♈	4:06 pm	**1:06 pm**	
☽♒ △ ☿♊	6:21 pm	**3:21 pm**	☽ v/c
☉ enters ♊	10:59 pm	**7:59 pm**	

21 Wed
3rd ♒

◗ 0 ♓ 24

☽ enters ♓	8:18 am	**5:18 am**	
☽♓ □ ☉♊	8:59 am	**5:59 am**	
☽♓ ☌ ♆♓	9:05 pm	**6:05 pm**	
☽♓ ⊼ ♂♎	11:45 pm	**8:45 pm**	

22 Thu
4th ♓

☽♓ ⚹ ♀♑	6:57 am	**3:57 am**	
☽♓ ☌ ♋♓	2:04 pm	**11:04 am**	
☽♓ △ ♃♋	4:14 pm	**1:14 pm**	
☽♓ △ ♄♏	5:05 pm	**2:05 pm**	
☽♓ □ ☿♊		11:25 pm	☽ v/c

FRI 23

4th ♓

☽♓ □ ☿♊ 2:25 am ☽ v/c
☽ enters ♈ 12:01 pm **9:01 am**
☽♈ ✶ ☉♊ 4:38 pm **1:38 pm**

OP: After Moon quares Mercury on Thursday/today until Moon enters Aries today. Short; good for night owls. (Pisces is one of the four signs in which the v/c Moon is a good thing. See page 77.)

SAT 24

4th ♈

☽♈ ☍ ♂♎ 4:07 am **1:07 am**
☽♈ □ ♇♑ 11:20 am **8:20 am**
♃♋ △ ♄♏ 1:47 pm **10:47 am**
☽♈ ☌ ♅♈ 2:52 pm **11:52 am**
☽♈ ⚻ ♄♏ 9:35 pm **6:35 pm**
☽♈ □ ♃♋ 9:44 pm **6:44 pm**

OP: After Moon squares Jupiter today until v/c Moon on Sunday. If you're hoping to meet someone new, wait two hours after the square to arrive wherever you're going. Some people may meet a new lover tonight.

SUN 25

4th ♈

☽♈ ☌ ♀♈ 10:06 am **7:06 am**
☽♈ ✶ ☿♊ 11:58 am **8:58 am** ☽ v/c
☽ enters ♉ 5:28 pm **2:28 pm**

Eastern Time plain / **Pacific Time bold**

APRIL

S	M	T	W	T	F	S
		1	2	3	4	5
6	7	8	9	10	11	12
13	14	15	16	17	18	19
20	21	22	23	24	25	26
27	28	29	30			

MAY

S	M	T	W	T	F	S
				1	2	3
4	5	6	7	8	9	10
11	12	13	14	15	16	17
18	19	20	21	22	23	24
25	26	27	28	29	30	31

JUNE

S	M	T	W	T	F	S
1	2	3	4	5	6	7
8	9	10	11	12	13	14
15	16	17	18	19	20	21
22	23	24	25	26	27	28
29	30					

MAY

26 MON
4th ♉
MEMORIAL DAY (OBSERVED)

☽ ♉ ✶ ♆ ♓	7:11 am	**4:11 am**	
☽ ♉ ⊼ ♂ ♎	10:23 am	**7:23 am**	
☽ ♉ △ ♀ ♑	5:30 pm	**2:30 pm**	
☽ ♉ ✶ ⚷ ♓		**10:28 pm**	

27 TUE
4th ♉

☽ ♉ ✶ ⚷ ♓	1:28 am		
☽ ♉ ☍ ♄ ♏	3:54 am	**12:54 am**	
☽ ♉ ✶ ♃ ♋	5:10 am	**2:10 am**	☽ v/c
☽ enters ♊		**9:47 pm**	

28 WED
4th ♉
● New Moon 7 ♊ 21

☽ enters ♊	12:47 am		
☿ ♊ ✶ ♀ ♈	9:58 am	**6:58 am**	
☽ ♊ ♂ ☉ ♊	2:40 pm	**11:40 am**	
☽ ♊ □ ♆ ♓	3:03 pm	**12:03 pm**	
☽ ♊ △ ♂ ♎	6:46 pm	**3:46 pm**	
☉ ♊ □ ♆ ♓	7:43 pm	**4:43 pm**	
♀ enters ♉	9:45 pm	**6:45 pm**	
☽ ♊ ⊼ ♀ ♑		**10:39 pm**	

29 THU
1st ♊

☽ ♊ ⊼ ♀ ♑	1:39 am		
☿ enters ♋	5:12 am	**2:12 am**	
☽ ♊ ✶ ♅ ♈	5:59 am	**2:59 am**	☽ v/c
☽ ♊ □ ⚷ ♓	10:06 am	**7:06 am**	
☽ ♊ ⊼ ♄ ♏	12:13 pm	**9:13 am**	

Mercury Note: Mercury enters its Storm (moving less than 40 minutes of arc per day) on Thursday, as it slows down before going retrograde. The Storm acts like the retrograde. Don't start any new projects now—just follow through with the items that are already on your plate. Write down new ideas with date and time they occurred.

☽ enters ⊗	10:13 am	**7:13 am**
☽⊗ ♂ ☿⊗	11:49 am	**8:49 am**
☽⊗ ✶ ♀ ♉	2:03 pm	**11:03 am**
☽⊗ △ ♆ ♓		**10:03 pm**

FRI 30
1st ♊

☽⊗ △ ♆ ♓	1:03 am	
☉♊ △ ♂⚎	4:01 am	**1:01 am**
☽⊗ □ ♂⚎	5:29 am	**2:29 am**
☽⊗ ☍ ♀♑	11:56 am	**8:56 am**
☽⊗ □ ♅♈	4:42 pm	**1:42 pm**
☽⊗ △ ⚷ ♓	8:53 pm	**5:53 pm**
☽⊗ △ ♄♏	10:39 pm	**7:39 pm**
☽⊗ ♂ ♃⊗		**11:32 pm** ☽ v/c

SAT 31
1st ⊗

OP: After Moon squares Saturn today until Moon enters Leo on Sunday. A great Saturday night to party, and a good Sunday for whatever you want to do with it. (Cancer is one of the four signs in which the v/c Moon is a good thing. See page 77.)

☽⊗ ♂ ♃⊗	2:32 am	☽ v/c
☽ enters ♌	9:43 pm	**6:43 pm**

SUN 1
1st ⊗

Eastern Time plain / **Pacific Time bold**

	MAY							JUNE							JULY					
S	M	T	W	T	F	S	S	M	T	W	T	F	S	S	M	T	W	T	F	S
				1	2	3	1	2	3	4	5	6	7			1	2	3	4	5
4	5	6	7	8	9	10	8	9	10	11	12	13	14	6	7	8	9	10	11	12
11	12	13	14	15	16	17	15	16	17	18	19	20	21	13	14	15	16	17	18	19
18	19	20	21	22	23	24	22	23	24	25	26	27	28	20	21	22	23	24	25	26
25	26	27	28	29	30	31	29	30						27	28	29	30	31		

June

2 Mon
1st ♌

☽♌ □ ♀♉	8:10 am	**5:10 am**
☽♌ ⚻ ♆♓	1:00 pm	**10:00 am**
☽♌ ⚹ ♂♎	6:17 pm	**3:17 pm**
☽♌ ⚹ ☉♊	10:54 pm	**7:54 pm**
☽♌ ⚻ ♇♑		**9:00 pm**

3 Tue
1st ♌

☽♌ ⚻ ♇♑	12:00 am	
☽♌ △ ♅♈	5:10 am	**2:10 am**
☽♌ ⚻ ⚷♓	9:19 am	**6:19 am**
☽♌ □ ♄♏	10:42 am	**7:42 am** ☽ v/c
☉♊ ⚻ ♇♑	12:18 pm	**9:18 am**

4 Wed
1st ♌

Shavuot

♀♉ ⚹ ♆♓	9:15 am	**6:15 am**
☽ enters ♍	10:20 am	**7:20 am**
☽♍ ⚹ ☿♋	4:11 pm	**1:11 pm**
☽♍ ☍ ♆♓		**10:37 pm**

5 Thu
1st ♍

◐ 15 ♍ 06

OP: After Moon squares Sun today until v/c Moon on Friday. If you have something important (begun before May 29) to wind up, you may want to work well into the night.

☽♍ ☍ ♆♓	1:37 am	
☽♍ △ ♀♉	3:24 am	**12:24 am**
☽♍ △ ♇♑	12:24 pm	**9:24 am**
☽♍ □ ☉♊	4:39 pm	**1:39 pm**
☽♍ ⚻ ♅♈	5:46 pm	**2:46 pm**
☽♍ ☍ ⚷♓	9:44 pm	**6:44 pm**
☽♍ ⚹ ♄♏	10:42 pm	**7:42 pm**

Mercury Note: Mercury goes retrograde on Saturday and remains so until July 1, after which it will still be in its Storm until July 9. Projects begun during this entire period may not work out as planned. It's best to use this time for review, editing, escrows, and so forth.

☽♍ ⚹ ♃☉	5:13 am	**2:13 am** ☽ v/c
☉♊ ⚹ ♅♈	7:20 am	**4:20 am**
☽ enters ♎	10:01 pm	**7:01 pm**

FRI 6
2nd ♍

☽♎ □ ☿☉	4:10 am	**1:10 am**
☿℞	7:56 am	**4:56 am**
♀♉ ⊼ ♂♎	8:10 am	**5:10 am**
☽♎ ⊼ ♆♓	12:42 pm	**9:42 am**
☽♎ ☌ ♂♎	7:31 pm	**4:31 pm**
☽♎ ⊼ ♀♉	8:29 pm	**5:29 pm**
☽♎ □ ♀♑	10:52 pm	**7:52 pm**

SAT 7
2nd ♎

☽♎ ☍ ♅♈	4:13 am	**1:13 am**
☽♎ △ ☉♊	7:44 am	**4:44 am**
☽♎ ⊼ ♄♓	7:52 am	**4:52 am**
☉♊ □ ♄♓	9:36 am	**6:36 am**
☽♎ □ ♃☉	3:47 pm	**12:47 pm** ☽ v/c
☉♊ ⊼ ♄♏	4:53 pm	**1:53 pm**
♀♉ △ ♀♑	9:40 pm	**6:40 pm**

SUN 8
2nd ♎

Eastern Time plain / **Pacific Time bold**

		MAY								JUNE								JULY			
S	M	T	W	T	F	S		S	M	T	W	T	F	S		S	M	T	W	T	F	S
				1	2	3		1	2	3	4	5	6	7				1	2	3	4	5
4	5	6	7	8	9	10		8	9	10	11	12	13	14		6	7	8	9	10	11	12
11	12	13	14	15	16	17		15	16	17	18	19	20	21		13	14	15	16	17	18	19
18	19	20	21	22	23	24		22	23	24	25	26	27	28		20	21	22	23	24	25	26
25	26	27	28	29	30	31		29	30							27	28	29	30	31		

9 Mon
2nd ♎

☽ enters ♏	6:38 am	**3:38 am**	
☽♏ △ ☿ ⊛	12:04 pm	**9:04 am**	
♆ℛ	3:51 pm	**12:51 pm**	
☽♏ △ ♆ ♓	8:21 pm	**5:21 pm**	

10 Tue
2nd ♏

OP: **After Moon conjoins Saturn until v/c Moon.** A few hours during which intense concentration can be very productive. Follow through on projects begun before May 29.

☽♏ ✶ ♀ ♑	5:43 am	**2:43 am**	
☽♏ ☍ ♀ ♉	8:49 am	**5:49 am**	
☽♏ ⊼ ♅ ♈	10:56 am	**7:56 am**	
☽♏ △ ♅ ♓	2:14 pm	**11:14 am**	
☽♏ ☌ ♄ ♏	2:30 pm	**11:30 am**	
☽♏ ⊼ ☉ ♊	6:07 pm	**3:07 pm**	
☽♏ △ ♃ ⊛	10:21 pm	**7:21 pm**	☽ v/c

11 Wed
2nd ♏

☽ enters ♐	11:23 am	**8:23 am**	
☽♐ ⊼ ☿ ⊛	3:37 pm	**12:37 pm**	
☽♐ □ ♆ ♓		**9:11 pm**	

12 Thu
2nd ♐

○ Full Moon 22 ♐ 06 (Pacific)

OP: **After Moon squares Neptune on Wednesday/today until Moon enters Capricorn on Friday.** Good for hard work and self-discipline, in dealing with projects begun before May 29. (Sagittarius is one of the four signs in which the v/c Moon is a good thing. See page 77.)

☽♐ □ ♆ ♓	12:11 am		
☽♐ ✶ ♂ ♎	7:56 am	**4:56 am**	
☽♐ △ ♅ ♈	1:59 pm	**10:59 am**	
☽♐ ⊼ ♀ ♉	4:24 pm	**1:24 pm**	
☽♐ □ ♅ ♓	5:01 pm	**2:01 pm**	
♀ ♉ ✶ ♅ ♓		**9:05 pm**	
♀ ♉ ☍ ♄ ♏		**9:09 pm**	
☽♐ ☍ ☉ ♊		**9:11 pm**	☽ v/c
☽♐ ⊼ ♃ ⊛		**10:23 pm**	
♄ ♏ △ ♅ ♓		**10:24 pm**	

♀♉ ✶ ⚷ ♓ 12:05 am
♀♉ ☍ ♄ ♏ 12:09 am
☽♐ ☍ ☉ ♊ 12:11 am ☽ v/c
☽♐ ☌ ♃ ♋ 1:23 am
♄♏ △ ⚷ ♓ 1:24 am
☽ enters ♑ 1:04 pm **10:04 am**
☽♑ ☍ ☿ ♋ 3:56 pm **12:56 pm**
☽♑ ✶ ♆ ♓ **10:22 pm**

Fri 13
2nd ♐
○ Full Moon 22 ♐ 06 (Eastern)

☽♑ ✶ ♆ ♓ 1:22 am
♂♎ □ ♀♑ 8:44 am **5:44 am**
☽♑ ☌ ♀♑ 9:43 am **6:43 am**
☽♑ □ ♂♎ 9:44 am **6:44 am**
☽♑ □ ♅ ♈ 2:50 pm **11:50 am**
☽♑ ✶ ♄♏ 5:34 pm **2:34 pm**
☽♑ ✶ ⚷ ♓ 5:43 pm **2:43 pm**
☽♑ △ ♀♉ 9:17 pm **6:17 pm**
☽♑ ☍ ♃ ♋ **11:35 pm ☽ v/c**

Sat 14
3rd ♑
Flag Day
OP: After Moon sextiles Saturn today (see "Translating Darkness" on page 80) until v/c Moon tonight/Sunday. This afternoon and evening are pleasant for socializing.

☽♑ ☍ ♃ ♋ 2:35 am ☽ v/c
☽♑ ⚹ ☉ ♊ 4:03 am **1:03 am**
☽ enters ≈ 1:27 pm **10:27 am**
☽≈ ⚹ ☿ ♋ 2:51 pm **11:51 am**

Sun 15
3rd ♑
Father's Day

Eastern Time plain / **Pacific Time bold**

	MAY							JUNE							JULY					
S	M	T	W	T	F	S	S	M	T	W	T	F	S	S	M	T	W	T	F	S
				1	2	3	1	2	3	4	5	6	7			1	2	3	4	5
4	5	6	7	8	9	10	8	9	10	11	12	13	14	6	7	8	9	10	11	12
11	12	13	14	15	16	17	15	16	17	18	19	20	21	13	14	15	16	17	18	19
18	19	20	21	22	23	24	22	23	24	25	26	27	28	20	21	22	23	24	25	26
25	26	27	28	29	30	31	29	30						27	28	29	30	31		

16 Mon
3rd ≈

☽≈ △ ♂⌐	11:07 am	**8:07 am**	
☽≈ ⚹ ♅♈	3:25 pm	**12:25 pm**	
☽≈ □ ♄♏	5:54 pm	**2:54 pm**	
☽≈ □ ♀♉		**11:09 pm**	

17 Tue
3rd ≈

OP: After Moon squares Venus on Monday/today until v/c Moon today. Early on today we can be extremely productive, as long as we stick to projects begun before May 29.

☽≈ □ ♀♉	2:09 am		
☽≈ ⚼ ♃⊛	3:59 am	**12:59 am**	
☿ enters ♊	6:04 am	**3:04 am**	
☽≈ △ ☉♊	8:12 am	**5:12 am**	
☽≈ △ ☿♊	2:07 pm	**11:07 am**	☽ v/c
☽ enters ♓	2:26 pm	**11:26 am**	

18 Wed
3rd ♓

☽♓ ☌ ♆♓	3:05 am	**12:05 am**
♀♉ ⚹ ♃⊛	5:16 am	**2:16 am**
☽♓ ⚹ ♀♑	11:41 am	**8:41 am**
☽♓ ⚼ ♂⌐	1:56 pm	**10:56 am**
☽♓ △ ♄♏	7:46 pm	**4:46 pm**
☽♓ ☌ ♇♓	8:19 pm	**5:19 pm**

19 Thu
3rd ♓

◐ 28 ♓ 24

☽♓ △ ♃⊛	7:15 am	**4:15 am**	
☽♓ ⚹ ♀♉	9:15 am	**6:15 am**	
☽♓ □ ☉♊	2:39 pm	**11:39 am**	
☽♓ □ ☿♊	3:05 pm	**12:05 pm**	☽ v/c
☽ enters ♈	5:26 pm	**2:26 pm**	
☉♊ ☌ ☿♊	6:50 pm	**3:50 pm**	

ᛉ ℞   8:44 am **5:44 am**
☽♈□ ♀♑   3:41 pm **12:41 pm**
☽♈☍ ♂♎   7:25 pm **4:25 pm**
☽♈☌ ♅♈   9:55 pm **6:55 pm**
☽♈⚻ ♄♏   **9:06 pm**

FRI 20
4th ♈

☽♈⚻ ♄♏ 12:06 am
☉ enters ♋ 6:51 am **3:51 am**
☽♈□ ♃♋ 1:13 pm **10:13 am**

☽♈✶ ☿♊ 6:24 pm **3:24 pm** ☽ v/c
☽ enters ♉ 11:03 pm **8:03 pm**
☽♉✶ ☉♋   **9:19 pm**

SAT 21
4th ♈
SUMMER SOLSTICE
LITHA
SUN ENTERS CANCER
OP: After Moon squares Jupiter until v/c Moon. Short, but with good energy.

☽♉✶ ☉♋ 12:19 am
☽♉✶ ♆♓ 12:57 pm **9:57 am**
☽♉△ ♀♑ 10:16 pm **7:16 pm**

SUN 22
4th ♉

Eastern Time plain / **Pacific Time bold**

	MAY								JUNE								JULY				
S	M	T	W	T	F	S		S	M	T	W	T	F	S		S	M	T	W	T	F	S
				1	2	3		1	2	3	4	5	6	7				1	2	3	4	5
4	5	6	7	8	9	10		8	9	10	11	12	13	14		6	7	8	9	10	11	12
11	12	13	14	15	16	17		15	16	17	18	19	20	21		13	14	15	16	17	18	19
18	19	20	21	22	23	24		22	23	24	25	26	27	28		20	21	22	23	24	25	26
25	26	27	28	29	30	31		29	30							27	28	29	30	31		

23 MON
4th ♉

OP: After Moon opposes Saturn today until Moon enters Gemini on Tuesday. During the day, follow through on projects begun before May 29. Then enjoy a delicious meal with friends or family this evening. (Taurus is one of the four signs in which the v/c Moon is a good thing. See page 77.)

☽♉ ⊼ ♂♎	3:45 am	**12:45 am**	
☽♉ ☍ ♄♏	6:59 am	**3:59 am**	
☽♉ ⚹ ⚷♓	7:57 am	**4:57 am**	
♀ enters ♊	8:33 am	**5:33 am**	
☽♉ ⚹ ♃♋	9:49 pm	**6:49 pm**	☽ v/c

24 TUE
4th ♉

OP: After Moon squares Neptune today until v/c Moon on Thursday. There's a lot of irritable and jumpy energy now as Mars opposes Uranus, but we can do good work and enjoy our friends in spite of it.

☽ enters ♊	7:05 am	**4:05 am**
☽♊ ♂ ♀♊	9:26 am	**6:26 am**
☽♊ □ ♆♓	9:29 pm	**6:29 pm**

25 WED
4th ♊

♂♎ ☍ ♅♈	4:26 am	**1:26 am**
☽♊ ⊼ ♇♑	7:04 am	**4:04 am**
☽♊ ⚹ ♅♈	2:15 pm	**11:15 am**
☽♊ △ ♂♎	2:31 pm	**11:31 am**
☽♊ ⊼ ♄♏	4:01 pm	**1:01 pm**
☽♊ □ ⚷♓	5:11 pm	**2:11 pm**

26 THU
4th ♊

☽♊ ♂ ☿♊	7:56 am	**4:56 am**	☽ v/c
☽ enters ♋	5:05 pm	**2:05 pm**	

Fri 27

4th ♋

● New Moon 5 ♋ 37

☽♋ ☌ ☉♋ 4:08 am **1:08 am**
☽♋ △ ♆♓ 7:53 am **4:53 am**
☽♋ ☍ ♇♑ 5:40 pm **2:40 pm**
☽♋ □ ♅♈ **10:16 pm**
☽♋ △ ♄♏ **11:48 pm**

Sat 28

1st ♋

Ramadan begins

☽♋ □ ♅♈ 1:16 am
☽♋ △ ♄♏ 2:48 am
☽♋ □ ♂♎ 3:19 am **12:19 am**
☽♋ △ ⚷♓ 4:09 am **1:09 am**
☽♋ ☌ ♃♋ 9:02 pm **6:02 pm** ☽ v/c

OP: After Moon squares Mars today until Moon enters Leo on Sunday. Today, we can make great progress on projects begun before May 29. Then enjoy the evening. (Cancer is one of the four signs in which the v/c Moon is a good thing. See page 77.)

Sun 29

1st ♋

☉♋ △ ♆♓ 3:22 am **12:22 am**
☽ enters ♌ 4:43 am **1:43 am**
♂♎ ⚻ ⚷♓ 5:10 am **2:10 am**
♀♊ □ ♆♓ 3:31 pm **12:31 pm**
☽♌ ⚻ ♆♓ 7:48 pm **4:48 pm**
☽♌ ⚹ ♀♊ 8:17 pm **5:17 pm**

Eastern Time plain / **Pacific Time bold**

MAY

S	M	T	W	T	F	S
				1	2	3
4	5	6	7	8	9	10
11	12	13	14	15	16	17
18	19	20	21	22	23	24
25	26	27	28	29	30	31

JUNE

S	M	T	W	T	F	S
1	2	3	4	5	6	7
8	9	10	11	12	13	14
15	16	17	18	19	20	21
22	23	24	25	26	27	28
29	30					

JULY

S	M	T	W	T	F	S
		1	2	3	4	5
6	7	8	9	10	11	12
13	14	15	16	17	18	19
20	21	22	23	24	25	26
27	28	29	30	31		

Mercury Note: Mercury goes direct on Tuesday but remains in its Storm, moving slowly until July 9. Until then, it is not yet time for new ideas to be workable.

30 MON
1st ♌

OP: After Moon sextiles Mars today (see "Translating Darkness" on page 80) until v/c Moon on Tuesday. Stick with projects already begun before May 29.

☽♌ ⊼ ♀♍	5:42 am	**2:42 am**	
☽♌ △ ♅♈	1:40 pm	**10:40 am**	
☽♌ □ ♄♏	2:58 pm	**11:58 am**	
☽♌ ⊼ ♆♓	4:28 pm	**1:28 pm**	
☽♌ ✶ ♂♎	5:42 pm	**2:42 pm**	

1 TUE
1st ♌

☽♌ ✶ ☿♊	6:00 am	**3:00 am**	☽ v/c
☿ D	8:50 am	**5:50 am**	
☽ enters ♍	5:24 pm	**2:24 pm**	

2 WED
1st ♍

☽♍ ☍ ♆♓	8:30 am	**5:30 am**
☽♍ ✶ ☉♋	3:19 pm	**12:19 pm**
☽♍ □ ♀♊	3:50 pm	**12:50 pm**
☽♍ △ ♀♑	6:20 pm	**3:20 pm**
☽♍ ⊼ ♅♈		**11:28 pm**

3 THU
1st ♍

OP: After Moon squares Mercury today until v/c Moon tonight/Friday. A short but potentially productive period.

☽♍ ⊼ ♅♈	2:28 am	
☽♍ ✶ ♄♏	3:32 am	**12:32 am**
☽♍ ☍ ♆♓	5:08 am	**2:08 am**
♀♊ ⊼ ♀♑	4:15 pm	**1:15 pm**
☽♍ □ ☿♊	7:01 pm	**4:01 pm**
☽♍ ✶ ♃♋		**9:21 pm** ☽ v/c

☽♍ ✶ ♃☺	12:21 am	☽ v/c
☉☺ ☌ ♀♈	4:03 am	**1:03 am**
☽ enters ♎	5:43 am	**2:43 am**
☽♎ ⊼ ♆♓	8:21 pm	**5:21 pm**

FRI 4
1st ♍
INDEPENDENCE DAY

☽♎ □ ♀♈	5:47 am	**2:47 am**
☽♎ □ ☉☺	7:59 am	**4:59 am**
☽♎ △ ♀♊	9:52 am	**6:52 am**
☽♎ ☍ ♅♈	1:46 pm	**10:46 am**
☽♎ ⊼ ♆♓	4:11 pm	**1:11 pm**
☽♎ ☌ ♂♎	9:31 pm	**6:31 pm**

SAT 5
1st ♎
◗ 13 ♎ 24

☽♎ △ ☿♊	6:52 am	**3:52 am**
☽♎ □ ♃☺	11:31 am	**8:31 am** ☽ v/c
☽ enters ♏	3:33 pm	**12:33 pm**
♀♊ ✶ ♅♈		**11:49 pm**

SUN 6
2nd ♎

Eastern Time plain / **Pacific Time bold**

	JUNE								JULY								AUGUST					
S	M	T	W	T	F	S		S	M	T	W	T	F	S		S	M	T	W	T	F	S
1	2	3	4	5	6	7			1	2	3	4	5								1	2
8	9	10	11	12	13	14		6	7	8	9	10	11	12		3	4	5	6	7	8	9
15	16	17	18	19	20	21		13	14	15	16	17	18	19		10	11	12	13	14	15	16
22	23	24	25	26	27	28		20	21	22	23	24	25	26		17	18	19	20	21	22	23
29	30							27	28	29	30	31				24	25	26	27	28	29	30
																31						

7 Mon
2nd ♏

OP: After Moon conjoins Saturn today until v/c Moon on Tuesday. The Sun square Uranus can bring new ideas, and we can be productive now.

♀Ⅱ ⚹ ♅♈	2:49 am	
☽♏ △ ♆♓	5:14 am	**2:14 am**
♀Ⅱ ⚻ ♄♏	10:09 am	**7:09 am**
☽♏ ⚹ ♇♑	1:59 pm	**10:59 am**
☽♏ △ ⊙♋	8:27 pm	**5:27 pm**
☽♏ ⚻ ♅♈	9:34 pm	**6:34 pm**
☽♏ ☌ ♄♏	10:12 pm	**7:12 pm**
☽♏ ⚻ ♀Ⅱ	11:23 pm	**8:23 pm**
☽♏ △ ♂♓	11:42 pm	**8:42 pm**
♀Ⅱ □ ♂♓		**11:47 pm**

8 Tue
2nd ♏

♀Ⅱ □ ♂♓	2:47 am	
⊙♋ □ ♅♈	12:23 pm	**9:23 am**
☽♏ ⚻ ☿Ⅱ	3:27 pm	**12:27 pm**
☽♏ △ ♃♋	6:32 pm	**3:32 pm** ☽ v/c
⊙♋ △ ♄♏	8:28 pm	**5:28 pm**
☽ enters ♐	9:24 pm	**6:24 pm**

9 Wed
2nd ♐

OP: After Moon squares Neptune today until Moon enters Capricorn on Thursday. Two good days for socializing as well as productive work. (Sagittarius is one of four signs in which the v/c Moon is a good thing. See page 77.)

☽♐ □ ♆♓	10:00 am	**7:00 am**
⊙♋ △ ♂♓	5:26 pm	**2:26 pm**
☽♐ △ ♅♈		**10:14 pm**

10 Thu
2nd ♐

☽♐ △ ♅♈	1:14 am	
☽♐ □ ♂♓	3:06 am	**12:06 am**
☽♐ ⚻ ⊙♋	3:47 am	**12:47 am**
☽♐ ☍ ♀Ⅱ	7:30 am	**4:30 am**
☽♐ ⚹ ♂♎	11:07 am	**8:07 am**
☽♐ ☍ ☿Ⅱ	8:19 pm	**5:19 pm** ☽ v/c
☽♐ ⚻ ♃♋	9:29 pm	**6:29 pm**
☽ enters ♑	11:24 pm	**8:24 pm**

☽♑ ⚹ ♆♓	11:12 am	**8:12 am**	
☽♑ ☌ ♀♑	6:48 pm	**3:48 pm**	
☽♑ □ ♅♈		**10:45 pm**	
☽♑ ⚹ ♄♏		**11:07 pm**	

Fri 11
2nd ♑

☽♑ □ ♅♈	1:45 am		
☽♑ ⚹ ♄♏	2:07 am		
☽♑ ⚹ ⚷♓	3:27 am	**12:27 am**	
☽♑ ☍ ☉♋	7:25 am	**4:25 am**	
☽♑ ⚻ ♀♊	11:52 am	**8:52 am**	
☽♑ □ ♂♎	12:42 pm	**9:42 am**	
☽♑ ☍ ♃♋	9:56 pm	**6:56 pm** ☽ v/c	
☽♑ ⚻ ☿♊	11:00 pm	**8:00 pm**	
☽ enters ♒	11:07 pm	**8:07 pm**	
☿ enters ♋		**9:45 pm**	

Sat 12
2nd ♑
○ Full Moon 20 ♑ 03

OP: After Moon squares Mars until v/c Moon. For most of the day, we have opportunities opening up. Now and during the next few OPs, look at the notes you made about new ideas that occurred to you while Mercury was retrograde and/or slow. How do those ideas look now?

☿ enters ♋	12:45 am		
♀♊ △ ♂♎	4:22 am	**1:22 am**	
☽♒ ⚹ ♅♈		**10:07 pm**	
☽♒ □ ♄♏		**10:26 pm**	

Sun 13
3rd ♒

Eastern Time plain / **Pacific Time bold**

	JUNE								JULY								AUGUST					
S	M	T	W	T	F	S		S	M	T	W	T	F	S		S	M	T	W	T	F	S
1	2	3	4	5	6	7			1	2	3	4	5							1	2
8	9	10	11	12	13	14		6	7	8	9	10	11	12		3	4	5	6	7	8	9
15	16	17	18	19	20	21		13	14	15	16	17	18	19		10	11	12	13	14	15	16
22	23	24	25	26	27	28		20	21	22	23	24	25	26		17	18	19	20	21	22	23
29	30							27	28	29	30	31				24	25	26	27	28	29	30
																31						

14 Mon
3rd ≈

☽≈ ⚹ ♅♈	1:07 am	
☽≈ □ ♄♏	1:26 am	
☽≈ ⚻ ☉♋	9:59 am	**6:59 am**
☽≈ △ ♂♎	1:37 pm	**10:37 am**
☽≈ △ ♀♊	3:23 pm	**12:23 pm** ☽ v/c
☽≈ ⚻ ♃♋	10:12 pm	**7:12 pm**
☽ enters ♓	10:40 pm	**7:40 pm**
☽♓ △ ☿♋		**11:07 pm**

15 Tue
3rd ♓

☽♓ △ ☿♋	2:07 am	
☽♓ ☌ ♆♓	10:25 am	**7:25 am**
☽♓ ⚹ ♀♑	6:08 pm	**3:08 pm**
☽♓ △ ♄♏		**10:48 pm**

16 Wed
3rd ♓

OP: After Moon squares Venus today until Moon enters Aries tonight/Thursday. Short, but good for artistic matters, meditation, and helping others. (Pisces is one of four signs in which the v/c Moon is a good thing. See page 77.)

☽♓ △ ♄♏	1:48 am	
☽♓ ☌ ♅♓	3:07 am	**12:07 am**
♃ enters ♌	6:30 am	**3:30 am**
☽♓ △ ☉♋	2:13 pm	**11:13 am**
☽♓ ⚻ ♂♎	4:16 pm	**1:16 pm**
☽♓ □ ♀♊	8:57 pm	**5:57 pm** ☽ v/c
☽ enters ♈		**9:07 pm**
☽♈ △ ♃♌		**9:24 pm**

17 Thu
3rd ♓

☽ enters ♈		12:07 am
☽♈ △ ♃♌		12:24 am
☽♈ □ ☿♋	8:26 am	**5:26 am**
☽♈ □ ♀♑	8:39 pm	**5:39 pm**

☽♈︎ ☌ ♅♈︎	4:37 am	**1:37 am**	
☽♈︎ ⚻ ♄♏︎	4:52 am	**1:52 am**	
♀ enters ♋︎	10:06 am	**7:06 am**	
☽♈︎ □ ☉♋︎	10:08 pm	**7:08 pm**	
☽♈︎ ☍ ♂︎♎︎	10:18 pm	**7:18 pm** ☽ v/c	
☿♋︎ △ ♆♓︎		**10:36 pm**	
☉♋︎ □ ♂︎♎︎		**11:32 pm**	

Fri 18
3rd ♈︎
◑ 26 ♈︎ 21

☿♋︎ △ ♆♓︎	1:36 am		
☉♋︎ □ ♂︎♎︎	2:32 am		
☽ enters ♉︎	4:43 am	**1:43 am**	
☽♉︎ □ ♃♌︎	5:54 am	**2:54 am**	
☽♉︎ ⚹ ♀♋︎	6:34 am	**3:34 am**	
☽♉︎ ⚹ ♆♓︎	5:49 pm	**2:49 pm**	
☽♉︎ ⚹ ☿♋︎	7:52 pm	**4:52 pm**	
☽♉︎ △ ♀♑︎		**11:31 pm**	

Sat 19
4th ♈︎

☽♉︎ △ ♀♑︎	2:31 am		
☽♉︎ ☍ ♄♏︎	11:21 am	**8:21 am**	
☽♉︎ ⚹ ⚸♓︎	12:41 pm	**9:41 am**	
♄ D	4:35 pm	**1:35 pm**	

Sun 20
4th ♉︎

OP: After Moon opposes Saturn today until Moon enters Gemini on Monday. We can get a lot done now. (Taurus is one of four signs in which the v/c Moon is a good thing. See page 77.)

Eastern Time plain / **Pacific Time bold**

	JUNE					
S	M	T	W	T	F	S
1	2	3	4	5	6	7
8	9	10	11	12	13	14
15	16	17	18	19	20	21
22	23	24	25	26	27	28
29	30					

	JULY					
S	M	T	W	T	F	S
		1	2	3	4	5
6	7	8	9	10	11	12
13	14	15	16	17	18	19
20	21	22	23	24	25	26
27	28	29	30	31		

	AUGUST					
S	M	T	W	T	F	S
					1	2
3	4	5	6	7	8	9
10	11	12	13	14	15	16
17	18	19	20	21	22	23
24	25	26	27	28	29	30
31						

July

21 Mon
4th ♉

☽♉ ⊼ ♂♎	8:06 am	**5:06 am**	
☽♉ ⚹ ☉♋	10:12 am	**7:12 am**	☽ v/c
☽ enters ♊	12:36 pm	**9:36 am**	
☽♊ ⚹ ♃♌	2:52 pm	**11:52 am**	
♅ ℞	10:53 pm	**7:53 pm**	
☽♊ □ ♆♓		**11:19 pm**	
☿♋ ☍ ♀♑		**11:49 pm**	

22 Tue
4th ♊
Sun enters Leo

☽♊ □ ♆♓	2:19 am		
☿♋ ☍ ♀♑	2:49 am		
☽♊ ⊼ ♀♑	11:24 am	**8:24 am**	
☉ enters ♌	5:41 pm	**2:41 pm**	
☽♊ ⚹ ♅♈	8:29 pm	**5:29 pm**	
☽♊ ⊼ ♄♏	8:45 pm	**5:45 pm**	
☽♊ □ ♂♓	10:01 pm	**7:01 pm**	

23 Wed
4th ♊

☽♊ △ ♂♎	8:53 pm	**5:53 pm**	☽ v/c
☽ enters ♋	10:59 pm	**7:59 pm**	

24 Thu
4th ♋

♀♋ △ ♆♓	7:09 am	**4:09 am**	
☽♋ △ ♆♓	1:03 pm	**10:03 am**	
☽♋ ☌ ♀♋	1:43 pm	**10:43 am**	
☉♌ ☌ ♃♌	4:44 pm	**1:44 pm**	
☿♋ □ ♅♈	8:07 pm	**5:07 pm**	
☿♋ △ ♄♏	10:11 pm	**7:11 pm**	
☽♋ ☍ ♀♑	10:23 pm	**7:23 pm**	

144

☿⊗ △ ♅ ♓ 5:42 am **2:42 am**
☽⊗ □ ♅ ♈ 7:49 am **4:49 am**
☽⊗ △ ♄ ♏ 8:08 am **5:08 am**

☽⊗ △ ♅ ♓ 9:15 am **6:15 am**
☽⊗ ☌ ☿⊗ 9:53 am **6:53 am** ☽ v/c
♂ enters ♏ 10:25 pm **7:25 pm**

Fri 25
4th ⊗
OP: After Moon trines Saturn today (see "Translating Darkness" on page 80) until Moon enters Leo on Saturday. Today can be a very productive day, and the evening can be pleasant for socializing. (Cancer is one of four signs in which the v/c Moon is a good thing. See page 77.)

☽ enters ♌ 10:55 am **7:55 am**
☽♌ □ ♂♏ 11:29 am **8:29 am**
☽♌ ☌ ♃♌ 3:33 pm **12:33 pm**
☽♌ ☌ ☉♌ 6:42 pm **3:42 pm**
☽♌ ⚻ ♆♓   **10:06 pm**

Sat 26
4th ⊗
● New Moon 3 ♌ 52

☽♌ ⚻ ♆♓ 1:06 am
☽♌ ⚻ ♀♑ 10:35 am **7:35 am**
☽♌ △ ♅♈ 8:14 pm **5:14 pm**
☽♌ □ ♄♏ 8:37 pm **5:37 pm** ☽ v/c
☽♌ ⚻ ♅♓ 9:33 pm **6:33 pm**
♀⊗ ☍ ♀♑   **11:39 pm**

Sun 27
1st ♌
RAMADAN ENDS

Eastern Time plain / **Pacific Time bold**

JUNE								JULY								AUGUST					
S	M	T	W	T	F	S		S	M	T	W	T	F	S		S	M	T	W	T	F	S
1	2	3	4	5	6	7				1	2	3	4	5							1	2
8	9	10	11	12	13	14		6	7	8	9	10	11	12		3	4	5	6	7	8	9
15	16	17	18	19	20	21		13	14	15	16	17	18	19		10	11	12	13	14	15	16
22	23	24	25	26	27	28		20	21	22	23	24	25	26		17	18	19	20	21	22	23
29	30							27	28	29	30	31				24	25	26	27	28	29	30
																31						

28 Mon
1st ♌

♀⊗ ☍ ♀♑	2:39 am	
☽ enters ♍	11:37 pm	**8:37 pm**

29 Tue
1st ♍

OP: After Moon trines Pluto today (see "Translating Darkness" on page 80) until v/c Moon on Thursday. All day Wednesday is good for getting things done.

☽♍ ✶ ♂♏	3:02 am	**12:02 am**
☽♍ ☍ ♆♓	1:46 pm	**10:46 am**
☽♍ △ ♀♑	11:15 pm	**8:15 pm**
☉♌ ⊼ ♆♓		**9:44 pm**

30 Wed
1st ♍

☉♌ ⊼ ♆♓	12:44 am	
☽♍ ✶ ♀⊗	4:26 am	**1:26 am**
☽♍ ⊼ ♅♈	8:59 am	**5:59 am**
☽♍ ✶ ♄♏	9:28 am	**6:28 am**
☽♍ ☍ ⚷♓	10:09 am	**7:09 am**

31 Thu
1st ♍

☽♍ ✶ ☿⊗	10:47 am	**7:47 am** ☽ v/c
☽ enters ♎	12:09 pm	**9:09 am**
☿ enters ♌	6:46 pm	**3:46 pm**
☽♎ ✶ ♃♌	7:02 pm	**4:02 pm**
♀⊗ □ ♅♈		**9:43 pm**
☽♎ ⊼ ♆♓		**10:57 pm**

♀⊗□ ♅♈ 12:43 am
☽♎⊼ ♆♓ 1:57 am
☽♎⚹ ☉♌ 6:16 am **3:16 am**
♀⊗△ ♄♏ 6:22 am **3:22 am**
♀⊗△ ⚷♓ 11:05 am **8:05 am**
☽♎□ ♀♑ 11:14 am **8:14 am**
♂♏□ ♃♌ 6:46 pm **3:46 pm**
☽♎☍ ♅♈ 8:45 pm **5:45 pm**
☽♎⊼ ⚷♓ 9:45 pm **6:45 pm**
☽♎□ ♀⊗ 10:58 pm **7:58 pm** ☽ v/c

FRI 1
1st ♎
LAMMAS

☿♌♂ ♃♌ 3:33 pm **12:33 pm**
☿♌□ ♂♏ 8:01 pm **5:01 pm**
☽ enters ♏ 10:57 pm **7:57 pm**

SAT 2
1st ♎

☽♏□ ♃♌ 6:33 am **3:33 am**
☽♏♂ ♂♏ 7:32 am **4:32 am**
☽♏□ ☿♌ 9:11 am **6:11 am**
☽♏△ ♆♓ 11:58 am **8:58 am**
☉♌⊼ ♀♑ 7:59 pm **4:59 pm**
☽♏⚹ ♀♑ 8:46 pm **5:46 pm**
☽♏□ ☉♌ 8:50 pm **5:50 pm**
☿♌⊼ ♆♓ **11:01 pm**

SUN 3
1st ♏
◐ 11 ♏ 36

Eastern Time plain / **Pacific Time bold**

		JULY				
S	M	T	W	T	F	S
		1	2	3	4	5
6	7	8	9	10	11	12
13	14	15	16	17	18	19
20	21	22	23	24	25	26
27	28	29	30	31		

		AUGUST				
S	M	T	W	T	F	S
					1	2
3	4	5	6	7	8	9
10	11	12	13	14	15	16
17	18	19	20	21	22	23
24	25	26	27	28	29	30
31						

		SEPTEMBER				
S	M	T	W	T	F	S
	1	2	3	4	5	6
7	8	9	10	11	12	13
14	15	16	17	18	19	20
21	22	23	24	25	26	27
28	29	30				

4 MON

2nd ♏

OP: After Moon conjoins Saturn until v/c Moon. The early part of the day is excellent for socializing, sales, and contacts.

☿♌ ⊼ ♆♓	2:01 am	
☽♏ ⊼ ♅♈	5:47 am	**2:47 am**
☽♏ ♂ ♄♏	6:29 am	**3:29 am**
☽♏ △ ♢♈	6:37 am	**3:37 am**
☽♏ △ ♀♋	1:43 pm	**10:43 am** ☽ v/c

5 TUE

2nd ♏

OP: After Moon squares Neptune today until Moon enters Capricorn on Thursday. Late today and all day Wednesday are good for either work or play. (Sagittarius is one of four signs in which the v/c Moon is a good thing. See page 77.)

☽ enters ♐	6:19 am	**3:19 am**
♄♏ △ ♢♓	12:09 pm	**9:09 am**
☽♐ △ ♃♌	2:17 pm	**11:17 am**
☽♐ □ ♆♓	6:19 pm	**3:19 pm**
☽♐ △ ☿♌		**10:33 pm**

6 WED

2nd ♐

☽♐ △ ☿♌	1:33 am	
☽♐ △ ☉♌	6:35 am	**3:35 am**
☿♌ ⊼ ♀♑	7:43 am	**4:43 am**
☽♐ △ ♅♈	10:52 am	**7:52 am** ☽ v/c
☽♐ □ ♢♓	11:33 am	**8:33 am**
☽♐ ⊼ ♀♋	11:09 pm	**8:09 pm**

7 THU

2nd ♐

♂♏ △♆♓	8:13 am	**5:13 am**
☽ enters ♑	9:38 am	**6:38 am**
☽♑ ⊼ ♃♌	5:49 pm	**2:49 pm**
☽♑ ⚹ ♆♓	8:43 pm	**5:43 pm**
☽♑ ⚹ ♂♏	9:15 pm	**6:15 pm**

FRI 8
2nd ♑

☽♑ ☌ ♇♑	4:22 am	**1:22 am**
☽♑ ⚻ ☿♌	11:37 am	**8:37 am**
☽♑ ⚻ ☉♌	11:40 am	**8:40 am**
☽♑ □ ♅♈	12:15 pm	**9:15 am**
☉♌ ☌ ☿♌	12:21 pm	**9:21 am**
☽♑ ⚹ ⚷♓	12:49 pm	**9:49 am**
☽♑ ⚹ ♄♏	1:08 pm	**10:08 am**
☿♌ △ ♅♈	4:14 pm	**1:14 pm**
☿♌ ⚻ ⚷♓	8:12 pm	**5:12 pm**
☉♌ △ ♅♈	8:36 pm	**5:36 pm**
☿♌ □ ♄♏	10:50 pm	**7:50 pm**

OP: After Moon squares Uranus today until v/c Moon on Saturday. Work hard during the day, then play in the evening.

SAT 9
2nd ♑

☽♑ ☍ ♀♋	4:09 am	**1:09 am** ☽ v/c
☉♌ ⚻ ⚷♓	4:49 am	**1:49 am**
☽ enters ♒	9:52 am	**6:52 am**
☉♌ □ ♄♏	11:10 am	**8:10 am**
☽♒ ☍ ♃♌	6:24 pm	**3:24 pm**
☽♒ □ ♂♏	10:51 pm	**7:51 pm**

SUN 10
2nd ♒
○ Full Moon 18 ♒ 02

☽♒ ⚹ ♅♈	11:31 am	**8:31 am**
☽♒ □ ♄♏	12:31 pm	**9:31 am**
☽♒ ☍ ☉♌	2:09 pm	**11:09 am**
☽♒ ☍ ☿♌	6:12 pm	**3:12 pm** ☽ v/c

OP: After Moon squares Saturn until v/c Moon. Short but potentially productive period.

Eastern Time plain / **Pacific Time bold**

JULY

S	M	T	W	T	F	S
		1	2	3	4	5
6	7	8	9	10	11	12
13	14	15	16	17	18	19
20	21	22	23	24	25	26
27	28	29	30	31		

AUGUST

S	M	T	W	T	F	S
					1	2
3	4	5	6	7	8	9
10	11	12	13	14	15	16
17	18	19	20	21	22	23
24	25	26	27	28	29	30
31						

SEPTEMBER

S	M	T	W	T	F	S
	1	2	3	4	5	6
7	8	9	10	11	12	13
14	15	16	17	18	19	20
21	22	23	24	25	26	27
28	29	30				

August

11 Mon
3rd ≈

☽≈ 🔭 ♀☋		7:19 am	**4:19 am**
☽ enters ♓		8:55 am	**5:55 am**
☽♓ 🔭 ♃♌		6:10 pm	**3:10 pm**
☽♓ ♂ ♅♓		7:26 pm	**4:26 pm**
☽♓ △ ♂♏		11:51 pm	**8:51 pm**
☽♓ ✳ ♀♑			**11:58 pm**

12 Tue
3rd ♓

OP: After Moon trines Saturn today (see "Translating Darkness" on page 80) until Moon enters Aries on Wednesday. Good for artistic matters, meditation, and helping others. (Pisces is one of four signs in which the v/c Moon is a good thing. See page 77.)

☽♓ ✳ ♀♑	2:58 am		
♀ enters ♌	3:24 am	**12:24 am**	
☽♓ ♂ ♅♓	11:14 am	**8:14 am**	
☽♓ △ ♄♏	12:01 pm	**9:01 am**	☽ v/c
☽♓ 🔭 ☉♌	4:50 pm	**1:50 pm**	
☽♓ 🔭 ☿♌		**10:07 pm**	

13 Wed
3rd ♓

☽♓ 🔭 ☿♌	1:07 am		
☽ enters ♈	9:00 am	**6:00 am**	
☽♈ △ ♀♌	11:43 am	**8:43 am**	
☽♈ △ ♃♌	7:27 pm	**4:27 pm**	
☽♈ 🔭 ♂♏		**11:46 pm**	

14 Thu
3rd ♈

OP: After Moon conjoins Uranus today until v/c Moon on Friday. We can accomplish a lot now.

☽♈ 🔭 ♂♏	2:46 am		
☽♈ □ ♀♑	3:54 am	**12:54 am**	
☽♈ ♂ ♅♈	12:14 pm	**9:14 am**	
☽♈ 🔭 ♄♏	1:41 pm	**10:41 am**	
☽♈ △ ☉♌	10:23 pm	**7:23 pm**	
♃♌ 🔭 ♆♓		**9:12 pm**	

Fri 15
3rd ♈

♃♌ ⚻ ♆♓	12:12 am	
♂♏ ⚹ ♇♑	5:29 am	**2:29 am**
☽♈ △ ☿♌	11:50 am	**8:50 am** ☽ v/c
☽ enters ♉	11:58 am	**8:58 am**
☿ enters ♍	12:44 pm	**9:44 am**
☽♉ □ ♀♌	7:57 pm	**4:57 pm**
☽♉ ⚹ ♆♓	11:35 pm	**8:35 pm**
☽♉ □ ♃♌		**9:01 pm**

Sat 16
3rd ♉

☽♉ □ ♃♌	12:01 am	
☽♉ △ ♇♑	8:11 am	**5:11 am**
☽♉ ☍ ♂♏	9:28 am	**6:28 am**
☽♉ ⚹ ⚷♓	5:25 pm	**2:25 pm**
☽♉ ☍ ♄♏	6:56 pm	**3:56 pm**

Sun 17
3rd ♉
◑ 24 ♉ 32

☽♉ □ ☉♌	8:26 am	**5:26 am** ☽ v/c
♀♌ ⚻ ♆♓	11:08 am	**8:08 am**
☽ enters ♊	6:41 pm	**3:41 pm**
♀♌ ☌ ♃♌		**10:21 pm**

Eastern Time plain / **Pacific Time bold**

JULY

S	M	T	W	T	F	S
		1	2	3	4	5
6	7	8	9	10	11	12
13	14	15	16	17	18	19
20	21	22	23	24	25	26
27	28	29	30	31		

AUGUST

S	M	T	W	T	F	S
					1	2
3	4	5	6	7	8	9
10	11	12	13	14	15	16
17	18	19	20	21	22	23
24	25	26	27	28	29	30
31						

SEPTEMBER

S	M	T	W	T	F	S
	1	2	3	4	5	6
7	8	9	10	11	12	13
14	15	16	17	18	19	20
21	22	23	24	25	26	27
28	29	30				

18 MON
4th ♊

OP: After Moon squares Neptune today until v/c Moon on Tuesday. Highly productive two days, although in the Last Quarter it's better to follow through on earlier plans than to start new projects.

♀♌ ♂ ♃♌	1:21 am	
☽♊ □ ☿♍	4:06 am	**1:06 am**
☽♊ □ ♆♌	7:00 am	**4:00 am**
☽♊ ⚹ ♃♌	8:33 am	**5:33 am**
☽♊ ⚹ ♀♌	9:12 am	**6:12 am**
☽♊ ⊼ ♀♑	4:12 pm	**1:12 pm**
☽♊ ⊼ ♂♏	8:30 pm	**5:30 pm**
☿♍ ☍ ♆♓	11:40 pm	**8:40 pm**
☽♊ ⚹ ♅♈		**10:41 pm**
☽♊ □ ♅♓		**10:54 pm**

19 TUE
4th ♊

☽♊ ⚹ ♅♈	1:41 am	
☽♊ □ ♅♓	1:54 am	
☽♊ ⊼ ♄♏	3:55 am	**12:55 am**
☽♊ ⚹ ☉♌	10:54 pm	**7:54 pm** ☽ v/c

20 WED
4th ♊

☽ enters ♋	4:45 am	**1:45 am**
☽♋ △ ♆♓	5:29 pm	**2:29 pm**
☽♋ ⚹ ☿♍		**9:59 pm**

21 THU
4th ♋

OP: After Moon squares Uranus today until Moon enters Leo on Friday. Same caution applies regarding the Last Quarter Moon—see Monday's note. (Cancer is another of four signs in which the v/c Moon is a good thing. See page 77.)

☽♋ ⚹ ☿♍	12:59 am	
☽♋ ☍ ♀♑	3:07 am	**12:07 am**
♀♌ ⊼ ♀♑	7:52 am	**4:52 am**
☽♋ △ ♂♏	10:48 am	**7:48 am**
☽♋ □ ♅♈	12:55 pm	**9:55 am**
☽♋ △ ♅♓	1:01 pm	**10:01 am**
☿♍ △ ♀♑	3:20 pm	**12:20 pm**
☽♋ △ ♄♏	3:34 pm	**12:34 pm** ☽ v/c

☽ enters ♌ 4:49 pm **1:49 pm**
☉ enters ♍ **9:46 pm**
♂♏ ⚹ ♅♈ **11:32 pm**

FRI 22
4th ♋
SUN ENTERS VIRGO (PACIFIC)

☉ enters ♍ 12:46 am
♂♏ ⚹ ♅♈ 2:32 am
♂♏ △ ⚷ ♓ 3:14 am **12:14 am**
☽♌ ⚻ ♆♓ 5:40 am **2:40 am**
☽♌ ☌ ♃♌ 9:47 am **6:47 am**
☽♌ ⚻ ♀♑ 3:30 pm **12:30 pm**
☽♌ ☌ ♀♌ 10:01 pm **7:01 pm**
☽♌ ⚻ ⚷ ♓ **10:22 pm**
☽♌ △ ♅♈ **10:22 pm**
☽♌ □ ♂♏ **11:40 pm**

SAT 23
4th ♌
SUN ENTERS VIRGO (EASTERN)

☽♌ ⚻ ⚷ ♓ 1:22 am
☽♌ △ ♅♈ 1:22 am
☽♌ □ ♂♏ 2:40 am
☽♌ □ ♄♏ 4:26 am **1:26 am** ☽ v/c
☿♍ ☍ ⚷ ♓ 9:55 am **6:55 am**
☿♍ ⚻ ♅♈ 10:01 am **7:01 am**

SUN 24
4th ♌

Eastern Time plain / **Pacific Time bold**

JULY								AUGUST								SEPTEMBER					
S	M	T	W	T	F	S		S	M	T	W	T	F	S		S	M	T	W	T	F	S
		1	2	3	4	5							1	2			1	2	3	4	5	6
6	7	8	9	10	11	12		3	4	5	6	7	8	9		7	8	9	10	11	12	13
13	14	15	16	17	18	19		10	11	12	13	14	15	16		14	15	16	17	18	19	20
20	21	22	23	24	25	26		17	18	19	20	21	22	23		21	22	23	24	25	26	27
27	28	29	30	31				24	25	26	27	28	29	30		28	29	30				
								31														

25 Mon
4th ♌
● New Moon 2 ♍ 19

☿♍ ✶ ♂♏	4:46 am	**1:46 am**
♀♌ ⊼ ♅ ♓	5:12 am	**2:12 am**
☽ enters ♍	5:33 am	**2:33 am**
♀♌ △ ♅ ♈	5:38 am	**2:38 am**
☿♍ ✶ ♄♏	8:29 am	**5:29 am**
☽♍ ♂ ☉♍	10:13 am	**7:13 am**
♂♏ ♂ ♄♏	3:30 pm	**12:30 pm**
☽♍ ♂ ♆♓	6:15 pm	**3:15 pm**

26 Tue
1st ♍

☽♍ △ ♀♑	4:08 am	**1:08 am**
☽♍ ♂ ♅ ♓	1:46 am	**10:46 am**
☽♍ ⊼ ♅ ♈	1:52 am	**10:52 am**
♀♌ □ ♄♏	2:22 pm	**11:22 am**
☽♍ ✶ ♄♏	5:20 pm	**2:20 pm**
☽♍ ✶ ♂♏	6:38 pm	**3:38 pm**
☽♍ ♂ ☿♍	10:29 pm	**7:29 pm** ☽ v/c

27 Wed
1st ♍

♀♌ □ ♂♏	11:46 am	**8:46 am**
☽ enters ♎	5:54 pm	**2:54 pm**

28 Thu
1st ♎

☽♎ ⊼ ♆♓	6:17 am	**3:17 am**
☽♎ ✶ ♃♌	12:44 pm	**9:44 am**
☽♎ □ ♀♑	4:03 pm	**1:03 pm**
☽♎ ⊼ ♅ ♓		**10:19 pm**
☽♎ ♂ ♅ ♈		**10:30 pm**

FRI 29
1st ♎

☽♎⚻ ⚷♓ 1:19 am
☽♎☍ ♅♈ 1:30 am
☉♍☍ ♆♓ 10:33 am **7:33 am**
☽♎⚹ ♀♌ 12:00 pm **9:00 am** ☽ v/c

OP: After Moon opposes Uranus on Thursday/today until v/c Moon today. Early risers can make use of this one.

SAT 30
1st ♎

☽ enters ♏ 4:53 am **1:53 am**
☽♏△ ♆♓ 4:42 pm **1:42 pm**
☽♏⚹ ☉♍ 7:16 pm **4:16 pm**
☽♏□ ♃♌ **9:00 pm**
☽♏⚹ ♇♑ **11:09 pm**

SUN 31
1st ♏

☽♏□ ♃♌ 12:00 am
☽♏⚹ ♇♑ 2:09 am
☽♏△ ⚷♓ 10:52 am **7:52 am**
☽♏⚻ ♅♈ 11:08 am **8:08 am**
☽♏☌ ♄♏ 3:10 pm **12:10 pm**
☽♏☌ ♂♏ 9:51 pm **6:51 pm**

Eastern Time plain / **Pacific Time bold**

JULY

S	M	T	W	T	F	S
		1	2	3	4	5
6	7	8	9	10	11	12
13	14	15	16	17	18	19
20	21	22	23	24	25	26
27	28	29	30	31		

AUGUST

S	M	T	W	T	F	S
					1	2
3	4	5	6	7	8	9
10	11	12	13	14	15	16
17	18	19	20	21	22	23
24	25	26	27	28	29	30
31						

SEPTEMBER

S	M	T	W	T	F	S
	1	2	3	4	5	6
7	8	9	10	11	12	13
14	15	16	17	18	19	20
21	22	23	24	25	26	27
28	29	30				

September

1 Mon

1st ♏

Labor Day

OP: After Moon squares Venus until v/c Moon. Only the truly dedicated self-employed are likely to make use of this on Labor Day!

☽♏□♀♌	3:17 am	**12:17 am**	
☽♏⚹☿♍	11:40 am	**8:40 am**	☽ v/c
☽ enters ♐	1:17 pm	**10:17 am**	
☽♐□♆♓		**9:19 pm**	
☿ enters ♎		**10:38 pm**	

2 Tue

1st ♐

◐ 9 ♐ 55

OP: After Moon squares Sun today until Moon enters Capricorn on Wednesday. The Moon in Sagittarius can get a lot done, and can be tempted to party as well. (Sagittarius is one of four signs in which the v/c Moon is a good thing. See page 77.)

☽♐□♆♓	12:19 am	
☿ enters ♎	1:38 am	
☽♐□☉♍	7:11 am	**4:11 am**
☽♐△♃♌	8:10 am	**5:10 am**
☽♐□⚷♓	5:20 pm	**2:20 pm**
☽♐△♅♈	5:38 pm	**2:38 pm**

3 Wed

2nd ♐

☉♍△♇♑	12:10 pm	**9:10 am**	
☽♐△♀♌	2:06 pm	**11:06 am**	☽ v/c
☽ enters ♑	6:15 pm	**3:15 pm**	
☽♑□☿♎	11:04 pm	**8:04 pm**	

4 Thu

2nd ♑

☽♑⚹♆♓	4:28 am	**1:28 am**
☽♑⚻♃♌	12:41 pm	**9:41 am**
☽♑☌♇♑	12:56 pm	**9:56 am**
☽♑△☉♍	2:44 pm	**11:44 am**
☽♑⚹⚷♓	8:21 pm	**5:21 pm**
☽♑□♅♈	8:41 pm	**5:41 pm**
☽♑⚹♄♏		**9:57 pm**

FRI 5
2nd ♑

☽♑ ⚹ ♄♏ 12:57 am
♃♌ ⚻ ♇♑ 6:23 am **3:23 am**
☽♑ ⚹ ♂♏ 11:08 am **8:08 am** ☽ v/c
♀ enters ♍ 1:07 pm **10:07 am**
☽ enters ♒ 7:59 pm **4:59 pm**
☽♒ ⚻ ♀♍ 8:36 pm **5:36 pm**

SAT 6
2nd ♒

☿♎ ⚻ ♆♓ 3:01 am **12:01 am**
☽♒ △ ☿♎ 5:52 am **2:52 am**
☽♒ ☍ ♃♌ 2:11 pm **11:11 am**
☽♒ ⚻ ☉♍ 6:50 pm **3:50 pm**
☽♒ ⚹ ♅♈ 9:05 pm **6:05 pm**
☽♒ □ ♄♏ **10:32 pm**

SUN 7
2nd ♒

☽♒ □ ♄♏ 1:32 am
☽♒ □ ♂♏ 1:19 pm **10:19 am** ☽ v/c
☽ enters ♓ 7:47 pm **4:47 pm**
☉♍ ☍ ⚷♓ 10:44 pm **7:44 pm**
☽♓ ☍ ♀♍ **9:38 pm**

Eastern Time plain / **Pacific Time bold**

AUGUST

S	M	T	W	T	F	S
					1	2
3	4	5	6	7	8	9
10	11	12	13	14	15	16
17	18	19	20	21	22	23
24	25	26	27	28	29	30
31						

SEPTEMBER

S	M	T	W	T	F	S
	1	2	3	4	5	6
7	8	9	10	11	12	13
14	15	16	17	18	19	20
21	22	23	24	25	26	27
28	29	30				

OCTOBER

S	M	T	W	T	F	S
			1	2	3	4
5	6	7	8	9	10	11
12	13	14	15	16	17	18
19	20	21	22	23	24	25
26	27	28	29	30	31	

8 MON
2nd ♓

○ Full Moon 16 ♓ 19

OP: After Moon conjoins Neptune today until Moon enters Aries on Tuesday. Good for artistic matters, meditation, and helping others. (Pisces is one of four signs in which the v/c Moon is a good thing. See page 77.)

☽♓ ☍ ♀♍	12:38 am	
☉♍ ⚼ ♅♈	4:47 am	**1:47 am**
☽♓ ☌ ♆♓	5:08 am	**2:08 am**
☽♓ ⚻ ☿♎	10:21 am	**7:21 am**
☽♓ ⚹ ♇♈	1:16 pm	**10:16 am**
☽♓ ⚻ ♃♌	2:22 pm	**11:22 am**
☽♓ ☌ ♅♈	8:06 pm	**5:06 pm**
☽♓ ☍ ☉♍	9:38 pm	**6:38 pm**
☽♓ △ ♄♏		**10:18 pm**

9 TUE
3rd ♓

☽♓ △ ♄♏	1:18 am	
☽♓ △ ♂♏	3:10 pm	**12:10 pm** ☽ v/c
☿♎ □ ♀♈	6:40 pm	**3:40 pm**
☽ enters ♈	7:33 pm	**4:33 pm**

10 WED
3rd ♈

☽♈ ⚻ ♀♍	4:54 am	**1:54 am**
♀♍ ☍ ♆♓	6:51 am	**3:51 am**
☽♈ □ ♀♈	1:31 pm	**10:31 am**
☿♎ ⚹ ♃♌	2:37 pm	**11:37 am**
☽♈ △ ♃♌	3:22 pm	**12:22 pm**
☽♈ ☍ ☿♎	3:26 pm	**12:26 pm**
☽♈ ☌ ♅♈	8:58 pm	**5:58 pm** ☽ v/c
☽♈ ⚻ ☉♍		**10:45 pm**
☽♈ ⚻ ♄♏		**11:20 pm**

11 THU
3rd ♈

☽♈ ⚻ ☉♍	1:45 am	
☽♈ ⚻ ♄♏	2:20 am	
☉♍ ⚹ ♄♏	11:03 am	**8:03 am**
☽♈ ⚻ ♂♏	7:04 pm	**4:04 pm**
☽ enters ♉	9:17 pm	**6:17 pm**

☽ ♉ ⚹ ♆ ♓	7:16 am	**4:16 am**
☽ ♉ △ ♀ ♍	12:09 pm	**9:09 am**
☽ ♉ △ ♀ ♑	4:22 pm	**1:22 pm**
☽ ♉ □ ♃ ♌	7:06 pm	**4:06 pm**
☿ ♎ ⚻ ⚷ ♓	10:26 pm	**7:26 pm**
☽ ♉ ⚹ ⚷ ♓	11:39 pm	**8:39 pm**
☽ ♉ ⚻ ☿ ♎	11:47 pm	**8:47 pm**

FRI 12
3rd ♉

☿ ♎ ☍ ♅ ♈	4:16 am	**1:16 am**
☽ ♉ ☍ ♄ ♏	6:24 am	**3:24 am**
☽ ♉ △ ☉ ♍	9:31 am	**6:31 am** ☽ v/c
♂ enters ♐	5:57 pm	**2:57 pm**
☽ enters ♊		**11:26 pm**
☽ ♊ ☍ ♂ ♐		**11:53 pm**

SAT 13
3rd ♉

OP: After Moon opposes Saturn today until Moon enters Gemini tonight/Sunday. The pleasure-loving Moon in Taurus is always a great time for socializing, especially combined with food! (Taurus is one of four signs in which the v/c Moon is a good thing. See page 77.)

☽ enters ♊	2:26 am	
☽ ♊ ☍ ♂ ♐	2:53 am	
♀ ♍ △ ♀ ♑	10:35 am	**7:35 am**
☽ ♊ □ ♆ ♓	1:04 pm	**10:04 am**
☽ ♊ ⚻ ♀ ♑	10:56 pm	**7:56 pm**
☽ ♊ □ ♀ ♍		**9:16 pm**
☽ ♊ ⚹ ♃ ♌		**11:45 pm**

SUN 14
3rd ♉

Eastern Time plain / **Pacific Time bold**

AUGUST								SEPTEMBER								OCTOBER					
S	M	T	W	T	F	S		S	M	T	W	T	F	S		S	M	T	W	T	F	S
					1	2			1	2	3	4	5	6					1	2	3	4
3	4	5	6	7	8	9		7	8	9	10	11	12	13		5	6	7	8	9	10	11
10	11	12	13	14	15	16		14	15	16	17	18	19	20		12	13	14	15	16	17	18
17	18	19	20	21	22	23		21	22	23	24	25	26	27		19	20	21	22	23	24	25
24	25	26	27	28	29	30		28	29	30						26	27	28	29	30	31	
31																						

15 Mon
3rd ♊
☾ 23 ♊ 09

☽♊ □ ♀♍	12:16 am	
☽♊ ✶ ♃♌	2:45 am	
☽♊ □ ♅♓	6:34 am	**3:34 am**
☽♊ ✶ ♅♈	7:13 am	**4:13 am**
☽♊ △ ☿♎	12:52 pm	**9:52 am**
☽♊ ⊼ ♄♏	2:22 pm	**11:22 am**
☽♊ □ ☉♍	10:05 pm	**7:05 pm** ☽ v/c

16 Tue
4th ♊

☽ enters ♋	11:24 am	**8:24 am**
☽♋ ⊼ ♂♐	3:11 pm	**12:11 pm**
☽♋ △ ♆♓	10:34 pm	**7:34 pm**

17 Wed
4th ♋

☽♋ ☍ ♀♑	9:05 am	**6:05 am**
♀♍ ☍ ♅♓	2:31 pm	**11:31 am**
☽♋ △ ♅♓	4:55 pm	**1:55 pm**
☽♋ ✶ ♀♍	5:12 pm	**2:12 pm**
☽♋ □ ♅♈	5:38 pm	**2:38 pm**
♀♍ ⊼ ♅♈	9:20 pm	**6:20 pm**
☽♋ △ ♄♏		**10:44 pm**

18 Thu
4th ♋

OP: After Moon squares Mercury until Moon enters Leo. Highly productive day, although in the Last Quarter it's better to follow through on earlier plans than to start new projects. (Cancer is one of four signs in which the v/c Moon is a good thing. See page 77.)

☽♋ △ ♄♏	1:44 am	
☽♋ □ ☿♎	6:00 am	**3:00 am**
☽♋ ✶ ☉♍	2:38 pm	**11:38 am** ☽ v/c
☽ enters ♌	11:10 pm	**8:10 pm**

Fri 19
4th ♌

☽♌ △ ♂♐	6:41 am	**3:41 am**
☽♌ ⚻ ♆♓	10:32 am	**7:32 am**
☽♌ ⚻ ♇♑	9:25 pm	**6:25 pm**

Sat 20
4th ♌

☽♌ ☌ ♃♌	3:29 am	**12:29 am**
☽♌ ⚻ ⚷♓	5:10 am	**2:10 am**
☽♌ △ ♅♈	5:57 am	**2:57 am**
☽♌ □ ♄♏	2:47 pm	**11:47 am**
☽♌ ⚹ ☿♎		**9:33 pm** ☽ v/c

OP: After Moon squares Saturn today until v/c Moon tonight/Sunday. Good for following through on plans made before the Moon entered its Last Quarter.

Sun 21
4th ♌

UN International Day of Peace

☽♌ ⚹ ☿♎	12:33 am	☽ v/c
♀♍ ⚹ ♄♏	9:03 am	**6:03 am**
☽ enters ♍	11:54 am	**8:54 am**
☽♍ □ ♂♐	11:05 pm	**8:05 pm**
☽♍ ☍ ♆♓	11:07 pm	**8:07 pm**
♂♐ □ ♆♓	11:39 pm	**8:39 pm**

Eastern Time plain / **Pacific Time bold**

AUGUST

S	M	T	W	T	F	S
					1	2
3	4	5	6	7	8	9
10	11	12	13	14	15	16
17	18	19	20	21	22	23
24	25	26	27	28	29	30
31						

SEPTEMBER

S	M	T	W	T	F	S
	1	2	3	4	5	6
7	8	9	10	11	12	13
14	15	16	17	18	19	20
21	22	23	24	25	26	27
28	29	30				

OCTOBER

S	M	T	W	T	F	S
			1	2	3	4
5	6	7	8	9	10	11
12	13	14	15	16	17	18
19	20	21	22	23	24	25
26	27	28	29	30	31	

22 Mon

4th ♍
Fall Equinox
Mabon
Sun enters Libra

☽♍ △ ♇♑	10:04 am	**7:04 am**
☽♍ ☍ ⚷♓	5:31 pm	**2:31 pm**
☽♍ ⊼ ♅♈	6:19 pm	**3:19 pm**
♇D	8:36 pm	**5:36 pm**
☉ enters ♎	10:29 pm	**7:29 pm**

23 Tue

4th ♍
● New Moon 1 ♎ 08 (Pacific)

☽♍ ⚹ ♄♏	3:41 am	**12:41 am**
☽♍ ☌ ♀♍	8:15 am	**5:15 am** ☽ v/c
♃♌ ⊼ ⚷♓	6:04 pm	**3:04 pm**
☽ enters ♎	11:59 pm	**8:59 pm**
☽♎ ☌ ☉♎		**11:14 pm**

24 Wed

4th ♎
● New Moon 1 ♎ 08 (Eastern)

☽♎ ☌ ☉♎	2:14 am	
☽♎ ⊼ ♆♓	10:51 am	**7:51 am**
☽♎ ⚹ ♂♐	2:31 pm	**11:31 am**
☽♎ □ ♇♑	9:39 pm	**6:39 pm**

25 Thu

1st ♎
Rosh Hashanah

OP: After Moon opposes Uranus today until v/c Moon on Friday. After the Moon leaves the Sun's beams today (about 12:42 pm EDT/9:42 am PDT), we can get a great deal done. Excellent for tactful communication.

☽♎ ⊼ ⚷♓	4:42 am	**1:42 am**
☽♎ ⚹ ♃♌	5:21 am	**2:21 am**
☽♎ ☍ ♅♈	5:30 am	**2:30 am**
♃♌ △ ♅♈	2:19 pm	**11:19 am**

Mercury Note: Mercury enters its Storm (moving less than 40 minutes of arc per day) on Friday, as it slows down before going retrograde. The Storm acts like the retrograde. Don't start any new projects now—just follow through with the items that are already on your plate. Write down new ideas with date and time they occurred.

☽⚼♂ ☿⚼	8:39 am	**5:39 am**	☽ v/c
☽ enters ♏	10:29 am	**7:29 am**	
☽♏△ Ψ♓	8:53 pm	**5:53 pm**	

FRI 26
1st ⚼

☽♏ ⚹ ♀♆	7:25 am	**4:25 am**
☽♏ △ ♅♓	2:00 pm	**11:00 am**
☽♏ ⚻ ♅♈	2:48 pm	**11:48 am**
☽♏ □ ♃♌	3:39 pm	**12:39 pm**
☿ enters ♏	6:39 pm	**3:39 pm**
☽♏ ♂ ♄♏		**9:46 pm**

SAT 27
1st ♏

☽♏ ♂ ♄♏	12:46 am		
☉⚼⚻ Ψ♓	10:52 am	**7:52 am**	
☽♏ ⚹ ♀♍	4:31 pm	**1:31 pm**	☽ v/c
☽ enters ♐	6:50 pm	**3:50 pm**	

SUN 28
1st ♏

OP: After Moon conjoins Saturn on Saturday/today until v/c Moon today. Good for either work or socializing.

Eastern Time plain / **Pacific Time bold**

	AUGUST					
S	M	T	W	T	F	S
					1	2
3	4	5	6	7	8	9
10	11	12	13	14	15	16
17	18	19	20	21	22	23
24	25	26	27	28	29	30
31						

	SEPTEMBER					
S	M	T	W	T	F	S
	1	2	3	4	5	6
7	8	9	10	11	12	13
14	15	16	17	18	19	20
21	22	23	24	25	26	27
28	29	30				

	OCTOBER					
S	M	T	W	T	F	S
			1	2	3	4
5	6	7	8	9	10	11
12	13	14	15	16	17	18
19	20	21	22	23	24	25
26	27	28	29	30	31	

29 Mon
1st ♐

OP: After Moon trines Uranus today (see "Translating Darkness" on page 80) until Moon enters Capricorn on Tuesday/Wednesday. Most of Tuesday is great for either work or play. (Sagittarius is one of four signs in which the v/c Moon is a good thing. See page 77.)

☽♐ □ ♆♓	4:42 am	**1:42 am**
☽♐ ⚹ ☉♎	6:10 am	**3:10 am**
☽♐ ☌ ♂♐	2:34 pm	**11:34 am**
♀ enters ♎	4:52 pm	**1:52 pm**
☽♐ □ ⚷♓	9:00 pm	**6:00 pm**
☽♐ △ ♅♈	9:47 pm	**6:47 pm**
☽♐ △ ♃♌	11:29 pm	**8:29 pm** ☽ v/c

30 Tue
1st ♐

☽ enters ♑		**9:41 pm**

1 Wed
1st ♐
◐ 8 ♑ 33

☽ enters ♑	12:41 am	
☽♑ ⚹ ☿♏	3:37 am	**12:37 am**
☽♑ □ ♀♎	3:51 am	**12:51 am**
☽♑ ⚹ ♆♓	9:59 am	**6:59 am**
☽♑ □ ☉♎	3:33 pm	**12:33 pm**
☽♑ ☌ ♇♑	7:48 pm	**4:48 pm**
☽♑ ⚹ ⚷♓		**10:27 pm**
☽♑ □ ♅♈		**11:11 pm**

2 Thu
2nd ♑

☽♑ ⚹ ⚷♓	1:27 am	
☽♑ □ ♅♈	2:11 am	
☽♑ ⚻ ♃♌	4:37 am	**1:37 am**
☽♑ ⚹ ♄♏	12:18 pm	**9:18 am** ☽ v/c

Mercury Note: Mercury goes retrograde on Saturday and remains so until October 25, after which it will still be in its Storm until October 29. Projects begun during this entire period may not work out as planned. It's best to use this time for review, editing, escrows, and so forth.

☽ enters ≈	4:00 am	**1:00 am**
☽≈ □ ☿ ♏	7:43 am	**4:43 am**
☽≈ △ ♀︎♎	11:53 am	**8:53 am**
☽≈ △ ☉♎	9:55 pm	**6:55 pm**
♀︎♎ ⊼ ♆ ♓	10:35 pm	**7:35 pm**

FRI 3
2nd ♑

☽≈ ⚹ ♂ ♐	3:14 am	**12:14 am**
☉♎□♀︎♑	4:06 am	**1:06 am**
☽≈ ⚹ ♅ ♈	4:19 am	**1:19 am**
☽≈ ☍ ♃♌	7:22 am	**4:22 am**
♂♐ □ ♅ ♓	10:17 am	**7:17 am**
☿ ℞	1:02 pm	**10:02 am**
☽≈ □ ♄♏	2:32 pm	**11:32 am** ☽ v/c
♂♐△ ♅ ♈		**9:18 pm**

SAT 4
2nd ≈
YOM KIPPUR

♂♐△ ♅ ♈	12:18 am	
☽ enters ♓	5:24 am	**2:24 am**
☽♓ △ ☿ ♏	9:06 am	**6:06 am**
☽♓ ☌ ♆ ♓	1:56 pm	**10:56 am**
☽♓ ⊼ ♀︎♎	5:38 pm	**2:38 pm**
☽♓ ⚹ ♀︎♑	11:20 pm	**8:20 pm**
☽♓ ⊼ ☉♎		**11:23 pm**

SUN 5
2nd ≈

Eastern Time plain / **Pacific Time bold**

	SEPTEMBER								OCTOBER								NOVEMBER				
S	M	T	W	T	F	S		S	M	T	W	T	F	S		S	M	T	W	T	F	S
	1	2	3	4	5	6					1	2	3	4								1
7	8	9	10	11	12	13		5	6	7	8	9	10	11		2	3	4	5	6	7	8
14	15	16	17	18	19	20		12	13	14	15	16	17	18		9	10	11	12	13	14	15
21	22	23	24	25	26	27		19	20	21	22	23	24	25		16	17	18	19	20	21	22
28	29	30						26	27	28	29	30	31			23	24	25	26	27	28	29
																30						

October

6 Mon

2nd ♓

OP: After Moon trines Saturn today (see "Translating Darkness" on page 80) until Moon enters Aries on Tuesday. Good for artistic matters, meditation, and helping others. (Pisces is one of four signs in which the v/c Moon is a good thing. See page 77.)

☽♓ ⚻ ☉♎	2:23 am		
☽♓ ☌ ⚷♓	4:21 am	**1:21 am**	
☽♓ □ ♂♐	6:35 am	**3:35 am**	
☽♓ ⚻ ♃♌	8:46 am	**5:46 am**	
☽♓ △ ♄♏	3:38 pm	**12:38 pm**	☽ v/c

7 Tue

2nd ♓

☽ enters ♈	6:07 am	**3:07 am**	
☉♎ ⚻ ⚷♓	6:50 am	**3:50 am**	
☽♈ ⚻ ☿♏	9:04 am	**6:04 am**	
☉♎ ☍ ♅♈	4:58 pm	**1:58 pm**	
☽♈ ☍ ♀♎	10:58 pm	**7:58 pm**	
☽♈ □ ♇♑		**9:12 pm**	

8 Wed

2nd ♈

Total Lunar Eclipse | ○ Full Moon 15 ♈ 07

☽♈ □ ♇♑	12:12 am		
☽♈ ☌ ♅♈	5:52 am	**2:52 am**	
☽♈ ☍ ☉♎	6:51 am	**3:51 am**	
☽♈ △ ♂♐	10:05 am	**7:05 am**	
☽♈ △ ♃♌	10:20 am	**7:20 am**	☽ v/c
♀♎ □ ♇♑	1:33 pm	**10:33 am**	
♂♐ △ ♃♌	4:43 pm	**1:43 pm**	
☽♈ ⚻ ♄♏	5:10 pm	**2:10 pm**	

9 Thu

3rd ♈

Sukkot begins

☽ enters ♉	7:44 am	**4:44 am**	
☽♉ ☍ ☿♏	9:08 am	**6:08 am**	
☽♉ ⚹ ♆♓	4:30 pm	**1:30 pm**	
☽♉ △ ♇♑		**11:36 pm**	

☽ ♉ △ ♀ ♑	2:36 am	
☽ ♉ ⊼ ♀ ♎	6:14 am	**3:14 am**
☽ ♉ ✶ ♅ ♓	7:38 am	**4:38 am**
☿ enters ♎	1:26 pm	**10:26 am**
☽ ♉ ⊼ ☉ ♎	1:27 pm	**10:27 am**
☽ ♉ □ ♃ ♌	1:48 pm	**10:48 am**
☽ ♉ ⊼ ♂ ♐	3:44 pm	**12:44 pm**
☉ ♎ ✶ ♃ ♌	7:17 pm	**4:17 pm**
☽ ♉ ☌ ♄ ♏	8:49 pm	**5:49 pm** ☽ v/c
♀ ♎ ⊼ ♅ ♓	9:17 pm	**6:17 pm**

Fri 10
3rd ♉

OP: After Moon opposes Saturn today until Moon enters Gemini on Saturday. A great time to socialize, especially over a good meal. (Taurus is one of four signs in which the v/c Moon is a good thing. See page 75.)

♀ ♎ ☍ ♅ ♈	5:10 am	**2:10 am**
☽ ♉ ⊼ ☿ ♎	10:32 am	**7:32 am**
☽ enters ♊	11:51 am	**8:51 am**
☽ ♊ □ ♆ ♓	9:06 pm	**6:06 pm**

Sat 11
3rd ♉

☽ ♊ ⊼ ♀ ♑	8:00 am	**5:00 am**
☽ ♊ □ ♅ ♓	1:11 pm	**10:11 am**
☽ ♊ ✶ ♅ ♈	1:57 pm	**10:57 am**
☽ ♊ △ ♀ ♎	5:34 pm	**2:34 pm**
☽ ♊ ✶ ♃ ♌	8:35 pm	**5:35 pm**
☽ ♊ △ ☉ ♎		**9:04 pm**
☽ ♊ ☍ ♂ ♐		**10:12 pm**

Sun 12
3rd ♊

Eastern Time plain / **Pacific Time bold**

SEPTEMBER						
S	M	T	W	T	F	S
	1	2	3	4	5	6
7	8	9	10	11	12	13
14	15	16	17	18	19	20
21	22	23	24	25	26	27
28	29	30				

OCTOBER						
S	M	T	W	T	F	S
			1	2	3	4
5	6	7	8	9	10	11
12	13	14	15	16	17	18
19	20	21	22	23	24	25
26	27	28	29	30	31	

NOVEMBER						
S	M	T	W	T	F	S
						1
2	3	4	5	6	7	8
9	10	11	12	13	14	15
16	17	18	19	20	21	22
23	24	25	26	27	28	29
30						

October

13 Mon
3rd ♊

Columbus Day (observed)

OP: After Moon opposes Mars on Sunday/today until v/c Moon today. If you're working today, just follow through on projects begun before September 26, and aim to get everything important done early.

☽♊ △ ☉♎	12:04 am		
☽♊ ☍ ♂♐	1:12 am		
☽♊ ⚻ ♄♏	3:53 am	**12:53 am**	
☽♊ △ ☿♎	1:58 pm	**10:58 am**	☽ v/c
☽ enters ♋	7:30 pm	**4:30 pm**	

14 Tue
3rd ♋

♀♎ ✳ ♃♌	4:33 am	**1:33 am**
☽♋ △ ♆♓	5:18 am	**2:18 am**
☽♋ ☍ ♀♑	5:02 pm	**2:02 pm**
☽♋ △ ♅♓	10:20 pm	**7:20 pm**
☽♋ □ ♇♈	11:07 pm	**8:07 pm**

15 Wed
3rd ♋

◑ 22 ♋ 21

Sukkot ends

OP: After Moon squares Mercury today until Moon enters Leo on Thursday. If you need to follow up on earlier projects this evening, it will come easily. If you don't, then just get some rest. (Cancer is one of four signs in which the v/c Moon is a good thing. See page 77.)

☉♎ ✳ ♂♐	3:19 am	**12:19 am**
☽♋ □ ♀♎	9:46 am	**6:46 am**
☽♋ △ ♄♏	2:35 pm	**11:35 am**
☽♋ ⚻ ♂♐	2:55 pm	**11:55 am**
☽♋ □ ☉♎	3:12 pm	**12:12 pm**
☽♋ □ ☿♎	7:27 pm	**4:27 pm** ☽ v/c

16 Thu
4th ♋

☽ enters ♌	6:29 am	**3:29 am**
☽♌ ⚻ ♆♓	4:38 pm	**1:38 pm**
☉♎ ☌ ☿♎	4:40 pm	**1:40 pm**
☿♎ ✳ ♂♐	9:49 pm	**6:49 pm**

☽♌	⊼	♀♑	4:57 am	**1:57 am**	
☽♌	⊼	♅♓	10:11 am	**7:11 am**	
☽♌	△	♅♈	10:58 am	**7:58 am**	
☿♎	☌	♀♎	1:56 pm	**10:56 am**	
☽♌	☌	♃♌	8:05 pm	**5:05 pm**	
☽♌	✶	☿♎		**11:22 pm**	

☽♌	✶	☿♎	2:22 am		
☽♌	□	♄♏	3:34 am	**12:34 am**	
☽♌	✶	♀♎	5:13 am	**2:13 am**	
☽♌	△	♂♐	7:18 am	**4:18 am**	
☽♌	✶	☉♎	9:10 am	**6:10 am**	☽ v/c
☽ enters	♍		7:08 pm	**4:08 pm**	

Sat 18
4th ♌

OP: After Moon squares Saturn until v/c Moon. Good for night owls or early risers who really need to follow up on something begun before September 26.

☽♍	☍	♆♓	5:16 am	**2:16 am**	
☽♍	△	♀♑	5:41 am	**2:41 pm**	
☽♍	☍	♅♓	10:40 am	**7:40 pm**	
☽♍	⊼	♅♈	11:24 pm	**8:24 pm**	
♀♎	✶	♂♐		**10:18 pm**	

Sun 19
4th ♍

Eastern Time plain / **Pacific Time bold**

SEPTEMBER						
S	M	T	W	T	F	S
	1	2	3	4	5	6
7	8	9	10	11	12	13
14	15	16	17	18	19	20
21	22	23	24	25	26	27
28	29	30				

OCTOBER						
S	M	T	W	T	F	S
			1	2	3	4
5	6	7	8	9	10	11
12	13	14	15	16	17	18
19	20	21	22	23	24	25
26	27	28	29	30	31	

NOVEMBER						
S	M	T	W	T	F	S
						1
2	3	4	5	6	7	8
9	10	11	12	13	14	15
16	17	18	19	20	21	22
23	24	25	26	27	28	29
30						

20 Mon
4th ♍

♀⚎⚹♂♐	1:18 am	
☽♍⚹♄♏	4:32 pm	**1:32 pm**
☿⚹♃♌	4:38 pm	**1:38 pm**
☽♍□♂♐	11:30 pm	**8:30 pm ☽ v/c**

21 Tue
4th ♍

☽ enters ⚎	7:12 am	**4:12 am**
☽⚎⚻♆♓	4:59 pm	**1:59 pm**

22 Wed
4th ⚎

☽⚎□♀♑	5:09 am	**2:09 am**
☽⚎⚻♅♓	9:45 am	**6:45 am**
☽⚎☍♅♈	10:25 am	**7:25 am**
☽⚎♂☿⚎	5:25 pm	**2:25 pm**
☽⚎⚹♃♌	8:48 pm	**5:48 pm**

23 Thu
4th ⚎
Partial Solar Eclipse | ● New Moon 0 ♏ 15

☉ enters ♏	7:57 am	**4:57 am**
☽⚹♂♐	1:22 pm	**10:22 am ☽ v/c**
♀ enters ♏	4:52 pm	**1:52 pm**
☽ enters ♏	5:10 pm	**2:10 pm**
☽♏♂♀♏	5:12 pm	**2:12 pm**
☽♏♂☉♏	5:57 pm	**2:57 pm**
☽♏△♆♓		**11:28 pm**

Mercury Note: Mercury goes direct on Saturday but remains in its Storm, moving slowly until October 29. Until then, it is not yet time for new ideas to be workable.

☽♏△♆♓	2:28 am	
☽♏⚹♀♍	2:16 pm **11:16 am**	
☽♏△♅♓	6:28 pm **3:28 pm**	
☽♏⚻♅♈	7:03 pm **4:03 pm**	

FRI 24
1st ♏

☉♏♂♀♏	3:31 am **12:31 am**	
☽♏□♃♌	5:44 am **2:44 am**	
☽♏♂♄♏	12:11 pm **9:11 am** ☽ v/c	
☿D	3:17 pm **12:17 pm**	
☽ enters ♐	**9:40 pm**	

SAT 25
1st ♏
ISLAMIC NEW YEAR

☽ enters ♐	12:40 am	
♂ enters ♑	6:43 am **3:43 am**	
☽♐□♆♓	9:33 am **6:33 am**	
☽♐□♅♓	**9:51 pm**	
☽♐△♅♈	**10:22 pm**	

SUN 26
1st ♏

Eastern Time plain / **Pacific Time bold**

SEPTEMBER						
S	M	T	W	T	F	S
	1	2	3	4	5	6
7	8	9	10	11	12	13
14	15	16	17	18	19	20
21	22	23	24	25	26	27
28	29	30				

OCTOBER						
S	M	T	W	T	F	S
			1	2	3	4
5	6	7	8	9	10	11
12	13	14	15	16	17	18
19	20	21	22	23	24	25
26	27	28	29	30	31	

NOVEMBER						
S	M	T	W	T	F	S
						1
2	3	4	5	6	7	8
9	10	11	12	13	14	15
16	17	18	19	20	21	22
23	24	25	26	27	28	29
30						

27 Mon
1st ♐

OP: After Moon trines Uranus on Sunday/today (see "Translating Darkness" on page 80) until Moon enters Capricorn on Tuesday. Continue working on projects begun before September 26. (Sagittarius is one of four signs in which the v/c Moon is a good thing. See page 77.)

☽♐ □ ♅ ♓	12:51 am		
☽♐ △ ♅ ♈	1:22 am		
☽♐ ✶ ♀ ♎	7:10 am	**4:10 am**	
☽♐ △ ♃ ♌	12:18 pm	**9:18 am**	☽ v/c
♀♏ △ ♆ ♓	2:48 pm	**11:48 am**	

28 Tue
1st ♐

☉♏ △ ♆ ♓	5:49 am	**2:49 am**
☽ enters ♑	6:03 am	**3:03 am**
☽♑ ☌ ♂♑	8:45 am	**5:45 am**
☽♑ ✶ ♆ ♓	2:36 pm	**11:36 am**
☽♑ ✶ ☉♏	3:18 pm	**12:18 pm**
☽♑ ✶ ♀♏	5:00 pm	**2:00 pm**
☽♑ ☌ ♇♑		**10:47 pm**

29 Wed
1st ♑

OP: After Moon squares Mercury until v/c Moon. Now and during the next few OPs, look at the notes you made about new ideas that occurred to you while Mercury was retrograde and/or slow. How do those ideas look now?

☽♑ ☌ ♇♑	1:47 am	
☽♑ ✶ ♅ ♓	5:22 am	**2:22 am**
☽♑ □ ♅ ♈	5:50 am	**2:50 am**
☽♑ □ ☿ ♎	1:30 pm	**10:30 am**
☽♑ ⊼ ♃ ♌	5:02 pm	**2:02 pm**
☽♑ ✶ ♄♏	11:01 pm	**8:01 pm** ☽ v/c

30 Thu
1st ♑
◑ 7 ≈ 36

☽ enters ≈	9:52 am	**6:52 am**
☽≈ □ ☉♏	10:48 pm	**7:48 pm**
☽≈ □ ♀♏		**10:34 pm**

☽≈ □ ♀♏	1:34 am		
☽≈ ✶ ♅♈	8:57 am	**5:57 am**	
☽≈ △ ☿♎	7:41 pm	**4:41 pm**	
☽≈ ☍ ♃♌	8:29 pm	**5:29 pm**	
☽≈ □ ♄♏		**11:22 pm** ☽ v/c	

FRI 31
2nd ≈
HALLOWEEN
SAMHAIN

☽≈ □ ♄♏	2:22 am	☽ v/c	
☿♎ ✶ ♃♌	8:44 am	**5:44 am**	
☽ enters ♓	12:37 pm	**9:37 am**	
♀♏ ✶ ♀♈	7:09 pm	**4:09 pm**	
♂♏ ✶ ♆♓	7:43 pm	**4:43 pm**	
☽♓ ☌ ♆♓	8:46 pm	**5:46 pm**	
☽♓ ✶ ♂♈	8:49 pm	**5:49 pm**	

SAT 1
2nd ≈
ALL SAINTS' DAY
OP: After Moon sextiles Mars today (see "Translating Darkness" on page 80) until Moon enters Aries on Monday. Good for artistic matters, meditation, and helping others. (Pisces is one of the four signs in which the v/c Moon is a good thing. See page 77.)

☽♓ △ ☉♏	4:10 am	**1:10 am**	
☽♓ ✶ ♀♈	6:45 am	**3:45 am**	
☽♓ △ ♀♏	7:56 am	**4:56 am**	
☽♓ ☌ ♅♓	9:56 am	**6:56 am**	
☽♓ ⚻ ♃♌	10:13 pm	**7:13 pm**	
☽♓ ⚻ ☿♎		**10:04 pm**	

SUN 2
2nd ♓
DAYLIGHT SAVING TIME ENDS AT 2:00 AM

Eastern Time plain / **Pacific Time bold**

OCTOBER						
S	M	T	W	T	F	S
			1	2	3	4
5	6	7	8	9	10	11
12	13	14	15	16	17	18
19	20	21	22	23	24	25
26	27	28	29	30	31	

NOVEMBER						
S	M	T	W	T	F	S
						1
2	3	4	5	6	7	8
9	10	11	12	13	14	15
16	17	18	19	20	21	22
23	24	25	26	27	28	29
30						

DECEMBER						
S	M	T	W	T	F	S
	1	2	3	4	5	6
7	8	9	10	11	12	13
14	15	16	17	18	19	20
21	22	23	24	25	26	27
28	29	30	31			

3 MON

2nd ♓

Continuation of OP that began on Saturday.

☽♓ ⊼ ☿♎	1:04 am	
☽♓ △ ♄♏	4:05 am	**1:05 am** ☽ v/c
♀♏ △ ♂ ♓	6:27 am	**3:27 am**
♀♏ ⊼ ♅♈	10:04 am	**7:04 am**
☽ enters ♈	1:53 pm	**10:53 am**
☉♏ ⚹ ♀♑	5:51 pm	**2:51 pm**
☽♈ □ ♂♑		**9:52 pm**

4 TUE

2nd ♈

ELECTION DAY (GENERAL)

OP: After Moon conjoins Uranus today until v/c Moon on Wednesday. You may feel more energetic than you have in a while. Continue looking at the notes you made about new ideas that occurred to you while Mercury was retrograde and/or slow. How do those ideas look now?

☽♈ □ ♂♑	12:52 am	
☽♈ □ ♀♑	9:08 am	**6:08 am**
☽♈ ⊼ ☉♏	10:15 am	**7:15 am**
☽♈ ♂ ♅♈	12:29 pm	**9:29 am**
☽♈ ⊼ ♀♏	3:06 pm	**12:06 pm**
☽♈ △ ♃♌		**10:01 pm**

5 WED

2nd ♈

☽♈ △ ♃♌	1:01 am	
☽♈ ⊼ ♄♏	7:01 am	**4:01 am**
☽♈ ☍ ☿♎	8:25 am	**5:25 am** ☽ v/c
☉♏ △ ♃♓	1:20 pm	**10:20 am**
☽ enters ♉	4:33 pm	**1:33 pm**
☉♏ ⊼ ♅♈	4:59 pm	**1:59 pm**
☽♉ ⚹ ♆♓		**9:49 pm**

6 THU

2nd ♉

○ Full Moon 14 ♉ 26

☽♉ ⚹ ♆♓	12:49 am	
☽♉ △ ♂♑	6:39 am	**3:39 am**
☽♉ △ ♀♑	12:18 pm	**9:18 am**
☽♉ ⚹ ♃♓	3:19 pm	**12:19 pm**
☽♉ ☍ ☉♏	5:23 pm	**2:23 pm**
☽♉ ☍ ♀♏	11:31 pm	**8:31 pm**

174

☽ ♉ □ ♃ ♌	4:59 am	**1:59 am**
☽ ♉ ☍ ♄ ♏	11:17 am	**8:17 am** ☽ v/c
☽ ♉ ⚻ ☿ ♎	6:10 pm	**3:10 pm**
☽ enters ♊	8:45 pm	**5:45 pm**

FRI 7

3rd ♉

OP: After Moon opposes Saturn until Moon enters Gemini. Good for either work or play. (Taurus is one of the four signs in which the v/c Moon is a good thing. See page 77.)

☽ ♊ □ ♆ ♓	5:21 am	**2:21 am**
☽ ♊ ⚻ ♂ ♑	2:39 pm	**11:39 am**
☽ ♊ ⚻ ♀ ♑	5:30 pm	**2:30 pm**
☿ enters ♏	6:09 pm	**3:09 pm**
☽ ♊ □ ♇ ♓	8:31 pm	**5:31 pm**
☽ ♊ ⚹ ♅ ♈	8:42 pm	**5:42 pm**

SAT 8

3rd ♊

OP: After Moon sextiles Uranus today (see "Translating Darkness" on page 80) until v/c Moon on Sunday. Good mostly for night owls (Eastern time) and early risers (Pacific time).

☽ ♊ ⚻ ☉ ♏	3:10 am	**12:10 am**
☽ ♊ ⚻ ♀ ♏	10:56 am	**7:56 am**
☽ ♊ ⚹ ♃ ♌	11:22 am	**8:22 am** ☽ v/c
♀ ♏ □ ♃ ♌	3:41 pm	**12:41 pm**
☽ ♊ ⚻ ♄ ♏	6:08 pm	**3:08 pm**

SUN 9

3rd ♊

Eastern Time plain / **Pacific Time bold**

	OCTOBER					
S	M	T	W	T	F	S
			1	2	3	4
5	6	7	8	9	10	11
12	13	14	15	16	17	18
19	20	21	22	23	24	25
26	27	28	29	30	31	

	NOVEMBER					
S	M	T	W	T	F	S
						1
2	3	4	5	6	7	8
9	10	11	12	13	14	15
16	17	18	19	20	21	22
23	24	25	26	27	28	29
30						

	DECEMBER					
S	M	T	W	T	F	S
	1	2	3	4	5	6
7	8	9	10	11	12	13
14	15	16	17	18	19	20
21	22	23	24	25	26	27
28	29	30	31			

10 MON
3rd ♊

☽ enters ♋	3:38 am	**12:38 am**
☽♋ △ ☿♏	8:05 am	**5:05 am**
☽♋ △ ♆♓	12:44 pm	**9:44 am**
♂♑☌ ♇♑	6:06 pm	**3:06 pm**
☽♋ ☍ ♇♑		**10:44 pm**
☽♋ ☍ ♂♑		**11:13 pm**

11 TUE
3rd ♋

VETERANS DAY

OP: After Moon squares Uranus today until Moon enters Leo on Wednesday. If you don't take the holiday off, you can be extremely productive today. (Cancer is one of the four signs in which the v/c Moon is a good thing. See page 77.)

☽♋ ☍ ♇♑	1:44 am	
☽♋ ☍ ♂♑	2:13 am	
☽♋ △ ⚷♓	4:46 am	**1:46 am**
☽♋ □ ♅♈	4:53 am	**1:53 am**
☽♋ △ ☉♏	4:55 pm	**1:55 pm**
☿♏ △ ♆♓	10:38 pm	**7:38 pm**
☽♋ △ ♀♏		**11:38 pm**

12 WED
3rd ♋

☽♋ △ ♀♏	2:38 am	
☽♋ △ ♄♏	4:16 am	**1:16 am** ☽ v/c
☽ enters ♌	1:44 pm	**10:44 am**
♂♑ ✶ ⚷♓	7:37 pm	**4:37 pm**
♀♏ ☌ ♄♏	8:02 pm	**5:02 pm**
♂♑ □ ♅♈	8:29 pm	**5:29 pm**
☽♌ ⊼ ♆♓	11:18 pm	**8:18 pm**
☽♌ □ ☿♏		**11:57 pm**

13 THU
3rd ♌

☽♌ □ ☿♏	2:57 am	
☽♌ ⊼ ♇♑	1:03 pm	**10:03 am**
☽♌ ⊼ ⚷♓	4:02 pm	**1:02 pm**
☽♌ △ ♅♈	4:04 pm	**1:04 pm**
☽♌ ⊼ ♂♑	5:27 pm	**2:27 pm**
☉♏ □ ♃♌	10:05 pm	**7:05 pm**

☽♌ ☌ ♃♌ 9:18 am **6:18 am**
☽♌ □ ☉♏ 10:16 am **7:16 am**
☽♌ □ ♄♏ 5:03 pm **2:03 pm**
☽♌ □ ♀♏ 9:53 pm **6:53 pm** ☽ v/c
☽ enters ♍ **11:08 pm**

Fri **14**
3rd ♌
◐ 22 ♌ 10

☽ enters ♍ 2:08 am
☽♍ ☍ ♆♓ 11:52 am **8:52 am**
☽♍ ⚹ ☿♏ **9:49 pm**
☽♍ △ ♀♑ **10:53 pm**
♆ D **11:04 pm**

Sat **15**
4th ♌

OP: After Moon opposes Neptune today until v/c Moon on Monday. The Virgo Moon may want to get a lot done, weekend or not.

☽♍ ⚹ ☿♏ 12:49 am
☽♍ △ ♀♑ 1:53 am
♆ D 2:04 am
☽♍ ⚻ ♅♈ 4:38 am **1:38 am**
☽♍ ☍ ⚷♓ 4:42 am **1:42 am**
☿♏ ⚹ ♀♑ 8:57 am **5:57 am**
☽♍ △ ♂♑ 10:18 am **7:18 am**
♀ enters ♐ 2:03 pm **11:03 am**

Sun **16**
4th ♍

Eastern Time plain / **Pacific Time bold**

OCTOBER						
S	M	T	W	T	F	S
		1	2	3	4	
5	6	7	8	9	10	11
12	13	14	15	16	17	18
19	20	21	22	23	24	25
26	27	28	29	30	31	

NOVEMBER						
S	M	T	W	T	F	S
						1
2	3	4	5	6	7	8
9	10	11	12	13	14	15
16	17	18	19	20	21	22
23	24	25	26	27	28	29
30						

DECEMBER						
S	M	T	W	T	F	S
	1	2	3	4	5	6
7	8	9	10	11	12	13
14	15	16	17	18	19	20
21	22	23	24	25	26	27
28	29	30	31			

November

17 Mon
4th ♍

Continuation of OP that began on Saturday.

☽♍ ⚹ ☉♏	4:26 am	**1:26 am**
☿♏ ⃔ ♅♈	5:04 am	**2:04 am**
☿♏ △ ⚷♓	5:57 am	**2:57 am**
☽♍ ⚹ ♄♏	6:11 am	**3:11 am** ☽ v/c
☽ enters ♎	2:30 pm	**11:30 am**
☽♎ ⚹ ♀♐	5:19 pm	**2:19 pm**
☽♎ ⃔ ♆♓	11:59 pm	**8:59 pm**

18 Tue
4th ♎

OP: After Moon squares Mars today/Wednesday until v/c Moon on Wednesday. Strictly for night owls.

☉♏ ☌ ♄♏	3:50 am	**12:50 am**
☽♎ □ ♀♑	1:40 pm	**10:40 am**
☽♎ ☍ ♅♈	4:03 pm	**1:03 pm**
☽♎ ⃔ ⚷♓	4:14 pm	**1:14 pm**
☽♎ □ ♂♑		**10:30 pm**

19 Wed
4th ♎

☽♎ □ ♂♑	1:30 am	
☽♎ ⚹ ♃♌	9:25 am	**6:25 am** ☽ v/c
☽ enters ♏		**9:31 pm**

20 Thu
4th ♎

☽ enters ♏	12:31 am	
☽♏ △ ♆♓	9:30 am	**6:30 am**
♀♐ □ ♆♓	9:55 am	**6:55 am**
☽♏ ⚹ ♀♑	10:33 pm	**7:33 pm**
☽♏ ⃔ ♅♈		**9:34 pm**
☽♏ △ ⚷♓		**9:50 pm**

☽♏︎⚻ ♅♈︎	12:34 am	
☽♏︎△ ⚷♓︎	12:50 am	
☿♏︎✶ ♂♑︎	9:00 am	**6:00 am**
☽♏︎✶ ♂♑︎	1:02 pm	**10:02 am**
☽♏︎☌ ☿♏︎	1:19 pm	**10:19 am**
☽♏︎□ ♃♌︎	5:18 pm	**2:18 pm**
☽♏︎☌ ♄♏︎		**9:53 pm** ☽ v/c

Fri 21
4th ♏︎

☽♏︎☌ ♄♏︎	12:53 am	☽ v/c
☉ enters ♐︎	4:38 am	**1:38 am**
☽ enters ♐︎	7:19 am	**4:19 am**
☽♐︎☌ ☉♐︎	7:32 am	**4:32 am**
☽♐︎□ ♆♓︎	3:50 pm	**12:50 pm**
☽♐︎☌ ♀♐︎	9:17 pm	**6:17 pm**
☿♏︎□ ♃♌︎	11:43 pm	**8:43 pm**

Sat 22
4th ♏︎
● New Moon 0 ♐︎ 07
Sun enters Sagittarius

☽♐︎△ ♅♈︎	6:02 am	**3:02 am**
☽♐︎□ ⚷♓︎	6:22 am	**3:22 am**
⚷ D	6:45 am	**3:45 pm**
☽♐︎△ ♃♌︎	10:16 pm	**7:16 pm** ☽ v/c

Sun 23
1st ♐︎

OP: From Moon leaving Sun's beams (about 3:42 pm EST/
12:42 pm PST) until Moon enters Capricorn on Monday. In
the meantime, the rest of today is good for business and also for
spiritual/psychological growth. (Sagittarius is one of the four
signs in which the v/c Moon is a good thing. See page 77.)

Eastern Time plain / **Pacific Time bold**

OCTOBER							NOVEMBER							DECEMBER						
S	M	T	W	T	F	S	S	M	T	W	T	F	S	S	M	T	W	T	F	S
			1	2	3	4							1		1	2	3	4	5	6
5	6	7	8	9	10	11	2	3	4	5	6	7	8	7	8	9	10	11	12	13
12	13	14	15	16	17	18	9	10	11	12	13	14	15	14	15	16	17	18	19	20
19	20	21	22	23	24	25	16	17	18	19	20	21	22	21	22	23	24	25	26	27
26	27	28	29	30	31		23	24	25	26	27	28	29	28	29	30	31			
							30													

24 Mon
1st ♐
Continuation of OP that began on Sunday.

☽ enters ♑	11:31 am	**8:31 am**	
☽♑ ⚹ ♆♓	7:45 pm	**4:45 pm**	
♂♑ ⚻ ♃♌	7:55 pm	**4:55 pm**	

25 Tue
1st ♑

☽♑ ♂ ♀♑	7:55 am	**4:55 am**	
☽♑ ☐ ♅♈	9:25 am	**6:25 am**	
☽♑ ⚹ ♇♓	9:49 am	**6:49 am**	
☿♏ ♂ ♄♏	9:37 pm	**6:37 pm**	
☽♑ ⚻ ♃♌		**10:30 pm**	

26 Wed
1st ♑

☽♑ ⚻ ♃♌	1:30 am		
☽♑ ♂ ♂♑	3:06 am	**12:06 am**	
☽♑ ⚹ ♄♏	9:10 am	**6:10 am**	
☽♑ ⚹ ☿♏	10:30 am	**7:30 am**	☽ v/c
☽ enters ♒	2:23 pm	**11:23 am**	
♀♐ △ ♅♈	7:22 pm	**4:22 pm**	
☽♒ ⚹ ☉♐	10:28 pm	**7:28 pm**	
☉♐ ☐ ♆♓	11:19 pm	**8:19 pm**	
♀♐ ☐ ♇♓		**9:33 pm**	

27 Thu
1st ♒
Thanksgiving Day

♀♐ ☐ ♇♓	12:33 am		
☽♒ ⚹ ♅♈	12:00 pm	**9:00 am**	
☽♒ ⚹ ♀♐	1:38 pm	**10:38 am**	
☿ enters ♐	9:26 pm	**6:26 pm**	

Fri 28
1st ♒

☽♒ ☍ ♃♌ 4:16 am **1:16 am**
☽♒ □ ♄♏ 12:14 pm **9:14 am** ☽ v/c
☽ enters ♓ 5:03 pm **2:03 pm**
☽♓ □ ☿♐ 7:31 pm **4:31 pm**
☽♓ ☌ ♆♓ **10:16 pm**

Sat 29
1st ♓
◐ 7 ♓ 06

☽♓ ☌ ♆♓ 1:16 am
☽♓ □ ☉♐ 5:06 am **2:06 am**
☽♓ ⚹ ♇♑ 1:36 pm **10:36 am**
☽♓ ☌ ⚷♓ 3:20 pm **12:20 pm**
☽♓ □ ♀♐ 9:28 pm **6:28 pm**

OP: After Moon squares Venus today until Moon enters Aries on Sunday. Good for artistic matters, meditation, and helping others. (Pisces is one of the four signs in which the v/c Moon is a good thing. See page 77.)

Sun 30
2nd ♓

☽♓ ⚻ ♃♌ 7:23 am **4:23 am**
☽♓ ⚹ ♂♑ 2:41 pm **11:41 am**
☽♓ △ ♄♏ 3:47 pm **12:47 pm** ☽ v/c
☽ enters ♈ 8:14 pm **5:14 pm**
☿♐ □ ♆♓ 11:26 pm **8:26 pm**

Eastern Time plain / **Pacific Time bold**

OCTOBER

S	M	T	W	T	F	S
			1	2	3	4
5	6	7	8	9	10	11
12	13	14	15	16	17	18
19	20	21	22	23	24	25
26	27	28	29	30	31	

NOVEMBER

S	M	T	W	T	F	S
						1
2	3	4	5	6	7	8
9	10	11	12	13	14	15
16	17	18	19	20	21	22
23	24	25	26	27	28	29
30						

DECEMBER

S	M	T	W	T	F	S
	1	2	3	4	5	6
7	8	9	10	11	12	13
14	15	16	17	18	19	20
21	22	23	24	25	26	27
28	29	30	31			

December

1 Mon
2nd ♈

☽♈△☿♐	5:15 am	**2:15 am**
☽♈△☉♐	12:30 pm	**9:30 am**
♂♑⚹♄♏	2:00 pm	**11:00 am**
☽♈□♀♑	5:12 pm	**2:12 pm**
☽♈☌♅♈	6:12 pm	**3:12 pm**

2 Tue
2nd ♈

☽♈△♀♐	6:14 am	**3:14 am**
☽♈△♃♌	11:16 am	**8:16 am**
☽♈☌♄♏	8:10 pm	**5:10 pm**
☽♈□♂♑	9:42 pm	**6:42 pm** ☽ v/c
☽ enters ♉		**9:15 pm**

3 Wed
2nd ♈

☽ enters ♉	12:15 am	
☽♉⚹♆♓	8:49 am	**5:49 am**
☽♉☌☿♐	4:16 pm	**1:16 pm**
☽♉☌☉♐	9:04 pm	**6:04 pm**
☽♉△♀♑	9:46 pm	**6:46 pm**
☽♉⚹♅♓	11:23 pm	**8:23 pm**

4 Thu
2nd ♉

OP: After Moon opposes Saturn today/Friday until Moon enters Gemini on Friday. Short; good only for night owls. (Taurus is one of the four signs in which the v/c Moon is a good thing. See page 77.)

♀♐△♃♌	2:11 pm	**11:11 am**
☽♉□♃♌	4:12 pm	**1:12 pm**
☽♉☌♀♐	4:24 pm	**1:24 pm**
☉♐△♅♈	5:30 pm	**2:30 pm**
♂ enters ♒	6:57 pm	**3:57 pm**
☽♉☍♄♏		**10:45 pm** ☽ v/c

☽ ♉ ☍ ♄ ♏	1:45 am		☽ v/c

Fri 5
2nd ♉

☉ ♐ □ ☿ ♓	4:31 am	**1:31 am**	
☽ enters ♊	5:28 am	**2:28 am**	
☽ ♊ △ ♂ ♒	6:07 am	**3:07 am**	
☽ ♊ □ ♆ ♓	2:20 pm	**11:20 am**	
☿ ♐ △ ♅ ♈	10:44 pm	**7:44 pm**	

☽ ♊ ⚻ ♀ ♑	3:48 am	**12:48 am**	
☽ ♊ ✶ ♅ ♈	4:28 am	**1:28 am**	
☽ ♊ ☍ ☿ ♐	5:16 am	**2:16 am**	
☽ ♊ □ ☿ ♓	5:23 am	**2:23 am**	
☿ ♐ □ ☿ ♓	6:18 am	**3:18 am**	
☽ ♊ ☍ ☉ ♐	7:27 am	**4:27 am**	
☽ ♊ ✶ ♃ ♌	10:48 pm	**7:48 pm**	

Sat 6
2nd ♊
○ Full Moon 14 ♊ 18

OP: After Moon sextiles Uranus today (see "Translating Darkness" on page 80) until v/c Moon on Sunday. A really excellent Saturday for whatever you want to accomplish, which might include Christmas shopping, if you'd like to buy gifts that people will actually want to keep.

☽ ♊ ☍ ♀ ♐	4:52 am	**1:52 am**	☽ v/c
☽ ♊ ⚻ ♄ ♏	9:12 am	**6:12 am**	
☽ enters ♋	12:34 pm	**9:34 am**	
☽ ♋ ⚻ ♂ ♒	4:49 pm	**1:49 pm**	
☽ ♋ △ ♆ ♓	9:52 pm	**6:52 pm**	

Sun 7
3rd ♊

Eastern Time plain / **Pacific Time bold**

NOVEMBER						
S	M	T	W	T	F	S
						1
2	3	4	5	6	7	8
9	10	11	12	13	14	15
16	17	18	19	20	21	22
23	24	25	26	27	28	29
30						

DECEMBER						
S	M	T	W	T	F	S
	1	2	3	4	5	6
7	8	9	10	11	12	13
14	15	16	17	18	19	20
21	22	23	24	25	26	27
28	29	30	31			

JANUARY 2015						
S	M	T	W	T	F	S
				1	2	3
4	5	6	7	8	9	10
11	12	13	14	15	16	17
18	19	20	21	22	23	24
25	26	27	28	29	30	31

8 Mon
3rd ♋

OP: **After Moon squares Uranus today until Moon enters Leo on Tuesday.** We need to regard this apparent OP as experimental. The tradition does not state clearly whether translation of darkness (see page 80) can carry over an interval longer than 24 hours with no intervening aspect—a very rare occurrence. If it can, we'll have a learning experience rather than a genuine OP. (Cancer is one of the four signs in which the v/c Moon is a good thing. See page 77.)

☉✗ ♂	☿ ✗	4:51 am	**1:51 am**	
☽♋ ☍	♀ ♑	12:02 pm	**9:02 am**	
☽♋ □	♅ ♈	12:33 pm	**9:33 am**	
☽♋ △	♇ ♓	1:36 pm	**10:36 am**	
♃ ℞		3:41 pm	**12:41 pm**	
☽♋ ⊼	☉ ✗	8:42 pm	**5:42 pm**	
☽♋ ⊼	☿ ✗	9:30 pm	**6:30 pm**	

9 Tue
3rd ♋

☽♋ △	♄ ♏	7:14 pm	**4:14 pm**	☽ v/c
☽♋ ⊼	♀ ✗	8:42 pm	**5:42 pm**	
☽ enters ♌		10:14 pm	**7:14 pm**	

10 Wed
3rd ♌

☽♌ ☍	♂ ♒	6:38 am	**3:38 am**
☽♌ ⊼	♆ ♓	8:03 am	**5:03 am**
♀ enters ♑		11:42 am	**8:42 am**
☽♌ ⊼	♇ ♑	10:57 pm	**7:57 pm**
☽♌ △	♅ ♈	11:16 pm	**8:16 pm**
☽♌ ⊼	♅ ♓		**9:31 pm**

11 Thu
3rd ♌

☽♌ ⊼	♅ ♓	12:31 am	
☽♌ △	☉ ✗	1:20 pm	**10:20 am**
☽♌ △	☿ ✗	5:40 pm	**2:40 pm**
☽♌ ♂	♃ ♌	7:21 pm	**4:21 pm**

Uranus-Pluto Note: These two slow outer planets make the sixth exact square of their current series on Sunday/Monday. They will make seven exact squares in all from June 24, 2012, to March 16, 2015. Think of the 1930s and the 1960s all over again, with the appropriate changes. "History doesn't repeat itself, but it does rhyme."

☿✗ △ ♃♌	6:24 am	**3:24 am**
☽♌ □ ♄♏	7:48 am	**4:48 am** ☽ v/c
☽ enters ♍	10:19 am	**7:19 am**
☽♍ △ ♀♑	3:51 pm	**12:51 pm**
☽♍ ☍ ♆♓	8:28 pm	**5:28 pm**
☽♍ ⚻ ♂≈	11:12 pm	**8:12 pm**

Fri 12
3rd ♌

☽♍ △ ♀♑	11:47 am	**8:47 am**
☽♍ ⚻ ♅♈	11:54 am	**8:54 am**
☽♍ ☍ ⚷♓	1:17 pm	**10:17 am**

Sat 13
3rd ♍

☽♍ □ ☉✗	7:51 am	**4:51 am**
☉✗ △ ♃♌	10:56 am	**7:56 am**
♀♑ ✶ ♆♓	11:55 am	**8:55 am**
☽♍ □ ☿✗	3:47 pm	**12:47 pm**

☽♍ ✶ ♄♏	9:11 pm	**6:11 pm** ☽ v/c
☽ enters ♎	11:05 pm	**8:05 pm**
♅♈ □ ♀♑		**9:14 pm**

Sun 14
3rd ♍
◑ 22 ♍ 26

OP: After Moon squares Mercury until v/c Moon. Short but usable for many things, including Christmas shopping.

Eastern Time plain / **Pacific Time bold**

NOVEMBER								DECEMBER								JANUARY 2015					
S	M	T	W	T	F	S		S	M	T	W	T	F	S		S	M	T	W	T	F	S
						1			1	2	3	4	5	6						1	2	3
2	3	4	5	6	7	8		7	8	9	10	11	12	13		4	5	6	7	8	9	10
9	10	11	12	13	14	15		14	15	16	17	18	19	20		11	12	13	14	15	16	17
16	17	18	19	20	21	22		21	22	23	24	25	26	27		18	19	20	21	22	23	24
23	24	25	26	27	28	29		28	29	30	31					25	26	27	28	29	30	31
30																					

15 Mon
4th ♎

♅♈ □ ♇♑	12:14 am	
☽♎ ⚻ ♆♓	9:10 am	**6:10 am**
☽♎ □ ♀♑	11:37 am	**8:37 am**
☽♎ △ ♂♒	3:56 pm	**12:56 pm**
☽♎ ☍ ♅♈		**9:07 pm**
☽♎ □ ♇♑		**9:12 pm**
☽♎ ⚻ ⚷♓		**10:36 pm**

16 Tue
4th ♎

OP: After Moon squares Pluto on Monday/today until v/c Moon today/Wednesday. All day Tuesday is available to follow through on projects already underway, like maybe buying gifts that you've already decided on. However, the Last Quarter warns against starting new projects.

☽♎ ☍ ♅♈	12:07 am	
☽♎ □ ♇♑	12:12 am	
☽♎ ⚻ ⚷♓	1:36 am	
☽♎ ⚹ ♃♌	7:31 pm	**4:31 pm**
☿ enters ♑	10:53 pm	**7:53 pm**
☽♎ ⚹ ☉♐		**9:40 pm** ☽ v/c

17 Wed
4th ♎

Hanukkah begins

☽♎ ⚹ ☉♐	12:40 am	☽ v/c
☽ enters ♏	9:52 am	**6:52 am**
☽♏ ⚹ ☿♑	11:26 am	**8:26 am**
☽♏ △ ♆♓	7:29 pm	**4:29 pm**

18 Thu
4th ♏

☽♏ ⚹ ♀♑	3:59 am	**12:59 am**
☽♏ □ ♂♒	5:29 am	**2:29 am**
☽♏ ⚻ ♅♈	9:25 am	**6:25 am**
☽♏ ⚹ ♇♑	9:40 am	**6:40 am**
☽♏ △ ⚷♓	10:55 am	**7:55 am**

DECEMBER

☽♏︎ □ ♃♌︎	3:26 am	**12:26 am**
☽♏︎ ♂ ♄♏︎	4:11 pm	**1:11 pm** ☽ v/c
☽ enters ♐︎	4:55 pm	**1:55 pm**
☽♐︎ □ ♆♓︎		**10:56 pm**

FRI 19
4th ♏︎

☽♐︎ □ ♆♓︎	1:56 am	
☿♑︎ ⚹ ♆♓︎	4:31 am	**1:31 am**
♀♑︎ □ ♅♈︎	12:08 pm	**9:08 am**
☽♐︎ ⚹ ♂♒︎	2:23 pm	**11:23 am**
☽♐︎ △ ♅♈︎	2:52 pm	**11:52 am**
♀♑︎ ♂ ♀♑︎	4:09 pm	**1:09 pm**
☽♐︎ □ ♅♓︎	4:21 pm	**1:21 pm**
♂♒︎ ⚹ ♅♈︎	10:47 pm	**7:47 pm**

SAT 20
4th ♐︎

♀♑︎ ⚹ ♅♓︎	5:02 am	**2:02 am**
☽♐︎ △ ♃♌︎	7:34 am	**4:34 am** ☽ v/c
♅ D	5:45 pm	**2:45 pm**
☉ enters ♑︎	6:03 pm	**3:03 pm**
☽ enters ♑︎	8:25 pm	**5:25 pm**
☽♑︎ ♂ ☉♑︎	8:36 pm	**5:36 pm**

SUN 21
4th ♐︎
● New Moon 0 ♑︎ 06
WINTER SOLSTICE
YULE
SUN ENTERS CAPRICORN

Eastern Time plain / **Pacific Time bold**

NOVEMBER	DECEMBER	JANUARY 2015
S M T W T F S	S M T W T F S	S M T W T F S
1	1 2 3 4 5 6	1 2 3
2 3 4 5 6 7 8	7 8 9 10 11 12 13	4 5 6 7 8 9 10
9 10 11 12 13 14 15	14 15 16 17 18 19 20	11 12 13 14 15 16 17
16 17 18 19 20 21 22	21 22 23 24 25 26 27	18 19 20 21 22 23 24
23 24 25 26 27 28 29	28 29 30 31	25 26 27 28 29 30 31
30		

187

December

22 Mon
1st ♑

☽♑ ⚹ ♆♓	5:02 am	**2:02 am**	
☽♑ ☌ ☿♑	10:57 am	**7:57 am**	
☽♑ □ ♅♈	5:17 pm	**2:17 pm**	
☽♑ ☌ ♇♑	5:44 pm	**2:44 pm**	
☽♑ ⚹ ⚷♓	6:48 pm	**3:48 pm**	
☽♑ ☌ ♀♑	10:17 pm	**7:17 pm**	☽ v/c

23 Tue
1st ♑

☽♑ ⚻ ♃♌	9:13 am	**6:13 am**
♄ enters ♐	11:34 am	**8:34 am**
☽ enters ♒	9:52 pm	**6:52 pm**
☽♒ ⚹ ♄♐	9:57 pm	**6:57 pm**

24 Wed
1st ♒

Christmas Eve

Hanukkah ends

OP: After Moon conjoins Mars today until v/c Moon on Thursday. Have a pleasant Christmas Eve and Christmas Day!

☽♒ ⚹ ♅♈	6:26 pm	**3:26 pm**
☿♑ □ ♅♈	8:31 pm	**5:31 pm**
☽♒ ☌ ♂♒	11:36 pm	**8:36 pm**
☿♑ ☌ ♇♑		**10:53 pm**

25 Thu
1st ♒

Christmas Day

☿♑ ☌ ♇♑	1:53 am		
☽♒ ☍ ♃♌	10:11 am	**7:11 am**	☽ v/c
☿♑ ⚹ ⚷♓	11:29 am	**8:29 am**	
☽ enters ♓	11:07 pm	**8:07 pm**	
☽♓ □ ♄♐	11:33 pm	**8:33 pm**	

Fri 26
1st ♓
Kwanzaa begins

☽♓ ⚹ ☉♑	6:46 am	**3:46 am**
☽♓ ☌ ♆♓	7:50 am	**4:50 am**
☽♓ ⚹ ♇♑	8:46 pm	**5:46 pm**
☽♓ ☌ ⚷♓	9:48 pm	**6:48 pm**
☉♑ ⚹ ♆♓	10:10 pm	**7:10 pm**
☽♓ ⚹ ☿♑		**11:04 pm**

OP: After Moon sextiles Pluto today (see "Translating Darkness" on page 80) until Moon enters Aries on Saturday/Sunday. Good for artistic matters, meditation, and helping others. (Pisces is another of the four signs in which the v/c Moon is a good thing. See page 77.)

Sat 27
1st ♓

☽♓ ⚹ ☿♑	2:04 am	
☽♓ ⚹ ♀♑	10:44 am	**7:44 am** ☽ v/c
☽♓ ⚻ ♃♌	12:02 pm	**9:02 am**
♀♑ ⚻ ♃♌		**9:51 pm**
☽ enters ♈		**10:35 pm**
☽♈ △ ♄♐		**11:25 pm**

Sun 28
1st ♓
◐ 6 ♈ 56

♀♑ ⚻ ♃♌	12:51 am	
☽ enters ♈	1:35 am	
☽♈ △ ♄♐	2:25 am	
☽♈ □ ☉♑	1:31 pm	**10:31 am**
☽♈ ☌ ♅♈	11:19 pm	**8:19 pm**
☽♈ □ ♇♑		**9:09 pm**

Eastern Time plain / **Pacific Time bold**

NOVEMBER

S	M	T	W	T	F	S
						1
2	3	4	5	6	7	8
9	10	11	12	13	14	15
16	17	18	19	20	21	22
23	24	25	26	27	28	29
30						

DECEMBER

S	M	T	W	T	F	S
	1	2	3	4	5	6
7	8	9	10	11	12	13
14	15	16	17	18	19	20
21	22	23	24	25	26	27
28	29	30	31			

JANUARY 2015

S	M	T	W	T	F	S
				1	2	3
4	5	6	7	8	9	10
11	12	13	14	15	16	17
18	19	20	21	22	23	24
25	26	27	28	29	30	31

29 Mon
2nd ♈

☽♈ □ ♇♑	12:09 am	
☽♈ ⚹ ♂♒	10:54 am	**7:54 am**
☽♈ □ ☿♑	12:19 pm	**9:19 am**
☽♈ △ ♃♌	3:37 pm	**12:37 pm**
☽♈ □ ♀♑	7:46 pm	**4:46 pm** ☽ v/c

30 Tue
2nd ♈

☽ enters ♉	5:56 am	**2:56 am**
☽♉ ⚻ ♄♐	7:12 am	**4:12 am**
☽♉ ⚹ ♆♓	3:29 pm	**12:29 pm**
☿♑ ⚻ ♃♌	3:37 pm	**12:37 pm**
☽♉ △ ☉♑	10:40 pm	**7:40 pm**

31 Wed
2nd ♉

New Year's Eve

OP: After Moon squares Jupiter today until Moon enters Gemini on Thursday. Enjoy your New Year's Eve! Stay sober, or have a designated driver. (Taurus is one of the four signs in which the v/c Moon is a good thing. See page 77.)

☽♉ △ ♇♑	5:28 am	**2:28 am**
☽♉ ⚹ ⚷♓	6:34 am	**3:34 am**
☽♉ □ ♂♒	7:50 pm	**4:50 pm**
☽♉ □ ♃♌	9:04 pm	**6:04 pm**
☽♉ △ ☿♑		**10:18 pm**

1 Thu
2nd ♉

New Year's Day

☽♉ △ ☿♑	1:18 am	
☽♉ △ ♀♑	7:19 am	**4:19 am** ☽ v/c
☽ enters ♊	12:09 pm	**9:09 am**
☽♊ ☍ ♄♐	1:53 pm	**10:53 am**
♂♒ ☍ ♃♌	2:49 pm	**11:49 am**
☽♊ □ ♆♓	10:07 pm	**7:07 pm**

Blank Horoscope Chart

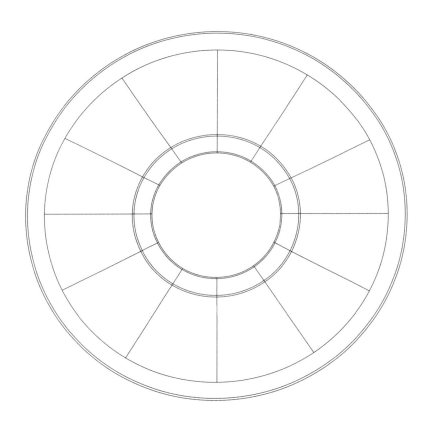

World Time Zones
Compared to Eastern Standard Time

(R)	EST (used in *Guide*)	(D)	Add 9 hours
(S)	CST/Subtract 1 hour	(D*)	Add 9.5 hours
(Q)	Add 1 hour	(E)	Add 10 hours
(P)	Add 2 hours	(E*)	Add 10.5 hours
(O)	Add 3 hours	(F)	Add 11 hours
(Z)	Add 5 hours	(F*)	Add 11.5 hours
(T)	MST/Subtract 2 hours	(G)	Add 12 hours
(U)	PST/Subtract 3 hours	(H)	Add 13 hours
(U*)	Subtract 3.5 hours	(I)	Add 14 hours
(V)	Subtract 4 hours	(I*)	Add 14.5 hours
(V*)	Subtract 4.5 hours	(K)	Add 15 hours
(W)	Subtract 5 hours	(K*)	Add 15.5 hours
(X)	Subtract 6 hours	(L)	Add 16 hours
(Y)	Subtract 7 hours	(L*)	Add 16.5 hours
(A)	Add 6 hours	(M)	Add 17 hours
(B)	Add 7 hours	(M*)	Add 18 hours
(C)	Add 8 hours	(P*)	Add 2.5 hours
(C*)	Add 8.5 hours		

Eastern Standard Time = Universal Time (Greenwich Mean Time) + or − the value from the table.

World Map of Time Zones

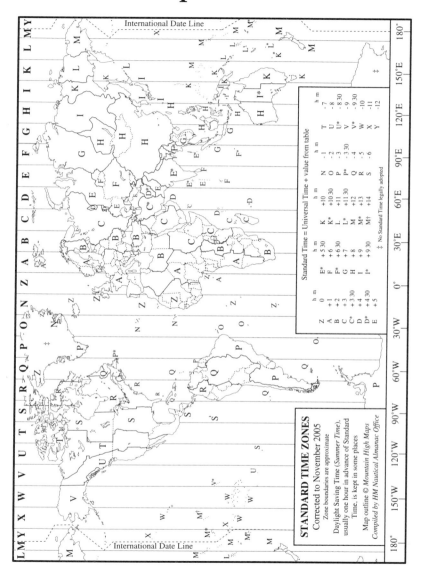

January 2014

DATE	SID.TIME	SUN	MOON	NODE	MERCURY	VENUS	MARS	JUPITER	SATURN	URANUS	NEPTUNE	PLUTO	CERES	PALLAS	JUNO	VESTA	CHIRON
1 W	6 42 17	10 ♑ 28 46	3 ♑ 48	5 ♏ 33 ℞	12 ♑ 05	26 ♑ 54 ℞	11 ♎ 39	16 ♋ 07 ℞	20 ♏ 21	8 ♈ 41	3 ♓ 14	11 ♑ 15	22 ♎ 01	13 ♍ 36	29 ♒ 52	18 ♎ 13	9 ♓ 58
2 Th	6 46 14	11 29 57	19 07	5 23	13 42	26 29	12 05	15 59	20 27	8 41	3 15	11 18	22 19	13 39	0 ♓ 18	18 33	10 01
3 F	6 50 10	12 31 08	4 ♒ 25	5 13	15 19	26 01	12 31	15 51	20 32	8 42	3 17	11 20	22 37	13 41	0 45	18 53	10 03
4 Sa	6 54 7	13 32 19	19 32	5 03	16 57	25 32	12 58	15 43	20 37	8 43	3 18	11 22	22 55	13 43	1 12	19 13	10 06
5 Su	6 58 3	14 33 29	4 ♓ 55	4 55	18 35	25 01	13 23	15 35	20 43	8 44	3 20	11 24	23 12	13 44	1 38	19 32	10 08
6 M	7 2 0	15 34 39	18 35	4 50	20 13	24 29	13 49	15 27	20 48	8 45	3 22	11 26	23 30	13 45 ℞	2 05	19 52	10 11
7 T	7 5 56	16 35 49	2 ♈ 25	4 47	21 52	23 55	14 14	15 18	20 53	8 46	3 23	11 28	23 47	13 45	2 32	20 11	10 13
8 W	7 9 53	17 36 58	15 46	4 46 D	23 31	23 20	14 39	15 10	20 58	8 47	3 25	11 30	24 04	13 44	2 59	20 30	10 16
9 Th	7 13 49	18 38 07	28 44	4 46 ℞	25 10	22 44	15 04	15 02	21 03	8 48	3 27	11 32	24 21	13 43	3 27	20 49	10 18
10 F	7 17 46	19 39 15	11 ♉ 20	4 46	26 50	22 08	15 29	14 54	21 08	8 49	3 29	11 34	24 37	13 41	3 54	21 07	10 21
11 Sa	7 21 43	20 40 23	23 41	4 45	28 30	21 31	15 53	14 46	21 12	8 51	3 30	11 36	24 53	13 39	4 21	21 26	10 24
12 Su	7 25 39	21 41 31	5 ♊ 50	4 41	0 ♒ 10	20 54	16 17	14 38	21 17	8 52	3 32	11 39	25 09	13 35	4 49	21 44	10 27
13 M	7 29 36	22 42 37	17 51	4 34	1 50	20 17	16 41	14 30	21 22	8 53	3 34	11 41	25 25	13 32	5 17	22 02	10 29
14 T	7 33 32	23 43 42	29 48	4 24	3 31	19 41	17 04	14 22	21 26	8 54	3 36	11 43	25 41	13 27	5 44	22 19	10 32
15 W	7 37 29	24 44 50	11 ♋ 42	4 11	5 12	19 05	17 27	14 14	21 31	8 56	3 38	11 45	25 56	13 22	6 12	22 37	10 35
16 Th	7 41 25	25 45 55	23 34	3 57	6 52	18 31	17 50	14 07	21 35	8 57	3 39	11 47	26 11	13 16	6 40	22 54	10 38
17 F	7 45 22	26 47 00	5 ♌ 27	3 42	8 32	17 57	18 13	13 59	21 40	8 59	3 41	11 49	26 26	13 10	7 08	23 11	10 41
18 Sa	7 49 18	27 48 04	17 21	3 27	10 13	17 25	18 35	13 51	21 44	9 00	3 43	11 51	26 40	13 03	7 37	23 27	10 44
19 Su	7 53 15	28 49 08	29 18	3 14	11 52	16 54	18 57	13 43	21 48	9 02	3 45	11 53	26 55	12 55	8 05	23 44	10 47
20 M	7 57 12	29 50 12	11 ♍ 20	3 04	13 31	16 25	19 18	13 36	21 52	9 04	3 47	11 55	27 09	12 47	8 33	24 00	10 50
21 T	8 1 8	0 ♒ 51 15	23 30	2 57	15 10	15 58	19 40	13 29	21 56	9 05	3 49	11 57	27 22	12 38	9 02	24 15	10 53
22 W	8 5 5	1 52 17	5 ♎ 49	2 52	16 47	15 33	20 01	13 21	22 00	9 07	3 51	11 59	27 36	12 28	9 31	24 31	10 56
23 Th	8 9 1	2 53 19	18 22	2 50	18 22	15 10	20 21	13 14	22 04	9 09	3 53	12 01	27 49	12 18	9 59	24 46	10 59
24 F	8 12 58	3 54 21	1 ♏ 14	2 50	19 56	14 50	20 41	13 07	22 07	9 11	3 55	12 03	28 02	12 08	10 28	25 01	11 03
25 Sa	8 16 54	4 55 22	14 28	2 50	21 28	14 32	21 01	13 00	22 11	9 12	3 57	12 05	28 14	11 56	10 57	25 16	11 06
26 Su	8 20 51	5 56 23	28 08	2 49	22 57	14 16	21 21	12 53	22 15	9 14	3 59	12 07	28 27	11 44	11 26	25 30	11 09
27 M	8 24 47	6 57 24	12 ♐ 16	2 45	24 23	14 03	21 40	12 46	22 18	9 16	4 01	12 09	28 39	11 32	11 55	25 44	11 12
28 T	8 28 44	7 58 23	26 52	2 39	25 46	13 52	21 59	12 39	22 22	9 18	4 03	12 11	28 50	11 19	12 25	25 58	11 16
29 W	8 32 41	8 59 22	11 ♑ 51	2 30	27 03	13 43	22 17	12 33	22 25	9 20	4 06	12 13	29 02	11 05	12 54	26 12	11 19
30 Th	8 36 37	10 00 21	27 06	2 20	28 16	13 38	22 35	12 26	22 28	9 22	4 08	12 15	29 13	10 51	13 23	26 25	11 22
31 F	8 40 34	11 01 18	12 ♒ 26	2 08	29 23	13 34 D	22 52	12 20	22 31	9 25	4 10	12 17	29 23	10 36	13 53	26 38	11 26

Tables are for midnight Greenwich Mean Time

February 2014

DATE	SID.TIME	SUN	MOON	NODE	MERCURY	VENUS	MARS	JUPITER	SATURN	URANUS	NEPTUNE	PLUTO	CERES	PALLAS	JUNO	VESTA	CHIRON
1 Sa	8 44 30	12≈02 14	27≈39	1♏,57℞	0♓23	13♑33	23♎09	12♋14℞	22♏,34	9♈27	4♓12	12♑19	29≈34	10♏21℞	14♓22	26♎50	11♓29
2 Su	8 48 27	13 03 10	12♓35	1 47	1 16	13 35	23 26	12 08	22 37	9 29	4 14	12 20	29 44	10 05	14 52	27 02	11 33
3 M	8 52 23	14 04 03	27 05	1 41	2 00	13 39	23 42	12 02	22 40	9 31	4 16	12 22	29 53	9 49	15 22	27 14	11 36
4 T	8 56 20	15 04 56	11♈07	1 37	2 35	13 45	23 58	11 56	22 43	9 33	4 18	12 24	0♏,02	9 33	15 52	27 25	11 39
5 W	9 0 16	16 05 47	24 38	1 35 D	3 01	13 54	24 13	11 50	22 45	9 36	4 21	12 26	0 11	9 16	16 22	27 36	11 43
6 Th	9 4 13	17 06 37	7♉41	1 35℞	3 16℞	14 04	24 28	11 45	22 48	9 38	4 23	12 28	0 20	8 58	16 52	27 47	11 47
7 F	9 8 10	18 07 25	20 21	1 36	3 20	14 17	24 42	11 40	22 50	9 41	4 25	12 30	0 28	8 41	17 22	27 57	11 50
8 Sa	9 12 6	19 08 12	2♊41	1 35	3 14	14 32	24 56	11 35	22 53	9 43	4 27	12 31	0 36	8 22	17 52	28 07	11 54
9 Su	9 16 3	20 08 58	14 48	1 32	2 56	14 49	25 09	11 30	22 55	9 45	4 29	12 33	0 44	8 04	18 22	28 17	11 57
10 M	9 19 59	21 09 42	26 45	1 26	2 28	15 08	25 22	11 25	22 57	9 48	4 32	12 35	0 51	7 45	18 53	28 26	12 01
11 T	9 23 56	22 10 24	8♋38	1 18	1 50	15 29	25 34	11 20	22 59	9 50	4 34	12 37	0 58	7 26	19 23	28 35	12 04
12 W	9 27 52	23 11 05	20 29	1 07	1 03	15 52	25 46	11 16	23 01	9 53	4 36	12 38	1 04	7 07	19 53	28 43	12 08
13 Th	9 31 49	24 11 44	2♌21	0 55	0 09	16 16	25 57	11 12	23 03	9 56	4 38	12 40	1 10	6 48	20 24	28 51	12 12
14 F	9 35 45	25 12 22	14 16	0 42	29≈08	16 43	26 07	11 08	23 05	9 58	4 41	12 42	1 16	6 28	20 55	28 59	12 15
15 Sa	9 39 42	26 12 58	26 16	0 29	28 02	17 10	26 17	11 04	23 06	10 01	4 43	12 43	1 21	6 08	21 25	29 06	12 19
16 Su	9 43 39	27 13 33	8♍22	0 18	26 54	17 40	26 27	11 00	23 08	10 04	4 45	12 45	1 26	5 48	21 56	29 13	12 23
17 M	9 47 35	28 14 06	20 34	0 09	25 45	18 11	26 36	10 57	23 09	10 06	4 47	12 47	1 31	5 28	22 27	29 19	12 26
18 T	9 51 32	29 14 38	2♎54	0 03	24 37	18 44	26 44	10 53	23 11	10 09	4 50	12 48	1 35	5 08	22 58	29 25	12 30
19 W	9 55 28	0♓15 09	15 24	29♎59	23 31	19 18	26 52	10 50	23 12	10 12	4 52	12 50	1 38	4 48	23 29	29 30	12 34
20 Th	9 59 25	1 15 38	28 06	29 58 D	22 30	19 53	26 59	10 47	23 13	10 15	4 54	12 51	1 42	4 28	24 00	29 35	12 38
21 F	10 3 21	2 16 06	11♏,03	29 58	21 33	20 30	27 05	10 44	23 14	10 18	4 56	12 53	1 45	4 07	24 31	29 40	12 41
22 Sa	10 7 18	3 16 33	24 17	29 59℞	20 43	21 08	27 11	10 42	23 15	10 20	4 59	12 54	1 47	3 47	25 03	29 44	12 45
23 Su	10 11 14	4 16 58	7♐51	0♏,00	20 00	21 47	27 16	10 40	23 16	10 23	5 01	12 56	1 49	3 27	25 34	29 47	12 49
24 M	10 15 11	5 17 22	21 47	29♎58	19 23	22 28	27 20	10 37	23 17	10 26	5 03	12 57	1 51	3 07	26 05	29 51	12 53
25 T	10 19 8	6 17 45	6♑06	29 55	18 54	23 09	27 24	10 35	23 17	10 29	5 06	12 59	1 52	2 47	26 37	29 53	12 56
26 W	10 23 4	7 18 07	20 45	29 49	18 33	23 52	27 27	10 34	23 18	10 32	5 08	13 00	1 53	2 28	27 08	29 56	13 00
27 Th	10 27 1	8 18 26	5≈39	29 42	18 18	24 35	27 29	10 32	23 18	10 35	5 10	13 01	1 53℞	2 08	27 40	29 57	13 04
28 F	10 30 57	9 18 45	20 41	29 34	18 11 D	25 20	27 31	10 31	23 19	10 38	5 12	13 03	1 53	1 49	28 11	29 59	13 08

March 2014

DATE	SID. TIME	SUN	MOON	NODE	MERCURY	VENUS	MARS	JUPITER	SATURN	URANUS	NEPTUNE	PLUTO	CERES	PALLAS	JUNO	VESTA	CHIRON
1 Sa	10 34 54	10✶19 01	5✶41	29♎26R	18♒10	26♑06	27♎32R	10♋29	23♏19	10♈41	5✶15	13♑04	1♏53	1♍30	28✶43	29♎59	13✶12
2 Su	10 38 50	11 19 16	20 30	29 19	18 16	26 52	27 32	10 28R	23 19R	10 44	5 17	13 05	1 52R	1 11R	29 15	0♏00R	13 15
3 M	10 42 47	12 19 29	4♈59	29 15	18 28	27 39	27 31	10 28	23 19	10 47	5 19	13 07	1 50	0 53	29 47	29♎59	13 19
4 T	10 46 43	13 19 40	19 04	29 12 D	18 46	28 27	27 30	10 27	23 19	10 51	5 21	13 08	1 48	0 35	0♈19	29 59	13 23
5 W	10 50 40	14 19 49	2♉41	29 12	19 09	29 16	27 28	10 27	23 19	10 54	5 24	13 09	1 46	0 17	0 51	29 58	13 27
6 Th	10 54 36	15 19 57	15 52	29 13	19 37	0♒06	27 25	10 27 D	23 18	10 57	5 26	13 10	1 44	29♌59	1 23	29 56	13 31
7 F	10 58 33	16 20 02	28 38	29 14	20 10	0 57	27 21	10 27	23 18	11 00	5 28	13 12	1 41	29 42	1 55	29 54	13 34
8 Sa	11 2 30	17 20 04	11♊03	29 15R	20 47	1 48	27 17	10 27	23 18	11 03	5 30	13 13	1 37	29 25	2 27	29 51	13 38
9 Su	11 6 26	18 20 05	23 13	29 16	21 29	2 40	27 12	10 27	23 17	11 06	5 33	13 14	1 33	29 09	2 59	29 48	13 42
10 M	11 10 23	19 20 04	5♋12	29 14	22 14	3 32	27 06	10 28	23 16	11 10	5 35	13 15	1 29	28 53	3 31	29 44	13 46
11 T	11 14 19	20 20 00	17 05	29 11	23 02	4 25	26 59	10 29	23 16	11 13	5 37	13 16	1 24	28 38	4 04	29 40	13 50
12 W	11 18 16	21 19 55	28 56	29 06	23 54	5 19	26 52	10 30	23 15	11 16	5 39	13 17	1 19	28 23	4 36	29 36	13 53
13 Th	11 22 12	22 19 47	10♌50	29 00	24 49	6 13	26 44	10 31	23 14	11 19	5 42	13 18	1 13	28 09	5 08	29 30	13 57
14 F	11 26 9	23 19 37	22 49	28 53	25 46	7 08	26 35	10 32	23 13	11 23	5 44	13 19	1 07	27 55	5 41	29 25	14 01
15 Sa	11 30 5	24 19 25	4♍55	28 46	26 48	8 04	26 25	10 34	23 11	11 26	5 46	13 20	1 01	27 41	6 13	29 19	14 05
16 Su	11 34 2	25 19 10	17 10	28 41	27 51	9 00	26 14	10 35	23 10	11 29	5 48	13 21	0 54	27 28	6 46	29 12	14 08
17 M	11 37 59	26 18 54	29 36	28 36	28 57	9 56	26 03	10 37	23 09	11 33	5 50	13 22	0 47	27 16	7 19	29 05	14 12
18 T	11 41 55	27 18 36	12♎13	28 33	0✶05	10 53	25 51	10 40	23 07	11 36	5 53	13 23	0 40	27 04	7 51	28 58	14 16
19 W	11 45 52	28 18 16	25 02	28 32 D	1 15	11 51	25 38	10 42	23 06	11 39	5 55	13 24	0 32	26 52	8 24	28 50	14 20
20 Th	11 49 48	29 17 54	8♏02	28 33	2 27	12 49	25 25	10 44	23 04	11 43	5 57	13 24	0 23	26 41	8 57	28 41	14 23
21 F	11 53 45	0♈17 30	21 16	28 34	3 41	13 47	25 10	10 47	23 02	11 46	5 59	13 25	0 15	26 31	9 30	28 33	14 27
22 Sa	11 57 41	1 17 05	4✗42	28 35	4 57	14 46	24 56	10 50	23 00	11 49	6 01	13 26	0 06	26 21	10 02	28 23	14 31
23 Su	12 1 38	2 16 38	18 23	28 37	6 15	15 45	24 40	10 53	22 58	11 53	6 03	13 27	29♎56	26 12	10 35	28 14	14 34
24 M	12 5 34	3 16 09	2♑18	28 37R	7 35	16 45	24 24	10 56	22 56	11 56	6 05	13 27	29 47	26 03	11 08	28 04	14 38
25 T	12 9 31	4 15 38	16 28	28 37	8 56	17 45	24 07	11 00	22 54	12 00	6 07	13 28	29 37	25 55	11 41	27 53	14 41
26 W	12 13 28	5 15 06	0♒49	28 35	10 19	18 45	23 49	11 03	22 52	12 03	6 09	13 29	29 26	25 48	12 14	27 42	14 45
27 Th	12 17 24	6 14 32	15 19	28 33	11 44	19 46	23 31	11 07	22 50	12 07	6 11	13 29	29 16	25 40	12 48	27 31	14 49
28 F	12 21 21	7 13 56	29 54	28 30	13 10	20 47	23 12	11 11	22 47	12 10	6 13	13 30	29 05	25 34	13 21	27 19	14 52
29 Sa	12 25 17	8 13 18	14✶27	28 27	14 38	21 48	22 53	11 15	22 45	12 13	6 15	13 30	28 53	25 28	13 54	27 07	14 56
30 Su	12 29 14	9 12 38	28 52	28 25	16 07	22 50	22 33	11 19	22 42	12 17	6 17	13 31	28 42	25 23	14 27	26 55	14 59
31 M	12 33 10	10 11 56	13♈04	28 23	17 38	23 52	22 13	11 24	22 40	12 20	6 19	13 31	28 30	25 18	15 00	26 42	15 03

Tables are for midnight Greenwich Mean Time

196

April 2014

DATE	SID.TIME	SUN	MOON	NODE	MERCURY	VENUS	MARS	JUPITER	SATURN	URANUS	NEPTUNE	PLUTO	CERES	PALLAS	JUNO	VESTA	CHIRON
1 T	12 37 7	11♈11 13	26♈58	28♎23 D	19♓10	24≈54	21♎52	11♋29	22♏37	12♈24	6♓21	13♑32	28≏18	25♌13	15♈34	26≏29	15♓06
2 W	12 41 3	12 10 27	10♉30	28 23	20 43	25 56	21 31 Rx	11 33	22 34 Rx	12 27	6 23	13 32	28 06 Rx	25 10 Rx	16 07	26 16 Rx	15 10
3 Th	12 45 0	13 09 39	23 40	28 24	22 19	26 59	21 09	11 38	22 31	12 30	6 25	13 33	27 54	25 06	16 41	26 02	15 13
4 F	12 48 56	14 08 49	6♊28	28 25	23 55	28 02	20 47	11 44	22 28	12 34	6 27	13 33	27 41	25 04	17 14	25 48	15 17
5 Sa	12 52 53	15 07 56	18 57	28 26	25 33	29 06	20 25	11 49	22 25	12 37	6 29	13 33	27 28	25 02	17 48	25 34	15 20
6 Su	12 56 50	16 07 01	1♋11	28 27	27 13	0♓09	20 02	11 54	22 22	12 41	6 31	13 34	27 15	25 00	18 21	25 20	15 24
7 M	13 0 46	17 06 04	13 13	28 28 Rx	28 54	1 13	19 40	12 00	22 19	12 44	6 33	13 34	27 02	24 59	18 55	25 06	15 27
8 T	13 4 43	18 05 05	25 08	28 28	0♈20	2 17	19 17	12 06	22 16	12 48	6 35	13 34	26 49	24 58 D	19 28	24 51	15 30
9 W	13 8 39	19 04 04	7♌01	28 27	2 20	3 21	18 54	12 12	22 12	12 51	6 36	13 34	26 36	24 58	20 02	24 36	15 34
10 Th	13 12 36	20 03 00	18 55	28 26	4 05	4 26	18 31	12 18	22 09	12 54	6 38	13 35	26 22	24 59	20 36	24 21	15 37
11 F	13 16 32	21 01 53	0♍57	28 25	5 52	5 30	18 08	12 24	22 05	12 58	6 40	13 35	26 09	24 59	21 10	24 06	15 40
12 Sa	13 20 29	22 00 45	13 08	28 23 Rx	7 41	6 35	17 45	12 30	22 02	13 01	6 42	13 35	25 55	25 01	21 43	23 51	15 43
13 Su	13 24 25	22 59 34	25 31	28 23	9 30	7 40	17 22	12 37	21 58	13 05	6 43	13 35	25 41	25 03	22 17	23 36	15 46
14 M	13 28 22	23 58 22	8♎16	28 23	11 22	8 46	16 59	12 44	21 54	13 08	6 45	13 35 Rx	25 28	25 05	22 51	23 21	15 50
15 T	13 32 19	24 57 07	21 04	28 23 D	13 15	9 51	16 36	12 51	21 51	13 11	6 47	13 35	25 14	25 08	23 25	23 06	15 53
16 W	13 36 15	25 55 50	4♏14	28 23	15 09	10 57	16 14	12 58	21 47	13 15	6 48	13 35	25 00	25 11	23 59	22 51	15 56
17 Th	13 40 12	26 54 32	17 39	28 23 Rx	17 05	12 03	15 52	13 05	21 43	13 18	6 50	13 35	24 47	25 15	24 33	22 36	15 59
18 F	13 44 8	27 53 11	1♐18	28 24	19 03	13 09	15 30	13 12	21 39	13 21	6 52	13 35	24 33	25 19	25 07	22 21	16 02
19 Sa	13 48 5	28 51 49	15 09	28 24	21 02	14 15	15 08	13 19	21 35	13 25	6 53	13 35	24 20	25 24	25 41	22 06	16 05
20 Su	13 52 1	29 50 25	29 09	28 23	23 02	15 21	14 47	13 27	21 31	13 28	6 55	13 34	24 06	25 29	26 15	21 51	16 08
21 M	13 55 58	0♉49 00	13♑16	28 23	25 04	16 28	14 26	13 34	21 27	13 31	6 56	13 34	23 53	25 34	26 49	21 36	16 11
22 T	13 59 54	1 47 32	27 27	28 23 D	27 07	17 34	14 05	13 42	21 23	13 35	6 58	13 34	23 39	25 40	27 23	21 21	16 14
23 W	14 3 51	2 46 04	11≈41	28 23	29 12	18 41	13 45	13 50	21 19	13 38	6 59	13 34	23 26	25 46	27 57	21 07	16 17
24 Th	14 7 48	3 44 33	25 54	28 23	1♉17	19 48	13 25	13 58	21 15	13 41	7 01	13 34	23 13	25 53	28 31	20 52	16 19
25 F	14 11 44	4 43 01	10♓05	28 24	3 24	20 55	13 06	14 06	21 11	13 45	7 02	13 33	23 00	26 00	29 05	20 38	16 22
26 Sa	14 15 41	5 41 28	24 10	28 24	5 31	22 02	12 48	14 15	21 06	13 48	7 04	13 33	22 48	26 07	29 40	20 24	16 25
27 Su	14 19 37	6 39 52	8♈06	28 25	7 40	23 10	12 30	14 23	21 02	13 51	7 05	13 33	22 35	26 15	0♉14	20 11	16 28
28 M	14 23 34	7 38 15	21 52	28 25 Rx	9 48	24 17	12 13	14 32	20 58	13 54	7 06	13 32	22 23	26 23	0 48	19 57	16 30
29 T	14 27 30	8 36 37	5♉23	28 25	11 57	25 25	11 56	14 40	20 54	13 57	7 08	13 32	22 11	26 32	1 23	19 44	16 33
30 W	14 31 27	9 34 56	18 39	28 25	14 06	26 32	11 40	14 49	20 49	14 01	7 09	13 31	21 59	26 41	1 57	19 32	16 36

DATE	SID.TIME	SUN	MOON	NODE	MERCURY	VENUS	MARS	JUPITER	SATURN	URANUS	NEPTUNE	PLUTO	CERES	PALLAS	JUNO	VESTA	CHIRON
1 Th	14 35 23	10 ♉ 33 14	1 ♊ 39	28 ♎ 23 Rx	16 ♉ 15	27 ♈ 40	11 ♎ 25	14 ♋ 58	20 ♏ 45	14 ♈ 04	7 ♓ 10	13 ♑ 31	21 ♎ 47	26 ♌ 50	2 ♉ 31	19 ♎ 19	16 ♓ 38
2 F	14 39 20	11 31 30	14 22	28 22	18 23	28 48	11 10 Rx	15 07	20 40 Rx	14 07	7 11	13 31 Rx	21 36 Rx	27 00	3 06	19 07 Rx	16 41
3 Sa	14 43 17	12 29 44	26 49	28 20	20 31	29 56	10 56	15 16	20 36	14 10	7 13	13 30	21 24	27 10	3 40	18 55	16 43
4 Su	14 47 13	13 27 56	9 ♋ 02	28 18	22 37	1 ♉ 04	10 43	15 25	20 32	14 13	7 14	13 29	21 14	27 20	4 15	18 44	16 46
5 M	14 51 10	14 26 06	21 05	28 16	24 42	2 13	10 31	15 35	20 27	14 16	7 15	13 29	21 03	27 31	4 49	18 33	16 48
6 T	14 55 6	15 24 15	3 ♌ 01	28 15	26 45	3 21	10 19	15 44	20 23	14 19	7 16	13 28	20 53	27 42	5 24	18 22	16 50
7 W	14 59 3	16 22 21	14 54	28 14 D	28 46	4 29	10 09	15 54	20 18	14 22	7 17	13 28	20 43	27 53	5 58	18 12	16 53
8 Th	15 2 59	17 20 25	26 48	28 15	0 ♊ 45	5 38	9 59	16 03	20 14	14 25	7 18	13 27	20 33	28 05	6 33	18 02	16 55
9 F	15 6 56	18 18 28	8 ♍ 50	28 16	2 41	6 46	9 50	16 13	20 09	14 28	7 19	13 26	20 24	28 17	7 07	17 53	16 57
10 Sa	15 10 52	19 16 28	21 02	28 17	4 34	7 55	9 41	16 23	20 05	14 31	7 20	13 26	20 15	28 29	7 42	17 44	16 59
11 Su	15 14 49	20 14 27	3 ♎ 30	28 19	6 25	9 04	9 34	16 33	20 00	14 34	7 21	13 25	20 06	28 41	8 16	17 36	17 01
12 M	15 18 45	21 12 24	16 16	28 20 Rx	8 13	10 13	9 27	16 43	19 56	14 37	7 22	13 24	19 58	28 54	8 51	17 28	17 04
13 T	15 22 42	22 10 19	29 23	28 20	9 57	11 22	9 21	16 53	19 51	14 40	7 23	13 23	19 50	29 07	9 25	17 20	17 06
14 W	15 26 39	23 08 12	12 ♏ 51	28 19	11 38	12 31	9 16	17 04	19 47	14 43	7 24	13 23	19 43	29 21	10 00	17 13	17 08
15 Th	15 30 35	24 06 04	26 40	28 18	13 16	13 40	9 11	17 14	19 42	14 46	7 25	13 22	19 35	29 34	10 35	17 06	17 10
16 F	15 34 32	25 03 55	10 ♐ 46	28 15	14 51	14 49	9 08	17 24	19 38	14 49	7 26	13 21	19 29	29 48	11 09	17 00	17 11
17 Sa	15 38 28	26 01 44	25 05	28 11	16 22	15 58	9 05	17 35	19 33	14 51	7 26	13 20	19 22	0 ♍ 02	11 44	16 54	17 13
18 Su	15 42 25	26 59 32	9 ♑ 31	28 07	17 50	17 07	9 03	17 45	19 29	14 54	7 27	13 19	19 16	0 17	12 19	16 49	17 15
19 M	15 46 21	27 57 19	24 00	28 03	19 13	18 17	9 02	17 56	19 24	14 57	7 28	13 18	19 10	0 31	12 54	16 45	17 17
20 T	15 50 18	28 55 05	8 ♒ 26	28 00	20 34	19 26	9 02 D	18 07	19 20	15 00	7 29	13 17	19 05	0 46	13 28	16 40	17 19
21 W	15 54 15	29 52 49	22 44	27 59 D	21 50	20 36	9 02	18 18	19 15	15 02	7 29	13 16	19 00	1 01	14 03	16 37	17 20
22 Th	15 58 11	0 ♊ 50 33	6 ♓ 52	27 59	23 03	21 46	9 03	18 29	19 11	15 05	7 30	13 15	18 56	1 16	14 38	16 34	17 22
23 F	16 2 8	1 48 15	20 48	28 00	24 12	22 55	9 05	18 40	19 07	15 07	7 31	13 14	18 52	1 32	15 13	16 31	17 23
24 Sa	16 6 4	2 45 56	4 ♈ 33	28 01	25 18	24 05	9 07	18 51	19 02	15 10	7 31	13 13	18 48	1 48	15 47	16 29	17 25
25 Su	16 10 1	3 43 37	18 04	28 03 Rx	26 19	25 15	9 11	19 02	18 58	15 13	7 32	13 12	18 45	2 04	16 22	16 27	17 26
26 M	16 13 57	4 41 16	1 ♉ 24	28 03	27 16	26 25	9 15	19 13	18 54	15 15	7 32	13 11	18 42	2 20	16 57	16 26	17 28
27 T	16 17 54	5 38 54	14 32	28 02	28 10	27 35	9 20	19 25	18 49	15 18	7 33	13 10	18 39	2 36	17 32	16 25 D	17 29
28 W	16 21 50	6 36 32	27 27	27 59	28 59	28 45	9 25	19 36	18 45	15 20	7 33	13 09	18 37	2 53	18 07	16 25	17 30
29 Th	16 25 47	7 34 08	10 ♊ 10	27 54	29 44	29 55	9 31	19 47	18 41	15 22	7 34	13 08	18 35	3 10	18 42	16 25	17 32
30 F	16 29 44	8 31 43	22 41	27 47	0 ♋ 25	1 ♉ 05	9 38	19 59	18 37	15 25	7 34	13 07	18 34	3 27	19 16	16 26	17 33
31 Sa	16 33 40	9 29 17	5 ♋ 00	27 40	1 01	2 15	9 46	20 11	18 33	15 27	7 34	13 05	18 33	3 44	19 51	16 27	17 34

Tables are for midnight Greenwich Mean Time

DATE	SID.TIME	SUN	MOON	NODE	MERCURY	VENUS	MARS	JUPITER	SATURN	URANUS	NEPTUNE	PLUTO	CERES	PALLAS	JUNO	VESTA	CHIRON
1 Su	16 37 37	10♊26 50	17♋09	27♎32R	1♋33	3♉25	9♎54	20♋22	18♏29	15♈29	7♓34	13♑04	18♎32D	4♍01	20♉26	16♎29	17♓35
2 M	16 41 33	11 24 21	29 09	27 25	2 01	4 36	10 03	20 34	18 25R	15 32	7 35	13 03R	18 32	4 19	21 01	16 31	17 36
3 T	16 45 30	12 21 51	11♌03	27 19	2 24	5 46	10 13	20 46	18 21	15 34	7 35	13 02	18 33	4 37	21 36	16 34	17 37
4 W	16 49 26	13 19 20	22 53	27 15	2 42	6 56	10 23	20 58	18 17	15 36	7 35	13 00	18 33	4 55	22 11	16 37	17 38
5 Th	16 53 23	14 16 48	4♍48	27 13D	2 56	8 07	10 34	21 10	18 13	15 38	7 35	12 59	18 34	5 13	22 46	16 41	17 39
6 F	16 57 19	15 14 14	16 47	27 13	3 05	9 17	10 45	21 22	18 10	15 40	7 36	12 58	18 36	5 31	23 20	16 45	17 40
7 Sa	17 1 16	16 11 40	28 58	27 13	3 09R	10 28	10 57	21 34	18 06	15 42	7 36	12 57	18 37	5 50	23 55	16 50	17 40
8 Su	17 5 13	17 09 04	11♎25	27 14	3 09	11 38	11 10	21 46	18 02	15 44	7 36	12 55	18 40	6 08	24 30	16 55	17 41
9 M	17 9 9	18 06 27	24 12	27 15R	3 05	12 49	11 23	21 58	17 59	15 46	7 36	12 54	18 42	6 27	25 05	17 00	17 42
10 T	17 13 6	19 03 49	7♏24	27 15	2 56	14 00	11 37	22 10	17 55	15 48	7 36	12 53	18 45	6 46	25 40	17 06	17 42
11 W	17 17 2	20 01 10	21 02	27 12	2 43	15 10	11 51	22 22	17 52	15 50	7 36	12 51	18 48	7 05	26 15	17 13	17 43
12 Th	17 20 59	20 58 30	5♐06	27 08	2 26	16 21	12 06	22 35	17 49	15 52	7 36	12 50	18 50	7 25	26 50	17 20	17 44
13 F	17 24 55	21 55 49	19 33	27 01	2 06	17 32	12 22	22 47	17 45	15 54	7 36	12 49	18 56	7 44	27 25	17 27	17 44
14 Sa	17 28 52	22 53 08	4♑16	26 54	1 42	18 43	12 38	22 59	17 42	15 56	7 35	12 47	19 01	8 04	27 59	17 35	17 44
15 Su	17 32 48	23 50 26	19 10	26 45	1 15	19 54	12 54	23 12	17 38	15 58	7 35	12 46	19 05	8 23	28 34	17 43	17 45
16 M	17 36 45	24 47 44	4≈03	26 37	0 45	21 05	13 11	23 24	17 35	15 59	7 35	12 44	19 10	8 43	29 09	17 51	17 45
17 T	17 40 42	25 45 01	18 49	26 31	0 14	22 16	13 29	23 37	17 32	16 01	7 35	12 43	19 16	9 03	29 44	18 00	17 45
18 W	17 44 38	26 42 18	3♓21	26 26	29♊41	23 27	13 47	23 49	17 29	16 03	7 35	12 42	19 22	9 23	0♊19	18 10	17 45
19 Th	17 48 35	27 39 34	17 35	26 26	29 07	24 38	14 05	24 02	17 26	16 04	7 34	12 40	19 28	9 43	0 54	18 19	17 45
20 F	17 52 31	28 36 50	1♈28	26 24D	28 32	25 49	14 24	24 15	17 23	16 06	7 34	12 39	19 34	10 04	1 28	18 30	17 46R
21 Sa	17 56 28	29 34 06	15 03	26 24R	27 58	27 00	14 44	24 27	17 21	16 07	7 34	12 37	19 41	10 24	2 03	18 40	17 46
22 Su	18 0 24	0♋31 22	28 20	26 25	27 25	28 11	15 03	24 40	17 18	16 09	7 33	12 36	19 48	10 45	2 38	18 51	17 45
23 M	18 4 21	1 28 38	11♉21	26 24	26 53	29 23	15 24	24 53	17 15	16 10	7 33	12 34	19 55	11 06	3 13	19 02	17 45
24 T	18 8 17	2 25 53	24 09	26 21	26 23	0♊34	15 45	25 06	17 13	16 11	7 33	12 33	20 03	11 27	3 48	19 14	17 45
25 W	18 12 14	3 23 09	6♊45	26 15	25 55	1 45	16 06	25 18	17 10	16 13	7 32	12 31	20 11	11 48	4 22	19 26	17 45
26 Th	18 16 11	4 20 24	19 12	26 06	25 31	2 57	16 27	25 31	17 08	16 14	7 32	12 30	20 20	12 09	4 57	19 39	17 45
27 F	18 20 7	5 17 39	1♋29	25 56	25 09	4 08	16 49	25 44	17 06	16 15	7 31	12 28	20 28	12 30	5 32	19 51	17 44
28 Sa	18 24 4	6 14 54	13 38	25 43	24 51	5 20	17 12	25 57	17 04	16 16	7 30	12 27	20 37	12 51	6 07	20 05	17 44
29 Su	18 28 0	7 12 08	25 40	25 31	24 38	6 31	17 35	26 10	17 01	16 18	7 30	12 25	20 47	13 13	6 41	20 18	17 44
30 M	18 31 57	8 09 23	7♌35	25 19	24 28	7 43	17 58	26 23	16 59	16 19	7 29	12 24	20 56	13 34	7 16	20 32	17 43

July 2014

DATE	SID.TIME	SUN	MOON	NODE	MERCURY	VENUS	MARS	JUPITER	SATURN	URANUS	NEPTUNE	PLUTO	CERES	PALLAS	JUNO	VESTA	CHIRON
1 T	18 35 53	9 ♋ 06 36	19 ♌ 27	25 ♎ 08 ℞	24 ♊ 24 D	8 ♊ 54	18 ♎ 21	26 ♋ 36	16 ♏ 58	16 ♈ 20	7 ♓ 29	12 ♑ 22	21 ♎ 06	13 ♍ 56	7 ♊ 51	20 ♎ 46	17 ♓ 43
2 W	18 39 50	10 03 50	1 ♍ 17	25 00 ℞	24 23	10 06	18 45	26 49	16 56 ℞	16 21	7 28 ℞	12 21 ℞	21 16	14 18	8 26	21 00	17 42 ℞
3 Th	18 43 46	11 01 03	13 09	24 54	24 28	11 18	19 10	27 02	16 54	16 22	7 27	12 19	21 27	14 40	9 00	21 15	17 41
4 F	18 47 43	11 58 16	25 07	24 51	24 38	12 29	19 34	27 15	16 52	16 23	7 27	12 18	21 37	15 02	9 35	21 30	17 41
5 Sa	18 51 40	12 55 28	7 ♎ 15	24 50 D	24 52	13 41	19 59	27 29	16 51	16 23	7 26	12 16	21 48	15 24	10 09	21 46	17 40
6 Su	18 55 36	13 52 41	19 39	24 50 ℞	25 12	14 53	20 25	27 42	16 49	16 24	7 25	12 15	21 59	15 46	10 44	22 02	17 39
7 M	18 59 33	14 49 53	2 ♏ 23	24 50	25 36	16 05	20 51	27 55	16 48	16 25	7 24	12 13	22 11	16 08	11 18	22 18	17 38
8 T	19 3 29	15 47 05	15 33	24 49	26 06	17 17	21 17	28 08	16 47	16 26	7 23	12 12	22 23	16 31	11 53	22 34	17 37
9 W	19 7 26	16 44 16	29 11	24 46	26 41	18 29	21 43	28 21	16 45	16 26	7 22	12 10	22 35	16 53	12 27	22 51	17 36
10 Th	19 11 22	17 41 28	13 ♐ 19	24 40	27 20	19 40	22 10	28 35	16 44	16 27	7 22	12 09	22 47	17 16	13 02	23 07	17 35
11 F	19 15 19	18 38 40	27 54	24 32	28 05	20 52	22 37	28 48	16 43	16 28	7 21	12 07	23 00	17 38	13 36	23 25	17 34
12 Sa	19 19 15	19 35 52	12 ♑ 51	24 21	28 54	22 04	23 04	29 01	16 42	16 28	7 20	12 06	23 12	18 01	14 11	23 42	17 33
13 Su	19 23 12	20 33 04	28 02	24 11	29 49	23 17	23 32	29 14	16 42	16 28	7 19	12 05	23 25	18 24	14 45	24 00	17 32
14 M	19 27 9	21 30 16	13 ♒ 15	24 00	0 ♋ 48	24 29	24 00	29 28	16 41	16 29	7 18	12 03	23 39	18 47	15 19	24 18	17 31
15 T	19 31 5	22 27 28	28 20	23 52	1 52	25 41	24 28	29 41	16 40	16 29	7 17	12 02	23 52	19 10	15 54	24 36	17 29
16 W	19 35 2	23 24 41	13 ♓ 09	23 46	3 00	26 53	24 57	29 54	16 40	16 30	7 16	12 00	24 06	19 33	16 28	24 55	17 28
17 Th	19 38 58	24 21 55	27 34	23 42	4 13	28 05	25 25	0 ♌ 07	16 39	16 30	7 15	11 59	24 20	19 56	17 02	25 13	17 27
18 F	19 42 55	25 19 09	11 ♈ 35	23 41 D	5 30	29 18	25 55	0 21	16 39	16 30	7 13	11 57	24 34	20 19	17 37	25 32	17 25
19 Sa	19 46 51	26 16 24	25 10	23 41 ℞	6 52	0 ♋ 30	26 24	0 34	16 39	16 30	7 12	11 56	24 48	20 42	18 11	25 52	17 24
20 Su	19 50 48	27 13 39	8 ♉ 22	23 40	8 19	1 42	26 54	0 47	16 39 D	16 30	7 11	11 54	25 03	21 06	18 45	26 11	17 22
21 M	19 54 44	28 10 56	21 15	23 39	9 49	2 55	27 23	1 01	16 39	16 31 ℞	7 10	11 53	25 17	21 29	19 19	26 31	17 21
22 T	19 58 41	29 08 13	3 ♊ 52	23 35	11 23	4 07	27 54	1 14	16 39	16 30	7 09	11 51	25 32	21 53	19 53	26 51	17 19
23 W	20 2 38	0 ♌ 05 31	16 16	23 29	13 02	5 20	28 24	1 27	16 39	16 30	7 08	11 50	25 47	22 16	20 27	27 11	17 18
24 Th	20 6 34	1 02 50	28 29	23 20	14 44	6 32	28 55	1 41	16 39	16 30	7 06	11 49	26 03	22 40	21 01	27 31	17 16
25 F	20 10 31	2 00 09	10 ♋ 35	23 09	16 30	7 45	29 26	1 54	16 40	16 30	7 05	11 47	26 18	23 04	21 35	27 52	17 14
26 Sa	20 14 27	2 57 30	22 35	22 55	18 19	8 57	29 57	2 07	16 40	16 30	7 04	11 46	26 34	23 27	22 09	28 13	17 12
27 Su	20 18 24	3 54 50	4 ♌ 30	22 42	20 11	10 10	0 ♏ 28	2 21	16 40	16 30	7 03	11 44	26 50	23 51	22 43	28 34	17 11
28 M	20 22 20	4 52 12	16 23	22 29	22 06	11 23	1 00	2 34	16 41	16 29	7 01	11 43	27 06	24 15	23 17	28 55	17 09
29 T	20 26 17	5 49 34	28 13	22 17	24 03	12 35	1 32	2 48	16 42	16 29	7 00	11 42	27 23	24 39	23 50	29 17	17 07
30 W	20 30 13	6 46 57	10 ♍ 04	22 08	26 02	13 48	2 04	3 01	16 43	16 29	6 59	11 40	27 39	25 03	24 24	29 38	17 05
31 Th	20 34 10	7 44 20	21 57	22 02	28 04	15 01	2 36	3 14	16 44	16 29	6 57	11 39	27 56	25 27	24 58	0 ♏ 00	17 03

Tables are for midnight Greenwich Mean Time

200

August 2014

DATE	SID.TIME	SUN	MOON	NODE	MERCURY	VENUS	MARS	JUPITER	SATURN	URANUS	NEPTUNE	PLUTO	CERES	PALLAS	JUNO	VESTA	CHIRON
1 F	20 38 7	8♌41 44	3♎56	21♎58R	0♌06	16♋14	3♏09	3♌27	16♏45	16♈01	6♓56	11♑38	28♎13	25♍51	25♊31	0♏22	17♓01
2 Sa	20 42 3	9 39 09	16 05	21 57 D	2 10	17 27	3 42	3 41	16 46	16 28R	6 54R	11 37R	28 30	26 16	26 05	0 45	16 59R
3 Su	20 46 0	10 36 34	28 28	21 57	4 15	18 40	4 15	3 54	16 47	16 27	6 53	11 35	28 47	26 40	26 38	1 07	16 57
4 M	20 49 56	11 34 00	11♏09	21 57R	6 20	19 52	4 48	4 07	16 48	16 26	6 52	11 34	29 04	27 04	27 12	1 30	16 55
5 T	20 53 53	12 31 27	24 14	21 57	8 25	21 05	5 22	4 21	16 50	16 26	6 50	11 33	29 22	27 29	27 45	1 53	16 52
6 W	20 57 49	13 28 54	7♐47	21 54	10 30	22 18	5 55	4 34	16 51	16 25	6 49	11 32	29 39	27 53	28 18	2 16	16 50
7 Th	21 1 46	14 26 22	21 49	21 50	12 35	23 32	6 29	4 47	16 53	16 24	6 47	11 30	29 57	28 18	28 52	2 39	16 48
8 F	21 5 42	15 23 51	6♑19	21 43	14 39	24 45	7 03	5 00	16 55	16 24	6 46	11 29	0♏15	28 42	29 25	3 02	16 46
9 Sa	21 9 39	16 21 21	21 14	21 35	16 42	25 58	7 37	5 14	16 57	16 23	6 44	11 28	0 33	29 07	29 58	3 26	16 43
10 Su	21 13 36	17 18 51	6♒27	21 25	18 45	27 11	8 12	5 27	16 58	16 22	6 43	11 27	0 52	29 32	0♋31	3 49	16 41
11 M	21 17 32	18 16 23	21 46	21 16	20 46	28 24	8 46	5 40	17 00	16 21	6 41	11 26	1 10	29 56	1 04	4 13	16 39
12 T	21 21 29	19 13 56	7♓01	21 09	22 46	29 37	9 21	5 53	17 02	16 20	6 40	11 25	1 29	0♎21	1 37	4 37	16 36
13 W	21 25 25	20 11 29	22 01	21 04	24 45	0♌51	9 56	6 06	17 05	16 19	6 38	11 23	1 47	0 46	2 10	5 01	16 34
14 Th	21 29 22	21 09 05	6♈39	21 01	26 43	2 04	10 32	6 19	17 07	16 18	6 36	11 22	2 06	1 11	2 43	5 26	16 31
15 F	21 33 18	22 06 41	20 50	21 00 D	28 40	3 17	11 07	6 32	17 09	16 17	6 35	11 21	2 25	1 36	3 15	5 50	16 29
16 Sa	21 37 15	23 04 19	4♉33	21 00	0♍35	4 31	11 42	6 45	17 12	16 16	6 33	11 20	2 44	2 01	3 48	6 15	16 26
17 Su	21 41 11	24 01 59	17 49	21 01R	2 28	5 44	12 18	6 58	17 14	16 15	6 32	11 19	3 03	2 26	4 21	6 40	16 24
18 M	21 45 8	24 59 40	0♊42	21 01	4 21	6 58	12 54	7 11	17 17	16 13	6 30	11 18	3 23	2 51	4 53	7 04	16 21
19 T	21 49 5	25 57 23	13 15	21 00	6 11	8 11	13 30	7 24	17 20	16 12	6 28	11 17	3 42	3 16	5 25	7 29	16 19
20 W	21 53 1	26 55 08	25 34	20 56	8 01	9 25	14 06	7 37	17 22	16 11	6 27	11 16	4 02	3 41	5 58	7 55	16 16
21 Th	21 56 58	27 52 54	7♋39	20 50	9 49	10 39	14 43	7 50	17 25	16 09	6 25	11 15	4 22	4 06	6 30	8 20	16 13
22 F	22 0 54	28 50 42	19 40	20 42	11 35	11 52	15 19	8 03	17 28	16 08	6 24	11 15	4 42	4 32	7 02	8 45	16 11
23 Sa	22 4 51	29 48 31	1♌34	20 33	13 21	13 06	15 56	8 16	17 31	16 07	6 22	11 14	5 02	4 57	7 34	9 11	16 08
24 Su	22 8 47	0♍46 22	13 26	20 23	15 04	14 20	16 33	8 29	17 35	16 05	6 20	11 13	5 22	5 22	8 06	9 37	16 05
25 M	22 12 44	1 44 14	25 17	20 14	16 47	15 33	17 10	8 41	17 38	16 04	6 19	11 12	5 42	5 48	8 38	10 03	16 03
26 T	22 16 40	2 42 08	7♍09	20 06	18 28	16 47	17 48	8 54	17 41	16 02	6 17	11 11	6 02	6 13	9 10	10 29	16 00
27 W	22 20 37	3 40 03	19 04	20 00	20 08	18 01	18 25	9 07	17 45	16 01	6 15	11 10	6 23	6 38	9 42	10 55	15 57
28 Th	22 24 34	4 37 59	1♎03	19 56	21 46	19 15	19 03	9 20	17 48	15 59	6 14	11 10	6 43	7 04	10 14	11 21	15 55
29 F	22 28 30	5 35 57	13 09	19 54 D	23 23	20 29	19 40	9 32	17 52	15 57	6 12	11 09	7 04	7 29	10 45	11 47	15 52
30 Sa	22 32 27	6 33 57	25 25	19 54	24 59	21 43	20 18	9 45	17 55	15 56	6 10	11 08	7 25	7 55	11 16	12 14	15 49
31 Su	22 36 23	7 31 58	7♏53	19 55	26 33	22 57	20 56	9 57	17 59	15 54	6 09	11 08	7 46	8 21	11 48	12 41	15 46

September 2014

DATE	SID.TIME	SUN	MOON	NODE	MERCURY	VENUS	MARS	JUPITER	SATURN	URANUS	NEPTUNE	PLUTO	CERES	PALLAS	JUNO	VESTA	CHIRON
1 M	22 40 20	8 ♍ 30 00	20 ♍ 38	19 ♎ 56	28 ♍ 07	24 ♌ 11	21 ♏ 34	10 ♌ 10	18 ♏ 03	15 ♈ 52	6 ♓ 07	11 ♑ 07	8 ♏ 07	8 ♎ 46	12 ♋ 19	13 ♏ 07	15 ♓ 43
2 T	22 44 16	9 28 04	3 ♐ 42	19 57 ℞	29 39	25 25	22 13	10 22	18 07	15 50 ℞	6 06 ℞	11 06 ℞	8 28	9 12	12 50	13 34	15 41 ℞
3 W	22 48 13	10 26 09	17 09	19 57	1 ♎ 01	26 39	22 51	10 34	18 11	15 49	6 04	11 06	8 49	9 38	13 21	14 01	15 38
4 Th	22 52 9	11 24 15	1 ♑ 02	19 56	2 39	27 53	23 30	10 47	18 15	15 47	6 02	11 05	9 10	10 03	13 52	14 28	15 35
5 F	22 56 6	12 22 23	15 20	19 53	4 07	29 07	24 09	10 59	18 19	15 45	6 01	11 05	9 32	10 29	14 23	14 55	15 32
6 Sa	23 0 2	13 20 32	0 ♒ 01	19 48	5 33	0 ♍ 21	24 47	11 11	18 23	15 43	5 59	11 04	9 53	10 55	14 54	15 23	15 29
7 Su	23 3 59	14 18 43	15 00	19 43	6 59	1 35	25 27	11 23	18 27	15 41	5 57	11 04	10 15	11 21	15 24	15 50	15 27
8 M	23 7 56	15 16 55	0 ♓ 08	19 38	8 23	2 50	26 06	11 36	18 32	15 39	5 56	11 03	10 36	11 47	15 55	16 17	15 24
9 T	23 11 52	16 15 09	15 17	19 34	9 46	4 04	26 45	11 48	18 36	15 37	5 54	11 03	10 58	12 13	16 25	16 45	15 21
10 W	23 15 49	17 13 25	0 ♈ 17	19 31	11 07	5 18	27 24	12 00	18 41	15 35	5 52	11 02	11 20	12 38	16 55	17 13	15 18
11 Th	23 19 45	18 11 42	14 58	19 30 D	12 27	6 33	28 04	12 12	18 45	15 33	5 51	11 02	11 42	13 04	17 25	17 40	15 15
12 F	23 23 42	19 10 02	29 15	19 30	13 45	7 47	28 44	12 23	18 50	15 31	5 49	11 02	12 04	13 30	17 55	18 08	15 13
13 Sa	23 27 38	20 08 23	13 ♉ 06	19 32	15 02	9 01	29 23	12 35	18 55	15 29	5 48	11 01	12 26	13 56	18 25	18 36	15 10
14 Su	23 31 35	21 06 47	26 29	19 33	16 17	10 16	0 ♐ 03	12 47	19 00	15 27	5 46	11 01	12 48	14 22	18 55	19 04	15 07
15 M	23 35 31	22 05 12	9 ♊ 27	19 34	17 31	11 30	0 43	12 59	19 04	15 24	5 45	11 01	13 10	14 48	19 25	19 32	15 04
16 T	23 39 28	23 03 40	22 04	19 35 ℞	18 42	12 45	1 24	13 10	19 09	15 22	5 43	11 01	13 32	15 14	19 54	20 01	15 01
17 W	23 43 25	24 02 10	4 ♋ 23	19 35	19 53	13 59	2 04	13 22	19 14	15 20	5 41	11 00	13 55	15 41	20 23	20 29	14 59
18 Th	23 47 21	25 00 43	16 29	19 33	21 01	15 14	2 44	13 33	19 19	15 18	5 40	11 00	14 17	16 07	20 53	20 57	14 56
19 F	23 51 18	25 59 17	28 26	19 30	22 07	16 28	3 25	13 45	19 25	15 16	5 38	11 00	14 40	16 33	21 22	21 26	14 53
20 Sa	23 55 14	26 57 53	10 ♌ 18	19 27	23 11	17 43	4 06	13 56	19 30	15 13	5 37	11 01	15 02	16 59	21 51	21 54	14 50
21 Su	23 59 11	27 56 32	22 09	19 23	24 12	18 57	4 47	14 07	19 35	15 11	5 35	11 00	15 25	17 25	22 19	22 23	14 48
22 M	0 3 7	28 55 13	4 ♍ 07	19 20	25 11	20 12	5 27	14 19	19 40	15 09	5 34	11 00	15 48	17 51	22 48	22 52	14 45
23 T	0 7 4	29 53 55	15 57	19 17	26 08	21 27	6 08	14 30	19 46	15 06	5 32	11 00 D	16 10	18 18	23 17	23 21	14 42
24 W	0 11 0	0 ♎ 52 40	27 59	19 15	27 01	22 41	6 50	14 41	19 51	15 04	5 31	11 00	16 33	18 44	23 45	23 49	14 40
25 Th	0 14 57	1 51 27	10 ♎ 09	19 14 D	27 52	23 56	7 31	14 52	19 57	15 02	5 30	11 00	16 56	19 10	24 13	24 18	14 37
26 F	0 18 54	2 50 15	22 29	19 13	28 39	25 11	8 12	15 03	20 02	14 59	5 28	11 00	17 19	19 37	24 41	24 48	14 34
27 Sa	0 22 50	3 49 06	4 ♏ 59	19 14	29 22	26 25	8 54	15 13	20 08	14 57	5 27	11 00	17 42	20 03	25 09	25 17	14 32
28 Su	0 26 47	4 47 58	17 41	19 15	0 ♎ 02	27 40	9 35	15 24	20 13	14 55	5 25	11 00	18 05	20 29	25 36	25 46	14 29
29 M	0 30 43	5 46 52	0 ♐ 38	19 16	0 37	28 55	10 17	15 35	20 19	14 52	5 24	11 00	18 28	20 56	26 04	26 15	14 27
30 T	0 34 40	6 45 48	13 50	19 17	1 08	0 ♎ 10	10 59	15 45	20 25	14 50	5 23	11 01	18 52	21 22	26 31	26 44	14 24

Tables are for midnight Greenwich Mean Time

202

October 2014

DATE	SID.TIME	SUN	MOON	NODE	MERCURY	VENUS	MARS	JUPITER	SATURN	URANUS	NEPTUNE	PLUTO	CERES	PALLAS	JUNO	VESTA	CHIRON
1 W	0 38 36	7≏44 46	27♐20	19≏18	1♏34	1≏25	11♐41	15♌56	20♏31	14♈47	5♓21	11♑01	19♏15	21≏48	26♋58	27♏14	14♓21
2 Th	0 42 33	8 43 46	11♑08	19 18 R	1 54	2 39	12 23	16 06	20 37	14 45 R	5 20 R	11 01	19 38	22 15	27 25	27 43	14 19 R
3 F	0 46 29	9 42 47	25 14	19 18	2 09	3 54	13 05	16 16	20 43	14 43	5 19	11 01	20 02	22 41	27 52	28 13	14 16
4 Sa	0 50 26	10 41 50	9≈37	19 17	2 17 R	5 09	13 47	16 26	20 49	14 40	5 17	11 02	20 25	23 08	28 19	28 43	14 14
5 Su	0 54 23	11 40 54	24 14	19 16	2 18	6 24	14 30	16 36	20 55	14 38	5 16	11 02	20 49	23 34	28 45	29 12	14 12
6 M	0 58 19	12 40 01	8♓59	19 15	2 13	7 39	15 12	16 46	21 01	14 35	5 15	11 02	21 12	24 01	29 11	29 42	14 09
7 T	1 2 16	13 39 09	23 47	19 15	1 59	8 54	15 55	16 56	21 07	14 33	5 14	11 03	21 36	24 27	29 37	0♐12	14 07
8 W	1 6 12	14 38 19	8♈30	19 14 D	1 38	10 09	16 37	17 06	21 13	14 31	5 12	11 03	22 00	24 54	0♌03	0 42	14 05
9 Th	1 10 9	15 37 31	23 01	19 14	1 09	11 24	17 20	17 16	21 19	14 28	5 11	11 04	22 23	25 20	0 29	1 12	14 02
10 F	1 14 5	16 36 45	7♉13	19 15	0 32	12 39	18 03	17 25	21 26	14 26	5 10	11 04	22 47	25 47	0 54	1 42	14 00
11 Sa	1 18 2	17 36 02	21 04	19 15	29≏47	13 54	18 46	17 35	21 32	14 23	5 09	11 05	23 11	26 13	1 19	2 12	13 58
12 Su	1 21 58	18 35 21	4♊31	19 15 R	28 54	15 09	19 29	17 44	21 38	14 21	5 08	11 05	23 35	26 40	1 44	2 42	13 56
13 M	1 25 55	19 34 42	17 34	19 15	27 55	16 24	20 12	17 53	21 45	14 18	5 07	11 06	23 59	27 06	2 09	3 12	13 53
14 T	1 29 51	20 34 05	0♋16	19 15	26 49	17 39	20 55	18 02	21 51	14 16	5 06	11 07	24 23	27 33	2 34	3 42	13 51
15 W	1 33 48	21 33 30	12 38	19 15 D	25 40	18 54	21 38	18 11	21 57	14 14	5 05	11 07	24 47	27 59	2 58	4 12	13 49
16 Th	1 37 45	22 32 58	24 46	19 15	24 27	20 09	22 22	18 20	22 04	14 11	5 04	11 08	25 11	28 26	3 22	4 43	13 47
17 F	1 41 41	23 32 28	6♌43	19 15	23 14	21 24	23 05	18 29	22 11	14 09	5 03	11 09	25 35	28 52	3 46	5 13	13 45
18 Sa	1 45 38	24 32 00	18 35	19 15	22 02	22 39	23 49	18 38	22 17	14 06	5 02	11 09	25 59	29 19	4 10	5 43	13 43
19 Su	1 49 34	25 31 35	0♍26	19 16	20 53	23 54	24 32	18 46	22 24	14 04	5 01	11 10	26 23	29 45	4 33	6 14	13 41
20 M	1 53 31	26 31 12	12 20	19 17	19 50	25 09	25 16	18 54	22 30	14 02	5 00	11 11	26 47	0♏12	4 56	6 44	13 40
21 T	1 57 27	27 30 51	24 21	19 17	18 54	26 24	26 00	19 03	22 37	13 59	4 59	11 12	27 11	0 39	5 19	7 15	13 38
22 W	2 1 24	28 30 32	6≏31	19 18	18 07	27 39	26 44	19 11	22 44	13 57	4 58	11 13	27 36	1 05	5 42	7 46	13 36
23 Th	2 5 20	29 30 15	18 54	19 18 R	17 30	28 55	27 28	19 19	22 51	13 55	4 58	11 14	28 00	1 32	6 04	8 16	13 34
24 F	2 9 17	0♏30 00	1♏30	19 18	17 04	0♍10	28 12	19 27	22 57	13 52	4 57	11 14	28 24	1 58	6 26	8 47	13 33
25 Sa	2 13 14	1 29 48	14 21	19 17	16 49 D	1 25	28 56	19 34	23 04	13 50	4 56	11 15	28 49	2 25	6 48	9 18	13 31
26 Su	2 17 10	2 29 37	27 26	19 16	16 46	2 40	29 40	19 42	23 11	13 48	4 55	11 16	29 13	2 51	7 09	9 49	13 29
27 M	2 21 7	3 29 28	10♐45	19 14	16 54	3 55	0♑25	19 50	23 18	13 46	4 55	11 17	29 37	3 18	7 31	10 19	13 28
28 T	2 25 3	4 29 21	24 16	19 12	17 12	5 11	1 09	19 57	23 25	13 43	4 54	11 18	0♐02	3 45	7 52	10 50	13 26
29 W	2 29 0	5 29 15	8♑00	19 10	17 40	6 26	1 53	20 04	23 32	13 41	4 53	11 19	0 26	4 11	8 12	11 21	13 25
30 Th	2 32 56	6 29 11	21 54	19 08	18 18	7 41	2 38	20 11	23 39	13 39	4 53	11 21	0 51	4 38	8 33	11 52	13 23
31 F	2 36 53	7 29 09	5≈57	19 08 D	19 04	8 56	3 22	20 18	23 45	13 37	4 52	11 22	1 15	5 04	8 53	12 23	13 22

DATE	SID.TIME	SUN	MOON	NODE	MERCURY	VENUS	MARS	JUPITER	SATURN	URANUS	NEPTUNE	PLUTO	CERES	PALLAS	JUNO	VESTA	CHIRON
1 Sa	2 40 49	8 ♏ 29 09	20 ≈ 08	19 ♎ 08	19 ♎ 57	10 ♏ 11	4 ♑ 07	20 ♌ 25	23 ♏ 52	13 ♈ 35	4 ♓ 52	11 ♑ 23	1 ♐ 40	5 ♏ 31	9 ♌ 13	12 ♐ 54	13 ♓ 21
2 Su	2 44 46	9 29 09	4 ♓ 24	19 09	20 57	11 27	4 52	20 31	23 59	13 32 ℞	4 51 ℞	11 24	2 05	5 58	9 32	13 26	13 20 ℞
3 M	2 48 43	10 29 12	18 44	19 11	22 03	12 42	5 37	20 38	24 06	13 30	4 51	11 25	2 29	6 24	9 51	13 57	13 18
4 T	2 52 39	11 29 16	3 ♈ 03	19 12	23 14	13 57	6 22	20 44	24 13	13 28	4 50	11 26	2 54	6 51	10 10	14 28	13 17
5 W	2 56 36	12 29 22	17 18	19 13 ℞	24 30	15 12	7 06	20 50	24 21	13 26	4 50	11 28	3 19	7 17	10 29	14 59	13 16
6 Th	3 0 32	13 29 29	1 ♉ 26	19 12	25 49	16 28	7 51	20 56	24 28	13 24	4 50	11 29	3 43	7 44	10 47	15 30	13 15
7 F	3 4 29	14 29 38	15 21	19 10	27 11	17 43	8 37	21 02	24 35	13 22	4 49	11 30	4 08	8 10	11 05	16 02	13 14
8 Sa	3 8 25	15 29 49	29 01	19 07	28 36	18 58	9 22	21 08	24 42	13 20	4 49	11 32	4 33	8 37	11 22	16 33	13 13
9 Su	3 12 22	16 30 02	12 ♊ 22	19 03	0 ♏ 03	20 13	10 07	21 13	24 49	13 18	4 49	11 33	4 57	9 03	11 40	17 04	13 12
10 M	3 16 18	17 30 17	25 24	18 58	1 32	21 29	10 52	21 19	24 56	13 16	4 49	11 34	5 22	9 30	11 56	17 36	13 11
11 T	3 20 15	18 30 33	8 ♋ 06	18 54	3 03	22 44	11 37	21 24	25 03	13 15	4 48	11 36	5 47	9 56	12 13	18 07	13 11
12 W	3 24 12	19 30 52	20 30	18 50	4 34	23 59	12 23	21 29	25 10	13 13	4 48	11 37	6 12	10 23	12 29	18 38	13 10
13 Th	3 28 8	20 31 12	2 ♌ 39	18 47	6 07	25 14	13 08	21 34	25 17	13 11	4 48	11 39	6 37	10 49	12 45	19 10	13 09
14 F	3 32 5	21 31 35	14 37	18 45 D	7 40	26 30	13 54	21 39	25 24	13 09	4 48	11 40	7 01	11 15	13 00	19 41	13 09
15 Sa	3 36 1	22 31 59	26 29	18 45	9 14	27 45	14 39	21 43	25 32	13 08	4 48	11 42	7 26	11 42	13 15	20 13	13 08
16 Su	3 39 58	23 32 25	8 ♍ 19	18 46	10 49	29 00	15 25	21 48	25 39	13 06	4 48 D	11 43	7 51	12 08	13 30	20 44	13 08
17 M	3 43 54	24 32 53	20 14	18 47	12 24	0 ♐ 16	16 10	21 52	25 46	13 04	4 48	11 45	8 16	12 35	13 44	21 16	13 07
18 T	3 47 51	25 33 23	2 ♎ 16	18 49	13 59	1 31	16 56	21 56	25 53	13 03	4 48	11 46	8 41	13 01	13 58	21 48	13 07
19 W	3 51 47	26 33 54	14 32	18 50 ℞	15 34	2 46	17 42	22 00	26 00	13 01	4 48	11 48	9 06	13 27	14 11	22 19	13 07
20 Th	3 55 44	27 34 28	27 05	18 50	17 09	4 01	18 28	22 03	26 07	12 59	4 48	11 49	9 31	13 54	14 24	22 51	13 06
21 F	3 59 40	28 35 03	9 ♏ 56	18 48	18 45	5 17	19 13	22 07	26 14	12 58	4 48	11 51	9 56	14 20	14 37	23 23	13 06
22 Sa	4 3 37	29 35 39	23 07	18 44	20 20	6 32	19 59	22 10	26 22	12 57	4 48	11 53	10 20	14 46	14 49	23 54	13 06
23 Su	4 7 34	0 ♐ 36 18	6 ♐ 36	18 38	21 55	7 47	20 45	22 13	26 29	12 55	4 49	11 54	10 45	15 13	15 00	24 26	13 06 D
24 M	4 11 30	1 36 57	20 23	18 31	23 30	9 03	21 31	22 16	26 36	12 54	4 49	11 56	11 10	15 39	15 12	24 58	13 06
25 T	4 15 27	2 37 38	4 ♑ 23	18 23	25 06	10 18	22 17	22 19	26 43	12 52	4 49	11 58	11 35	16 05	15 23	25 30	13 06
26 W	4 19 23	3 38 20	18 31	18 16	26 41	11 33	23 03	22 22	26 50	12 51	4 50	11 59	12 00	16 31	15 33	26 01	13 06
27 Th	4 23 20	4 39 04	2 ≈ 44	18 11	28 16	12 49	23 50	22 24	26 57	12 50	4 50	12 01	12 25	16 57	15 43	26 33	13 06
28 F	4 27 16	5 39 48	16 58	18 07	29 50	14 04	24 36	22 26	27 04	12 49	4 50	12 03	12 50	17 23	15 52	27 05	13 06
29 Sa	4 31 13	6 40 33	1 ♓ 09	18 05 D	1 ♐ 25	15 19	25 22	22 28	27 12	12 48	4 51	12 05	13 15	17 50	16 01	27 37	13 07
30 Su	4 35 10	7 41 19	15 16	18 05	3 00	16 35	26 08	22 30	27 19	12 46	4 51	12 06	13 40	18 16	16 10	28 09	13 07

Tables are for midnight Greenwich Mean Time

December 2014

DATE	SID.TIME	SUN	MOON	NODE	MERCURY	VENUS	MARS	JUPITER	SATURN	URANUS	NEPTUNE	PLUTO	CERES	PALLAS	JUNO	VESTA	CHIRON
1 M	4 39 6	8 ♐ 42 06	29 ♓ 17	18 ♎ 06 D	4 ♐ 34	17 ♐ 50	26 ♑ 55	22 ♌ 32	27 ♏ 26	12 ♈ 45	4 ♓ 52	12 ♑ 08	14 ♓ 05	18 ♏ 42	16 ♑ 18	28 ♏ 41	13 ♓ 07
2 T	4 43 3	9 42 54	13 ♈ 12	18 07 R	6 09	19 05	27 41	22 33	27 33	12 44 R	4 52	12 10	14 30	19 08	16 25	29 12	13 08
3 W	4 46 59	10 43 43	27 00	18 07	7 43	20 21	28 27	22 34	27 40	12 43	4 53	12 12	14 55	19 34	16 32	29 44	13 08
4 Th	4 50 56	11 44 33	10 ♉ 40	18 05	9 17	21 36	29 14	22 35	27 47	12 42	4 53	12 14	15 20	20 00	16 39	0 ♐ 16	13 09
5 F	4 54 52	12 45 24	24 10	18 00	10 52	22 51	0 ♒ 00	22 36	27 54	12 42	4 54	12 16	15 45	20 25	16 45	0 48	13 09
6 Sa	4 58 49	13 46 16	7 ♊ 29	17 52	12 26	24 06	0 47	22 37	28 01	12 41	4 55	12 17	16 10	20 51	16 50	1 20	13 10
7 Su	5 2 45	14 47 08	20 34	17 43	14 00	25 22	1 33	22 37	28 08	12 40	4 55	12 19	16 35	21 17	16 55	1 52	13 11
8 M	5 6 42	15 48 02	3 ♋ 25	17 32	15 34	26 37	2 20	22 38 R	28 15	12 39	4 56	12 21	17 00	21 43	17 00	2 24	13 11
9 T	5 10 39	16 48 57	16 01	17 21	17 09	27 52	3 06	22 38	28 22	12 39	4 57	12 23	17 24	22 09	17 04	2 56	13 12
10 W	5 14 35	17 49 54	28 21	17 10	18 43	29 08	3 53	22 37	28 28	12 38	4 58	12 25	17 49	22 34	17 08	3 28	13 13
11 Th	5 18 32	18 50 51	10 ♌ 29	17 02	20 17	0 ♑ 23	4 39	22 37	28 35	12 37	4 58	12 27	18 14	23 00	17 10	4 00	13 13
12 F	5 22 28	19 51 49	22 26	16 55	21 51	1 38	5 26	22 37	28 42	12 37	4 59	12 29	18 39	23 26	17 13	4 32	13 15
13 Sa	5 26 25	20 52 48	4 ♍ 17	16 51	23 26	2 53	6 13	22 36	28 49	12 36	5 00	12 31	19 04	23 51	17 15	5 04	13 16
14 Su	5 30 21	21 53 48	16 06	16 50 D	25 00	4 09	6 59	22 35	28 56	12 36	5 01	12 33	19 29	24 17	17 16	5 36	13 17
15 M	5 34 18	22 54 50	27 58	16 50	26 35	5 24	7 46	22 34	29 03	12 35	5 02	12 35	19 54	24 42	17 17	6 08	13 18
16 T	5 38 14	23 55 52	10 ♎ 00	16 50 R	28 10	6 39	8 33	22 33	29 09	12 35	5 03	12 37	20 19	25 08	17 17 R	6 40	13 20
17 W	5 42 11	24 56 55	22 15	16 50	29 45	7 55	9 20	22 31	29 16	12 35	5 04	12 39	20 43	25 33	17 17	7 12	13 21
18 Th	5 46 8	25 58 00	4 ♏ 50	16 49	1 ♑ 20	9 10	10 06	22 29	29 23	12 35	5 05	12 41	21 08	25 58	17 16	7 44	13 22
19 F	5 50 4	26 59 05	17 48	16 45	2 55	10 25	10 53	22 27	29 29	12 34	5 06	12 43	21 33	26 24	17 15	8 16	13 24
20 Sa	5 54 1	28 00 11	1 ♐ 11	16 38	4 30	11 40	11 40	22 25	29 36	12 34	5 07	12 45	21 58	26 49	17 13	8 48	13 25
21 Su	5 57 57	29 01 18	14 59	16 29	6 05	12 56	12 27	22 23	29 43	12 34 D	5 09	12 47	22 23	27 14	17 11	9 20	13 27
22 M	6 1 54	0 ♑ 02 25	29 09	16 18	7 41	14 11	13 14	22 21	29 49	12 34	5 10	12 49	22 47	27 39	17 08	9 52	13 28
23 T	6 5 50	1 03 33	13 ♑ 37	16 06	9 17	15 26	14 01	22 18	29 56	12 34	5 11	12 51	23 12	28 04	17 04	10 24	13 30
24 W	6 9 47	2 04 41	28 15	15 54	10 52	16 42	14 47	22 15	0 ♐ 02	12 34	5 12	12 53	23 37	28 29	17 00	10 57	13 31
25 Th	6 13 43	3 05 50	12 ♒ 55	15 45	12 28	17 57	15 34	22 12	0 08	12 34	5 13	12 55	24 02	28 54	16 55	11 29	13 33
26 F	6 17 40	4 06 58	27 31	15 38	14 04	19 12	16 21	22 09	0 15	12 35	5 15	12 57	24 26	29 19	16 50	12 01	13 35
27 Sa	6 21 37	5 08 07	11 ♓ 56	15 34	15 40	20 27	17 08	22 05	0 21	12 35	5 16	12 59	24 51	29 44	16 44	12 33	13 37
28 Su	6 25 33	6 09 16	26 09	15 32 D	17 16	21 43	17 55	22 02	0 27	12 35	5 17	13 02	25 16	0 ♐ 09	16 38	13 05	13 39
29 M	6 29 30	7 10 24	10 ♈ 06	15 32 R	18 52	22 58	18 42	21 58	0 34	12 35	5 19	13 04	25 40	0 34	16 32	13 37	13 40
30 T	6 33 26	8 11 33	23 50	15 32	20 28	24 13	19 29	21 54	0 40	12 36	5 20	13 06	26 05	0 58	16 24	14 09	13 42
31 W	6 37 23	9 12 41	7 ♉ 19	15 30	22 04	25 28	20 16	21 50	0 46	12 36	5 22	13 08	26 29	1 23	16 17	14 41	13 44

The Planetary Hours

The selection of an auspicious time for starting any activity is an important matter. Its existence tends to take on a nature corresponding to the conditions under which it was begun. Each hour is ruled by a planet, and the nature of any hour corresponds to the nature of the planet ruling it. The nature of the planetary hours is the same as the description of each of the planets. Uranus, Neptune, and Pluto are considered here as higher octaves of Mercury, Venus, and Mars.

Sunrise Hour	Sun	Mon	Tue	Wed	Thu	Fri	Sat
1	☉	☽	♂	☿	♃	♀	♄
2	♀	♄	☉	☽	♂	☿	♃
3	☿	♃	♀	♄	☉	☽	♂
4	☽	♂	☿	♃	♀	♄	☉
5	♄	☉	☽	♂	☿	♃	♀
6	♃	♀	♄	☉	☽	♂	☿
7	♂	☿	♃	♀	♄	☉	☽
8	☉	☽	♂	☿	♃	♀	♄
9	♀	♄	☉	☽	♂	☿	♃
10	☿	♃	♀	♄	☉	☽	♂
11	☽	♂	☿	♃	♀	♄	☉
12	♄	☉	☽	♂	☿	♃	♀

Sunset Hour	Sun	Mon	Tue	Wed	Thu	Fri	Sat
1	♃	♀	♄	☉	☽	♂	☿
2	♂	☿	♃	♀	♄	☉	☽
3	☉	☽	♂	☿	♃	♀	♄
4	♀	♄	☉	☽	♂	☿	♃
5	☿	♃	♀	♄	☉	☽	♂
6	☽	♂	☿	♃	♀	♄	☉
7	♄	☉	☽	♂	☿	♃	♀
8	♃	♀	♄	☉	☽	♂	☿
9	♂	☿	♃	♀	♄	☉	☽
10	☉	☽	♂	☿	♃	♀	♄
11	♀	♄	☉	☽	♂	☿	♃
12	☿	♃	♀	♄	☉	☽	♂

Table of Rising and Setting Signs

To find your approximate Ascendant, locate your Sun sign in the left column and determine the approximate time of your birth. Line up your Sun sign with birth time to find Ascendant. Note: This table will give you the approximate Ascendant only. To obtain your exact Ascendant you must consult your natal chart.

Sun Sign	6–8 AM	8–10 AM	10 AM–12 PM	12–2 PM	2–4 PM	4–6 PM
Aries	Taurus	Gemini	Cancer	Leo	Virgo	Libra
Taurus	Gemini	Cancer	Leo	Virgo	Libra	Scorpio
Gemini	Cancer	Leo	Virgo	Libra	Scorpio	Sagittarius
Cancer	Leo	Virgo	Libra	Scorpio	Sagittarius	Capricorn
Leo	Virgo	Libra	Scorpio	Sagittarius	Capricorn	Aquarius
Virgo	Libra	Scorpio	Sagittarius	Capricorn	Aquarius	Pisces
Libra	Scorpio	Sagittarius	Capricorn	Aquarius	Pisces	Aries
Scorpio	Sagittarius	Capricorn	Aquarius	Pisces	Aries	Taurus
Sagittarius	Capricorn	Aquarius	Pisces	Aries	Taurus	Gemini
Capricorn	Aquarius	Pisces	Aries	Taurus	Gemini	Cancer
Aquarius	Pisces	Aries	Taurus	Gemini	Cancer	Leo
Pisces	Aries	Taurus	Gemini	Cancer	Leo	Virgo

Sun Sign	6–8 PM	8–10 PM	10 PM–12 AM	12–2 AM	2–4 AM	4–6 AM
Aries	Scorpio	Sagittarius	Capricorn	Aquarius	Pisces	Aries
Taurus	Sagittarius	Capricorn	Aquarius	Pisces	Aries	Taurus
Gemini	Capricorn	Aquarius	Pisces	Aries	Taurus	Gemini
Cancer	Aquarius	Pisces	Aries	Taurus	Gemini	Cancer
Leo	Pisces	Aries	Taurus	Gemini	Cancer	Leo
Virgo	Aries	Taurus	Gemini	Cancer	Leo	Virgo
Libra	Taurus	Gemini	Cancer	Leo	Virgo	Libra
Scorpio	Gemini	Cancer	Leo	Virgo	Libra	Scorpio
Sagittarius	Cancer	Leo	Virgo	Libra	Scorpio	Sagittarius
Capricorn	Leo	Virgo	Libra	Scorpio	Sagittarius	Capricorn
Aquarius	Virgo	Libra	Scorpio	Sagittarius	Capricorn	Aquarius
Pisces	Libra	Scorpio	Sagittarius	Capricorn	Aquarius	Pisces

Notes